IMAGES
of America

TAYLOR COUNTY

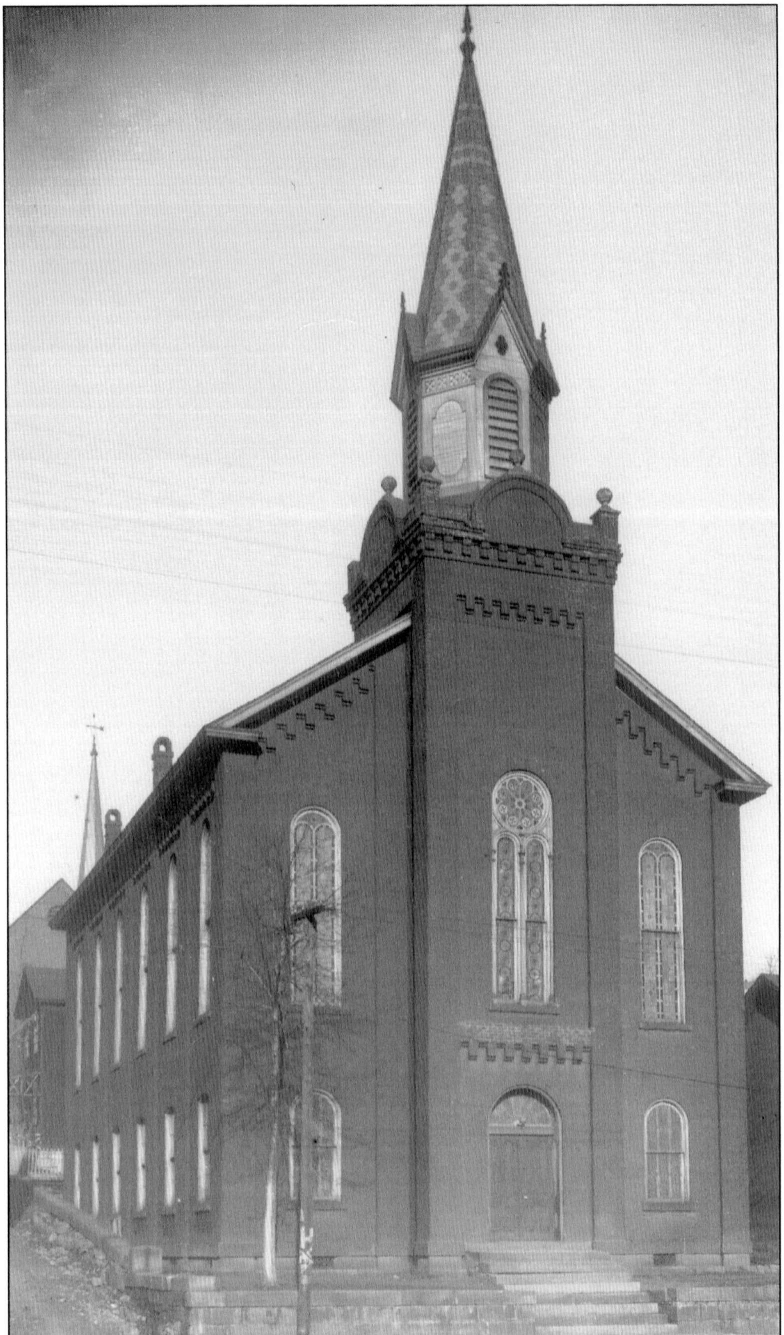

WHERE MOTHER'S DAY BEGAN. The first Mother's Day service was conducted May 10, 1908, at the Andrews Methodist Episcopal Church at the request of founder Anna Jarvis. This Grafton woman was successful in getting President Woodrow Wilson to sign a resolution in 1914, designating the second Sunday in May as Mother's Day. In 1962, this historic church became the International Mother's Day Shrine. A Mother's Day service continues to be held each year. (Photo courtesy of Peggy Robinson.)

IMAGES
of America

TAYLOR COUNTY

Prepared for
the Taylor County Historical and Genealogical Society
by

Darlene Ford
Marvin Gelhausen
Wayne McDevitt
Rick Reese
Peggy Robinson

ARCADIA
PUBLISHING

ISBN 978-0-7385-0588-6

Published by Arcadia Publishing
Charleston, South Carolina

Printed in the United States of America

Library of Congress Catalog Card Number: 00-108250

For all general information contact Arcadia Publishing at:
Telephone 843-853-2070
Fax 843-853-0044
E-Mail sales@arcadiapublishing.com
For customer service and orders:
Toll-Free 1-888-313-2665

Visit us on the Internet at www.arcadiapublishing.com

This book is dedicated to the Honorable John T. McGraw a prominent early resident of Grafton.(See McGraw's biographical sketch on p. 8.)

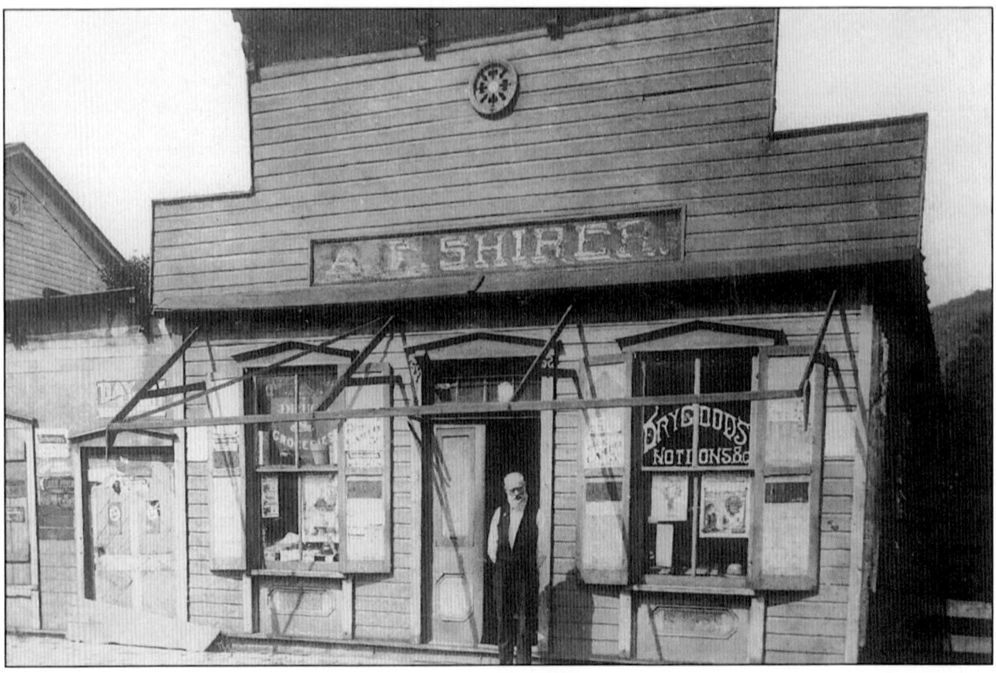

An Early Business. A.F. Shirer Drugs, Groceries, Drygoods, Notions & Co. was located at the north end of Pike Street. Shown is George Franis, one of the owners of the store. Jo Orr of Grafton also says her husband operated the store in the years before it was razed.

Contents

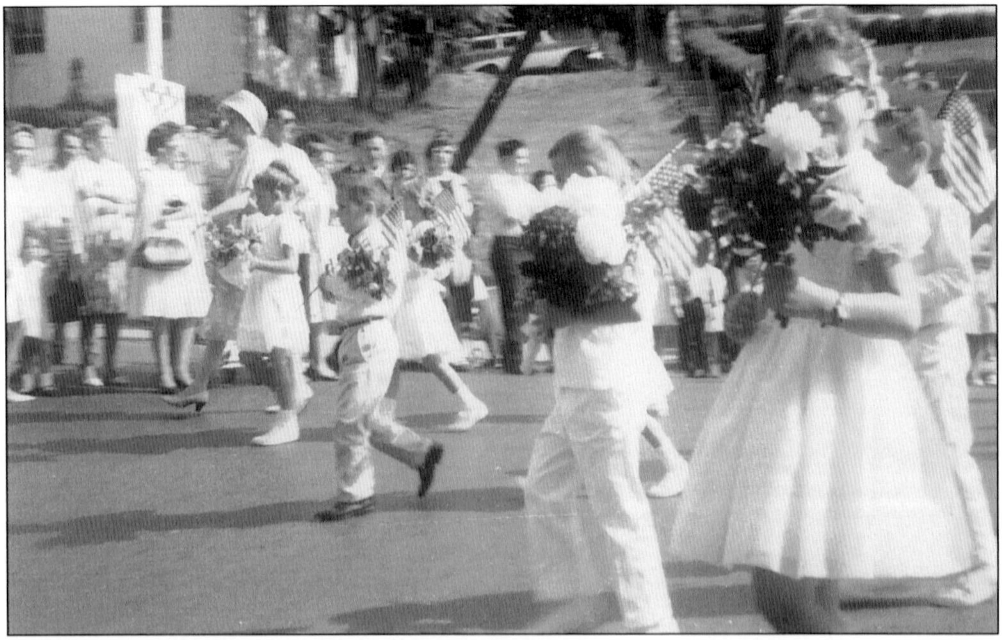

ACKNOWLEDGMENTS

Photos provided by individuals for publication in this book will include a notation that they are provided courtesy of the owner, unless the owner requested not to be identified. Most of the photos published without a notation are from the Taylor County Historical Collection of the Taylor County Historical and Genealogical Society. The collection is housed at the Taylor County Public Library. Individual contributors include the following: G. Thomas Bartlett III, Marguerite Baugh, the Bluemont Cemetery Historical Collection, James Bolliger, Rich Bord, the Department of the Army—Carlisle Barracks, PA, Harold (deceased) and Norma Fawcett, the Flemington High School Yearbook, Darlene Ford, Marvin Gelhausen, Lois Heflin, James Kerns, Oleda Kite, Betty Leuliette, Ruth Mason, Wayne McDevitt, Danny Moore, Leonard and Geneva Phelps, Rick Reese, Larry M. Richman, Peggy Robinson, Rita Jean Robinson, Martha Ann Rus, Paul Shaffer, Mary Susan Shafferman, the Taylor County Board of Education, Richard Utt, Thunder on the Tygart, Norma Wyckoff, and West Virginia University.

Several of the photos from individual presenters were scanned by G. Thomas Bartlett so actual photos would not have to be shipped to the printer. We thank Mr. Bartlett for his assistance with this project.

Historical information for the photo captions contained in this pictorial history of Taylor County was pulled from a number of reference sources, including the writings of late Taylor County historian Charles Brinkman; the *Taylor County History Book*, published by the Taylor County Historical and Genealogical Society; the 1972 *Historical Anecdotes of Early Taylor County* by the late Paul C. Bartlett; a 1910 Board of Trade publication entitled *Grafton, West Virginia, Best Town-Best State*; Flemington, WV, district history *We Were, We Are*, by Geneva Phelps; prior city directories of the city of Grafton; records at the Taylor County Clerk's office; and microfilm files at the Taylor County Public Library.

INTRODUCTION

Grafton, Taylor County, WV, has international acclaim as the birthplace of Mother's Day. Founder Anna Jarvis was born at the Webster community of Taylor County and her birthplace is now a museum. The International Mother's Day Shrine, where the first Mother's Day service was held on May 10, 1908, is listed as a National Historic Landmark.

Grafton, a railroad town, traces its roots to the arrival of the B&O Railroad in the mid-1800s. Generations of families found employment here with the railroad. The roundhouse and several other rail yard landmarks are gone, but the large B&O Station and the adjacent Willard Hotel from the early 1900s are in the early stages of renovation into the West Virginia Railroad Museum and other multi-use facilities. An early freight station also remains.

The first slaves to be set free may have been released here at the county jail in Pruntytown. Historians are just beginning efforts to verify this story, which has been passed down from generation to generation. West Virginia does have the distinction of being the only state created out of the Civil War. Taylor County served as a launching site for the first organized land skirmish at Philippi.

Taylor County also is a patriotic community. For more than 100 years, schoolchildren have marched each year to the Grafton National Cemetery to decorate the graves of fallen heroes.

This pictorial history features historical highlights from Taylor County and from Grafton's incorporation in 1856 to the city's honor by *Look* magazine as an All American City in 1963. Part of that honor came from a Womens March for Industry, after the area hit upon hard economic times in the late 1950s.

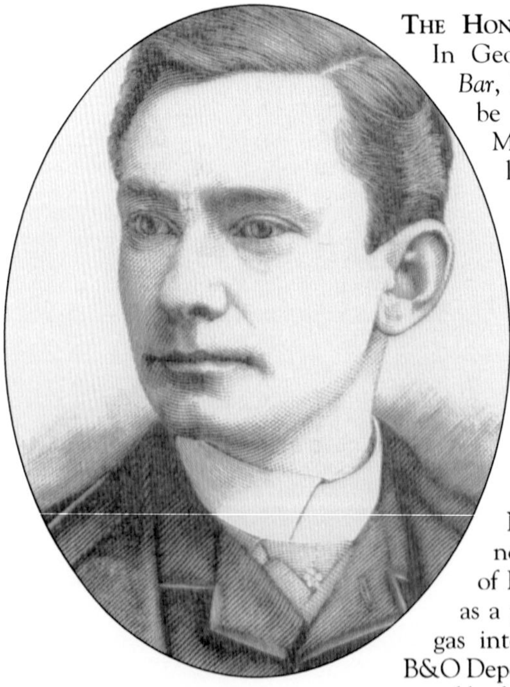

The Honorable John T. McGraw (1856–1920). In George W. Atkinson's 1919 book *Bench and Bar*, he writes, "No history of West Virginia can be truthfully written without giving Colonel McGraw prominent mention . . . He is a brilliant lawyer, a prominent politician, and a leading public spirited citizen." McGraw received a bachelor of laws from Yale University in 1876 and served as Taylor County's prosecuting attorney from 1881 to 1884. In 1882, he was appointed as an aide-de-camp with the rank of colonel on the staff of West Virginia Governor Jackson. In 1885, President Cleveland appointed him collector of internal revenue for the state of West Virginia. McGraw was an ardent Democrat and a personal friend of William Jennings Bryan. In 1912, he gave one of the speeches to nominate Thomas Woodrow Wilson to the office of President, and afterward often was mentioned as a possible cabinet member. He brought natural gas into Grafton, was instrumental in getting the B&O Depot and Hotel, purchased a professional baseball team, and built the street railroad system for Grafton. He also owned several coal mines in the western section of Taylor County. The failure in 1915 of his Grafton Bank and of his eyesight started his downfall, caused in part by his years of altruism. With the passing of time, we now are able to appreciate him for the good he did for society.

The Honorable Norman F. Kendall. Author Howard H. Wolfe referred to Norman F. Kendall as "the world's greatest authority on the history of Mother's Day." Kendall was an educator, writer of history, a banker, and a business-community leader. He held many positions, including serving as a member of the board of education of the Taylor County school system. He was a principal and assistant superintendent of the West Virginia Industrial School for Boys at Pruntytown. He wrote the book *A History of Mother's Day*, authored *The Kendall Journal* (a genealogy paper), had hundreds of articles published in newspapers and magazines, and authored a serial, *Early History of Taylor County*, that was published in *The Grafton News*. He assisted in the organization of four banks that served Grafton and Taylor County, and was active for 27 years in the banking business. He served two terms as mayor of Fetterman, was president of the Grafton Chamber of Commerce, and represented the Grafton-Taylor County area in the West Virginia Legislature during 1927–28.

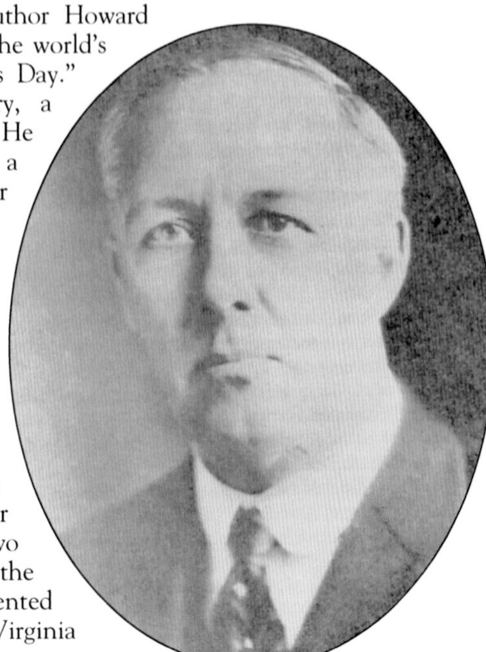

One

Mother's Day

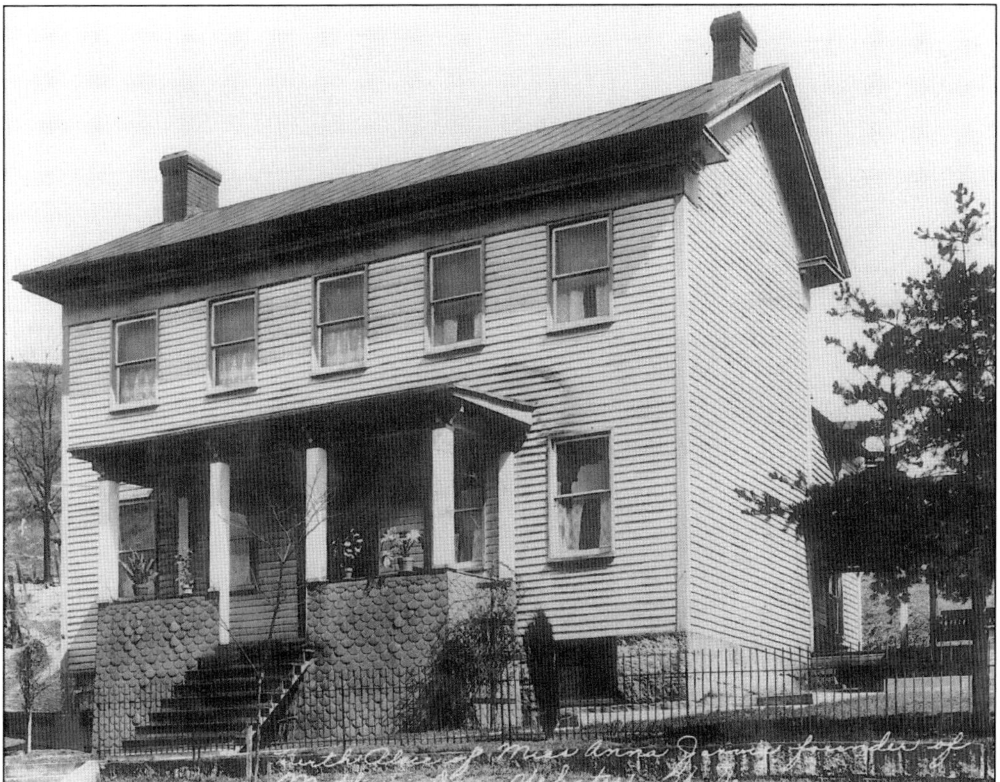

Birthplace of Mother's Day Founder. The Anna Jarvis Birthplace Museum at Webster in Taylor County has been restored to its Civil War-era appearance. Built by Granville Jarvis in 1854, the Jarvis family occupied the home until 1865. Anna Jarvis, founder of Mother's Day, was born in the upstairs left-hand bedroom. Taylor County historians say Gen. George B. McClellan used the lower right-hand room as his office in mid-1861. Acreage across Route 250 from the home has been developed into the Ocean Pearl Felton Historical Park. (Photo courtesy of Thunder on the Tygart.)

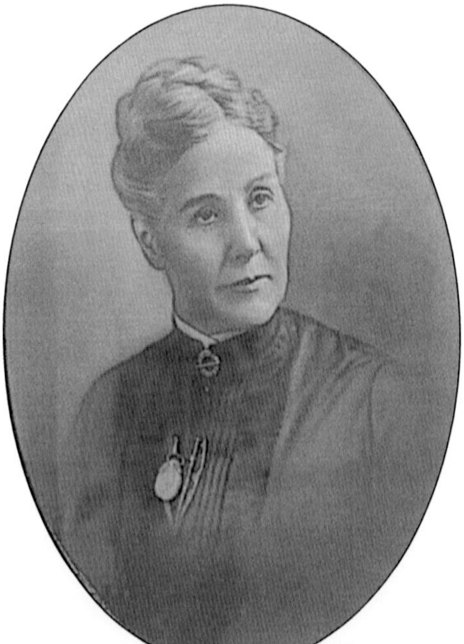 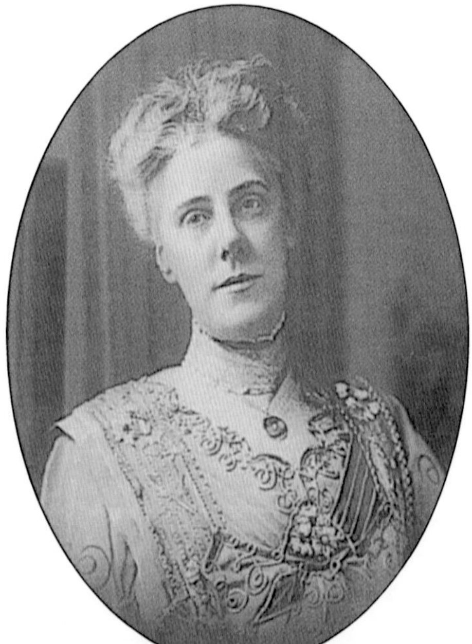

MOTHER AND DAUGHTER. Anna Reeves Jarvis (left) was the first mother honored by Mother's Day. Her daughter, Anna Jarvis (right), founded the holiday. (Photos courtesy of Peggy Robinson.)

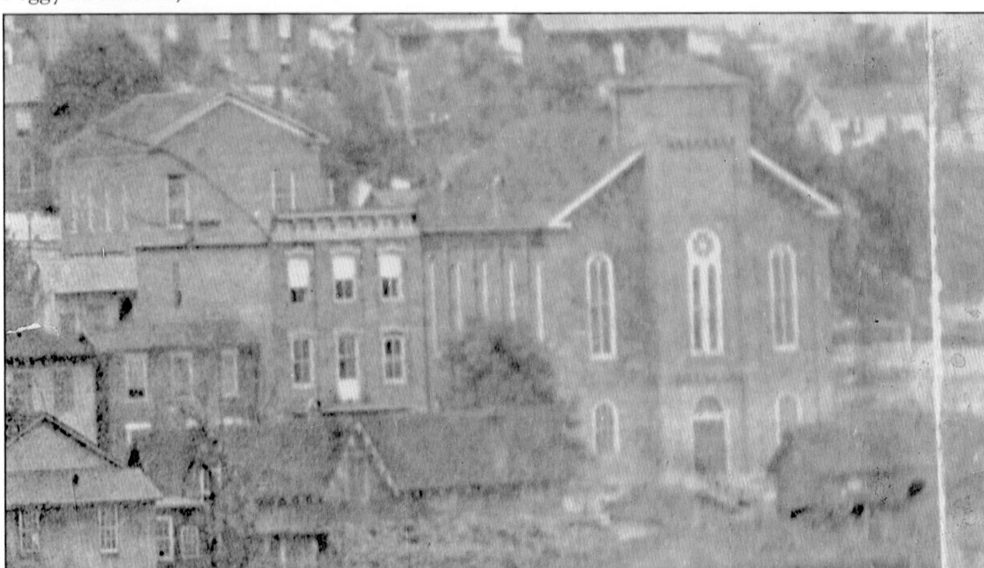

HISTORY OF THE CHURCH. Construction began in 1872 on Andrews Methodist Episcopal Church. The first service in the handmade brick structure was conducted on January 26, 1873. The service was on the lower or first floor in the lecture room as the sanctuary had not adequately been furnished for use. The formal dedication of the sanctuary occurred on March 16, 1873. Bishop Edward Gayer Andrews presided. Members pledged $3,800 and they were so pleased with the service and the future outlook for the congregation that they officially named the church for the bishop. (Photo courtesy of James Bolliger.)

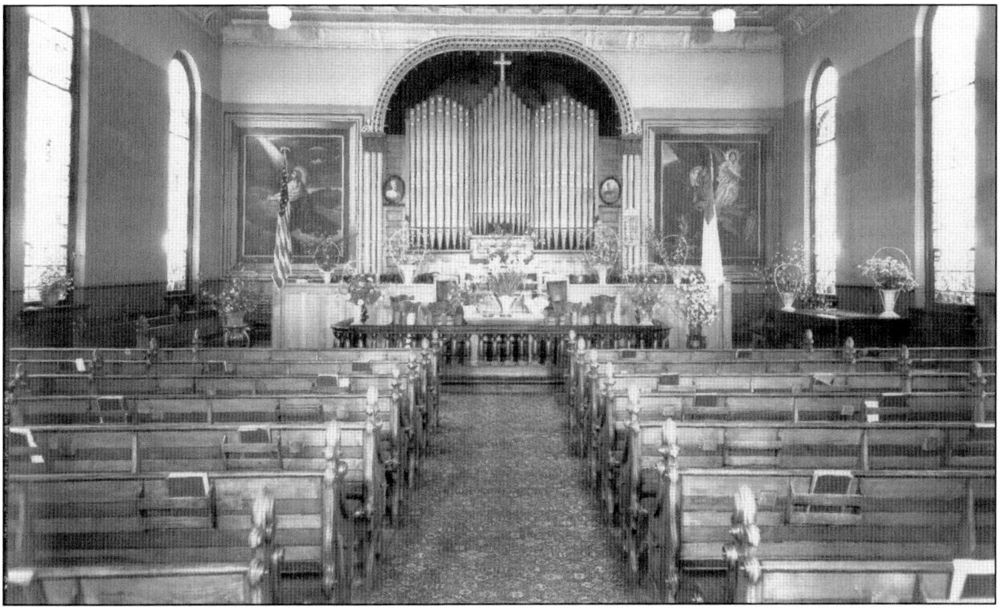

Interior of the Mother's Day Shrine. In 1903, stained-glass windows replaced the original plain glass windows. Several of the windows were donated as memorials. The sanctuary also features large 7.5-by-11.5-foot oil paintings in full color, placed between the windows and on each side of the altar. The artist was George Blaney. The works of art, dating from about 1910, were unveiled as they were completed. In addition to tours, the church is now primarily used for the annual Mother's Day service and weddings.

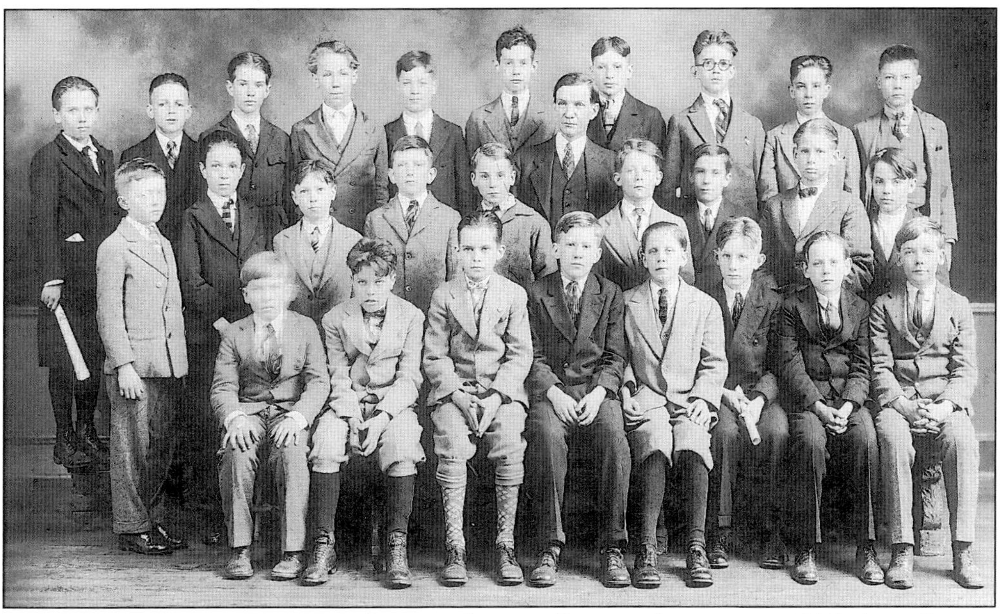

Andrews Methodist Episcopal Church Sunday School Class from 1917. Anna Reeves Jarvis, the first honored mother, and Anna Jarvis, the daughter and founder of Mother's Day, each taught Sunday school at Andrews Church. The mother taught for more than a quarter of a century and was superintendent of the children's department. A Jarvis Memorial Sunday School Class was organized on Sunday, May 7, 1911.

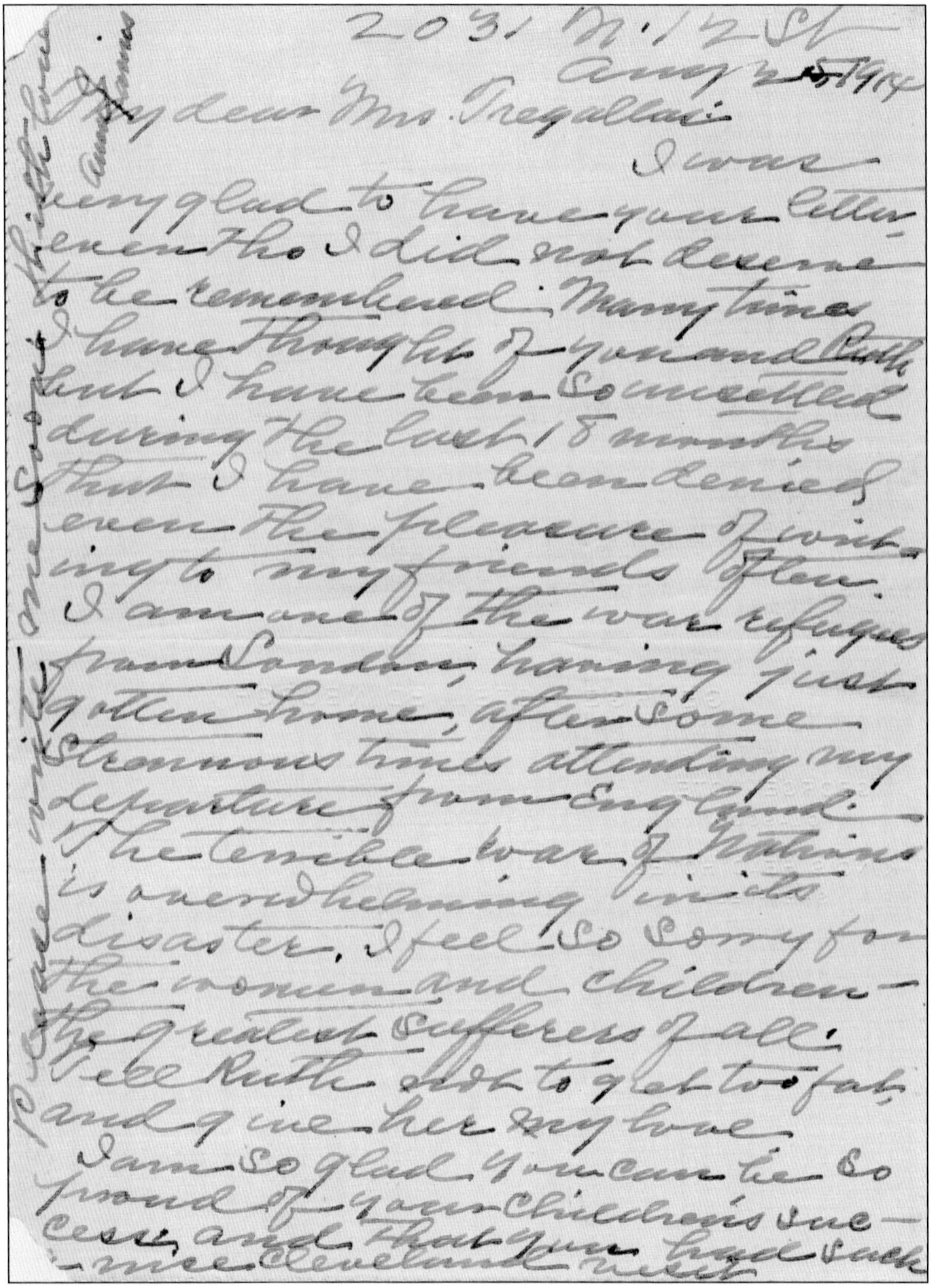

2031 N. 12 St
Aug 25 1914

My dear Mrs. Tregallas:

I was very glad to have your letter even tho I did not deserve to be remembered. Many times I have thought of you and Ruth but I have been so unsettled during the last 18 months that I have been denied even the pleasure of writing to my friends often.

I am one of the war refugees from London, having just gotten home, after some strenuous times attending my departure from England. The terrible war of Nations is overwhelming in its disaster. I feel so sorry for the women and children — the greatest sufferers of all. Tell Ruth not to get too fat, and give her my love.

I am so glad you can be so proud of your children's success, and that you had such a nice Cleveland visit

Please write me soon [illegible]
Anna Jarvis

A Special Letter. Anna Jarvis sent this handwritten letter from Philadelphia, PA, to a Grafton resident. Note her signature in the upper left-hand corner. (Photo courtesy of Peggy Robinson.)

Two

Railroading and Public Transportation

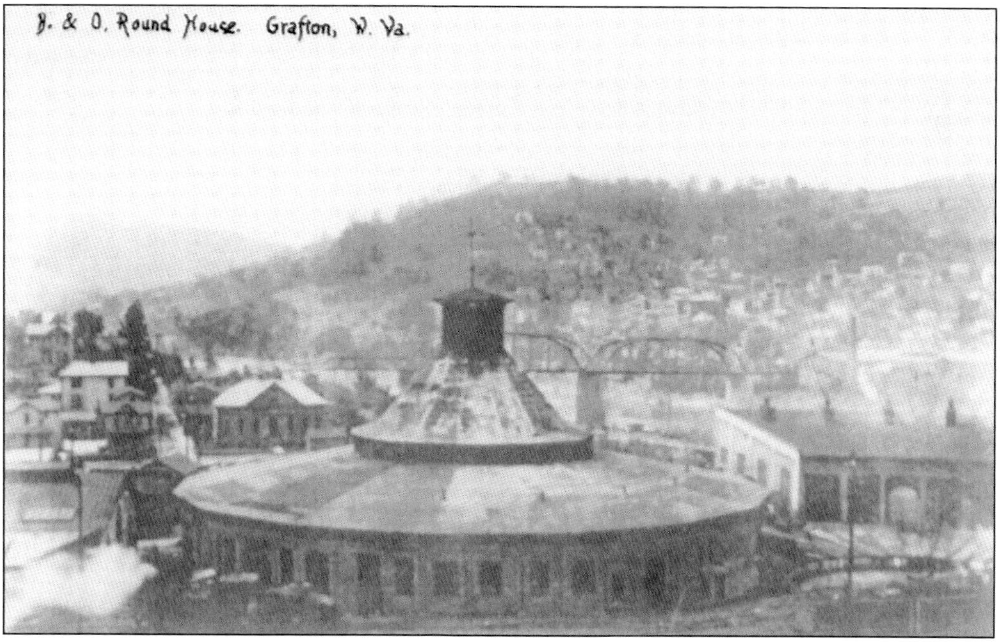

Railroad Heritage. Grafton started its growth as a city after the B&O Railroad arrived. For many years, Grafton was a hub of railroad operations and generations of families found employment working on the railroad. This postcard view of the Grafton rail yards shows both the 1868 roundhouse and a newer half-circle roundhouse that was built in 1910. Also shown is the rail yard turntable. The 1868 brick octagonal roundhouse was built to replace the outdated 1853 half-roundhouse built by the Northwest Virginia Railroad. The 1868 roundhouse was razed in 1911. Additions were made to the half-circle roundhouse in 1919 and in 1930. During the 1930 addition, workers dismantled the old footbridge as it was determined to be unsafe. A new footbridge was constructed and it was attached to the roof of the new roundhouse addition. In 1994, the half-circle roundhouse was demolished and the attached footbridge was dismantled for safety/esthetic reasons. Both roundhouses shown have since been razed. Today, a new rail office building has been constructed in the rail yards. The old turntable remains, and the B&O Station and Willard Hotel are in the early stages of renovation into a rail museum and multi-use facilities. (Photo courtesy of Wayne McDevitt.)

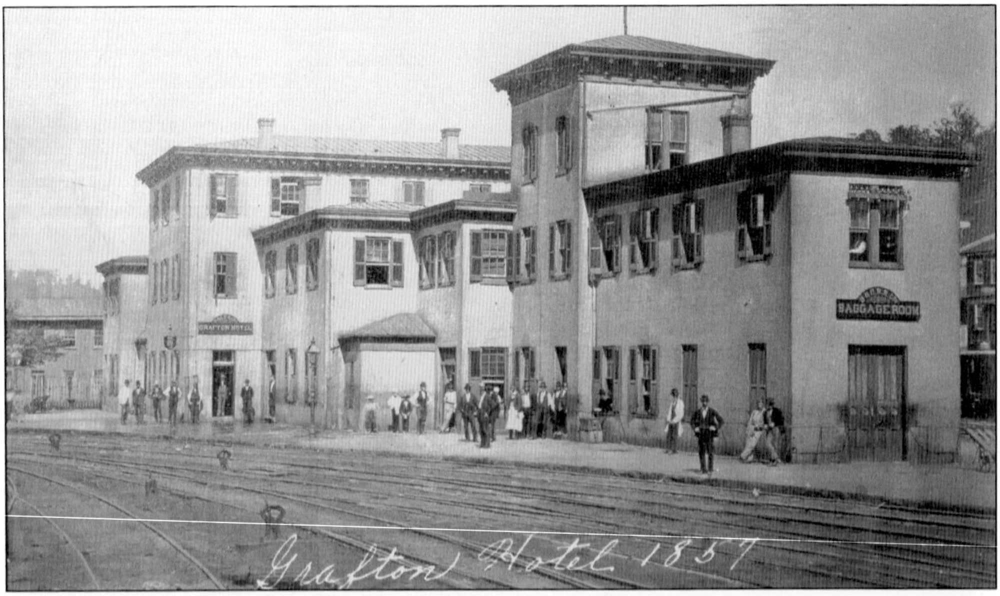

Grafton Hotel, 1857. The B&O Railroad's first hotel for passengers coming through Grafton was located on a triangular plot on the western edge of the Grafton rail yard. A new B&O Station and adjacent hotel were constructed along East Main Street. The passenger station was dedicated on August 11, 1911, and the Willard Hotel officially opened with an elaborate dinner on April 17, 1912. (Photo courtesy of James Bolliger.)

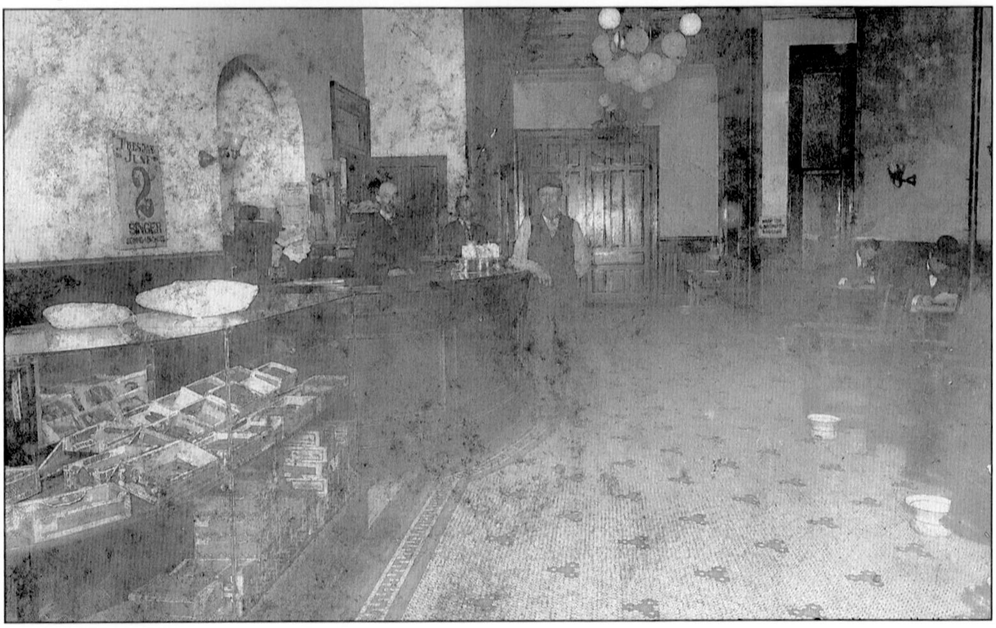

Grand Old Hotel. The first B&O hotel at Grafton was a prominent and imposing structure serving the travel needs of early visitors to Grafton and Taylor County. Built in 1857, it was located between the Wheeling and Parkersburg branches of the rail lines. The lobby area of the hotel also served as the Grafton depot. In the early 1900s, residents could walk across the railroad foot bridge and go down steps to the hotel. During September/October, 1948, the old Grafton Hotel, popularly called "the old beanery," was razed.

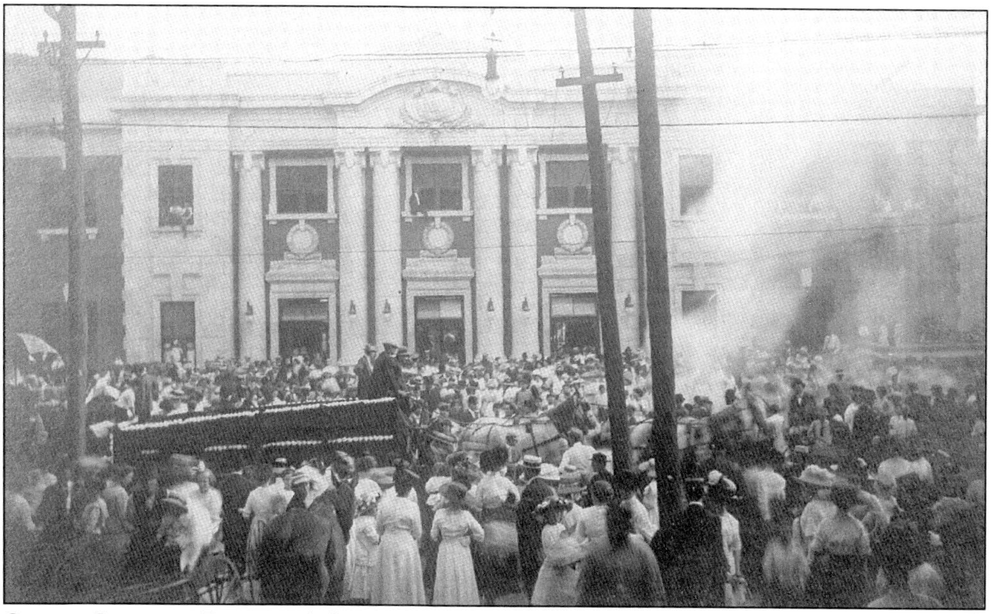

Grand Opening. From its dedication on August 11, 1911, until the mid-1970s, the B&O Station was a hub of activity, not only for the railroad but also for Grafton. At one time, 33 passenger trains a day arrived and departed from the station. Every five minutes, buses departed from the station. The main offices were on the second floor. An elegant passenger lobby area with marble columns housed the ticket office and a news stand. On the platform level was the baggage department, and the railroad postal department. (Photo courtesy of Danny Moore.)

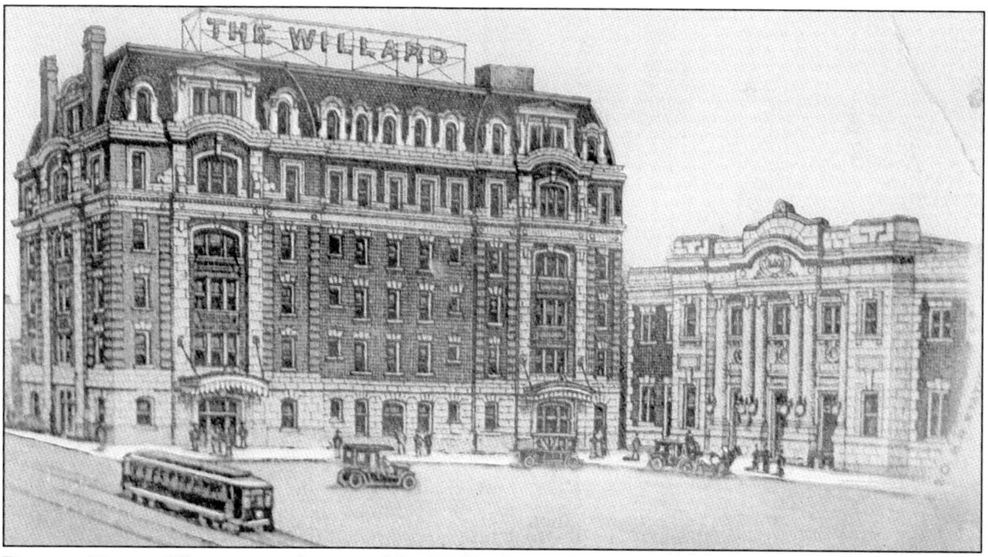

Bygone Years. This postcard view of the Willard Hotel and B&O Station also shows a streetcar traveling along Main Street. The Willard was named for Daniel Willard, president of the B&O Railroad at the time. At the time of its construction, it was one of the most elegant hotels in the state. M.A. Long of Baltimore was the architect, and J.J. Walsh and Sons, also of Baltimore, were the builders of both the hotel and station. The construction cost of the hotel was $75,000. (Photo courtesy of Rick Reese.)

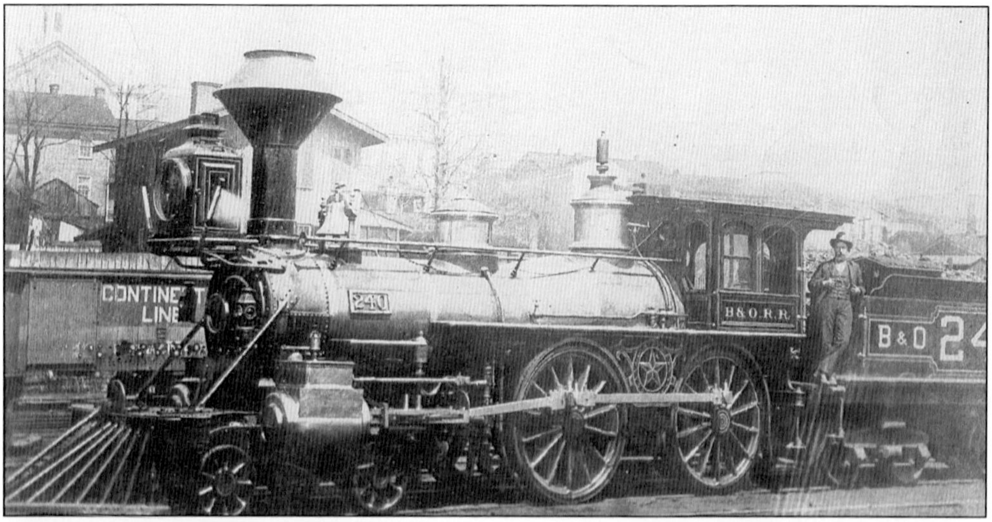

The Iron Horses. While the earliest settlers of present-day Grafton and Taylor County arrived on foot, horseback, or by wagon, real growth came as track was laid and trains began carrying people and goods into the area. Steam trains of various styles and designs served Grafton for many years, before giving way to the diesel engines. This photo has the name John H. Gigley written across it. Thomas McGraw, who came with the first construction train of the B&O, opened a store on Railroad Street on May 1, 1852. (Photo courtesy of James Bolliger.)

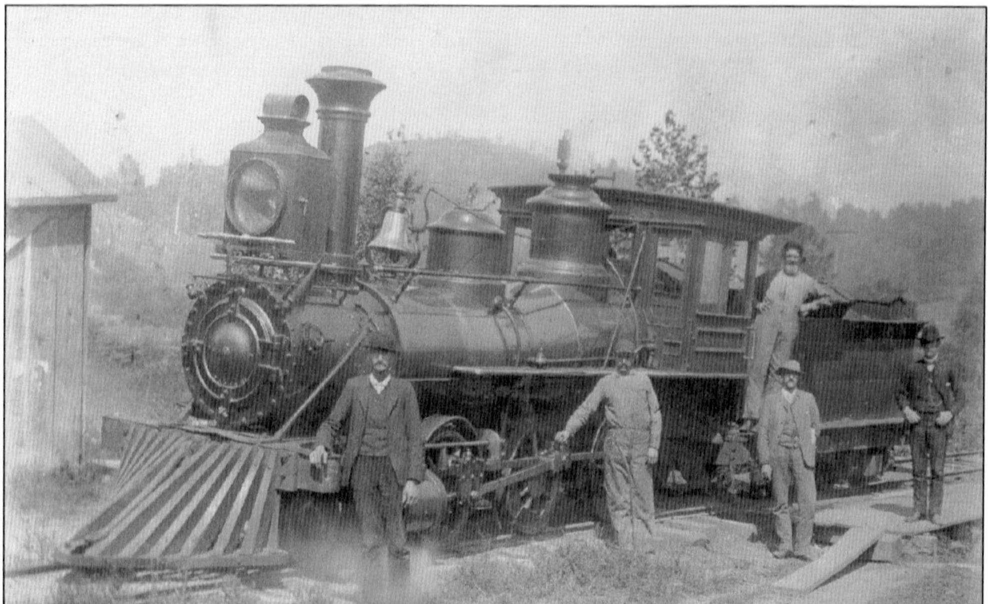

The G&G Railroad. The Grafton and Greenbrier Railroad was organized in 1882. Its tracks, originally narrow-gauged until taken over by the B&O, ran along the Tygart River from Grafton to Belington. Original plans were for the line to go all the way to Greenbrier, but it was never finished beyond Belington. Part of this rail line was relocated for construction of the Tygart Dam. In this photo, the man at the front of the train is not identified. The other four men are Bernard Wilmoth, Jake Blocker, Billy Graham, and Jas Flanagan. (Photo courtesy of James Bolliger.)

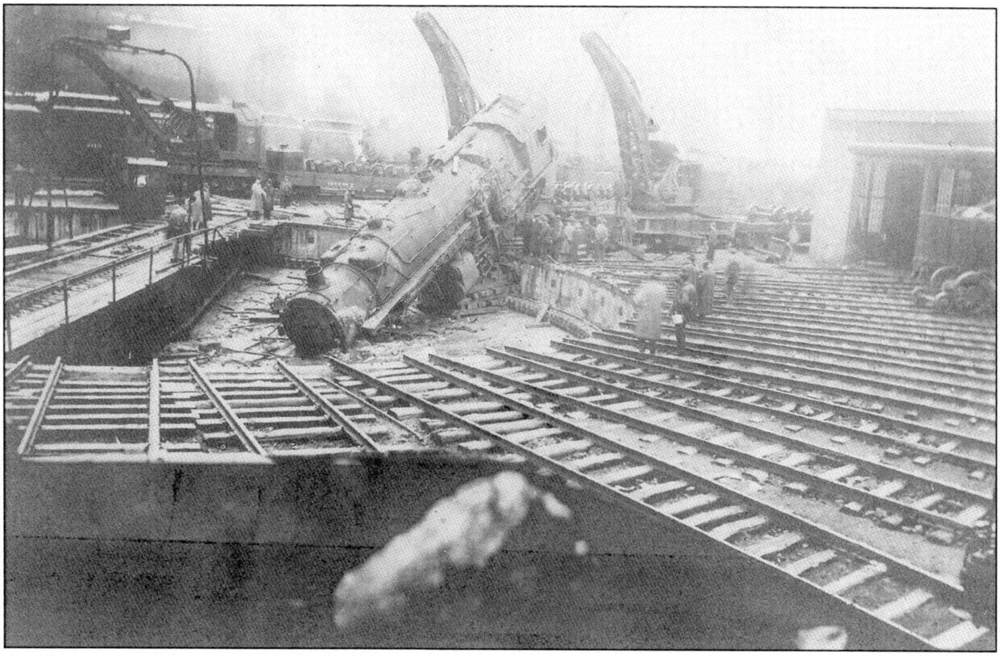

AN UNUSUAL WRECK. While the Grafton rail yards have seen their share of train wrecks over the years, it was unusual to see this: an engine in the pit of the turntable, having apparently failed to stop in time. A large number of workers are shown as two rail cranes have been brought in to begin the task of getting the damaged engine back up out of the pit and onto the tracks. The turntable is one of the last early rail items that remains in the Grafton rail yard. (Photo courtesy of Rick Reese.)

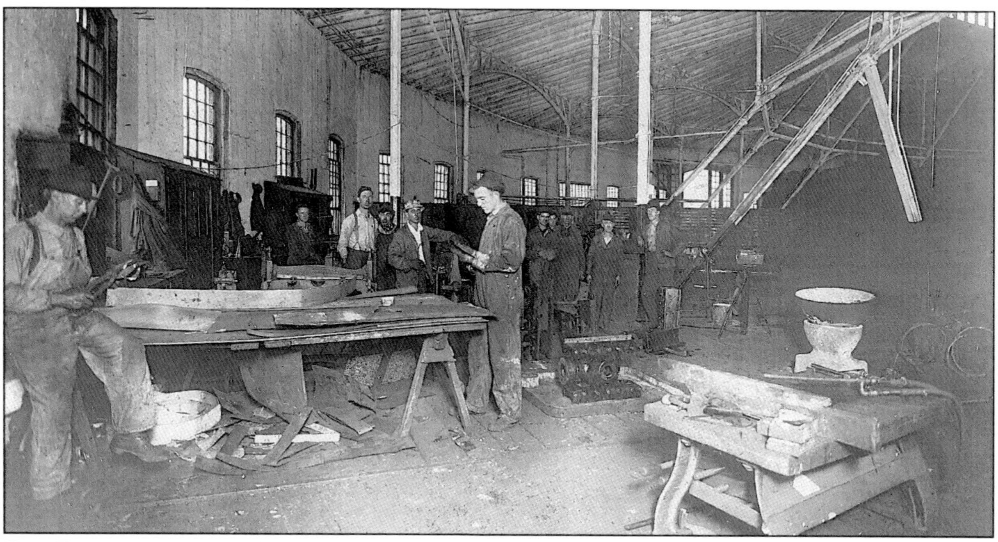

THE RAILROAD SHOP. This crew of railroad workers is shown in the pipe shop located in the former B&O Roundhouse that was a landmark of the Grafton B&O rail yards for many years. Only the turntable of the old roundhouse remains today. In its earliest years, the railroad had some facilities at Fetterman. However, as expansion needs arose, the railroad found the asking price too high for additional acreage, and a decision was made to build at what is now Grafton, as better-priced acreage could be obtained.

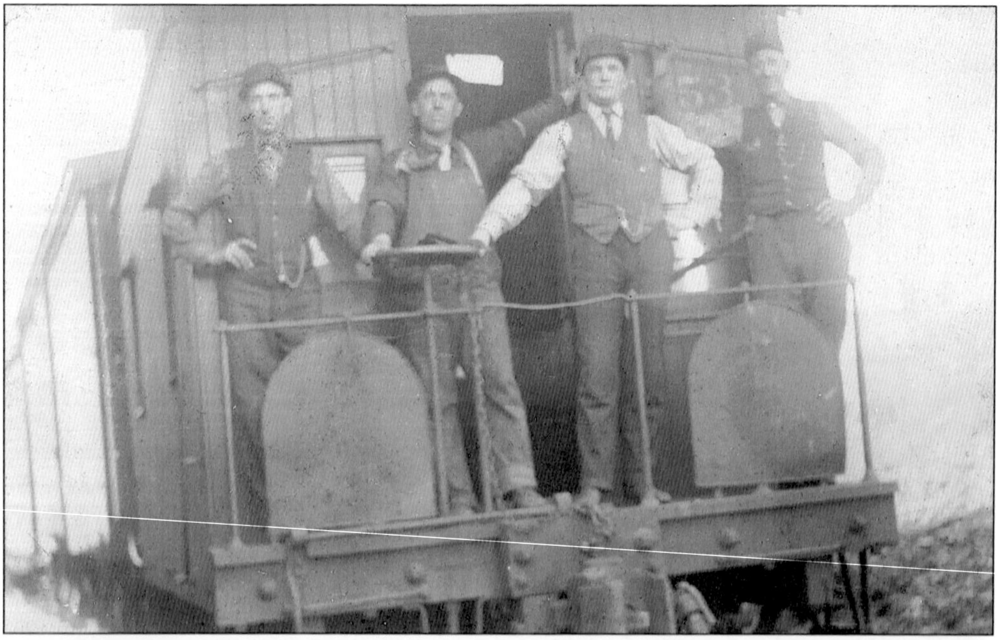

An Old Caboose. Time changes many things and such was the case with the once familiar caboose that was usually the last car on any train passing through. Trains today operate without cabooses. Shown above are Harter Robinson, Charles Putnam, Bernard Hoffman, and J. Malone. An old caboose has been placed on a vacant Main Street lot, across the street from First Community Bank and the Taylor County Courthouse. The lot is now known as Heritage Park. The caboose is ADA accessible and open for tours. (Photo courtesy of Peggy Robinson.)

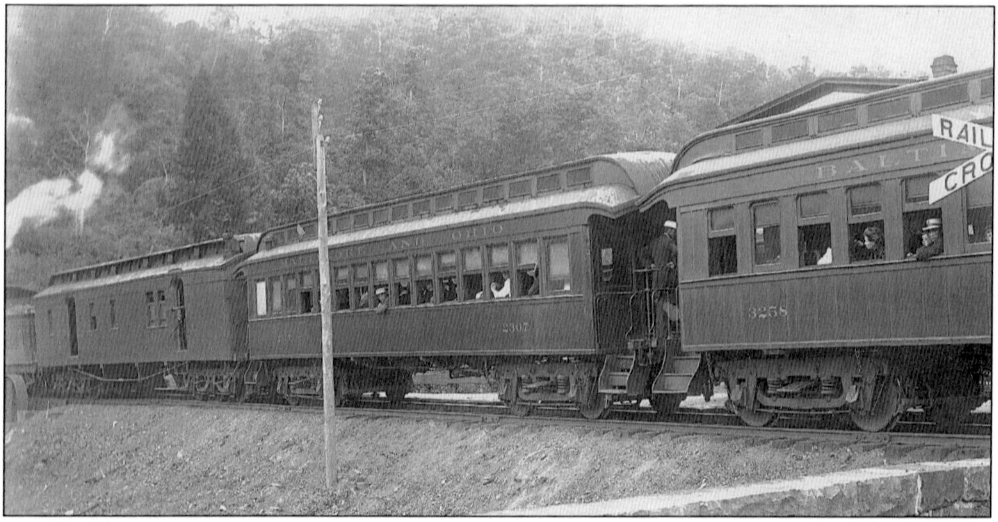

Rail Passenger Service. For many years, railroad passenger service was the most modern form of transportation. Residents of Baltimore, MD, frequently took the train to Grafton, staying in one of our early hotels and dining in Latrobe Street restaurants. This train ran between Grafton and Belington and service was discontinued on August 5, 1937, as construction was starting on the Tygart Dam. The B&O Railroad ended passenger service on May 1, 1971, when Engine No. 12 made a final run out of Grafton. (Photo courtesy of Peggy Robinson.)

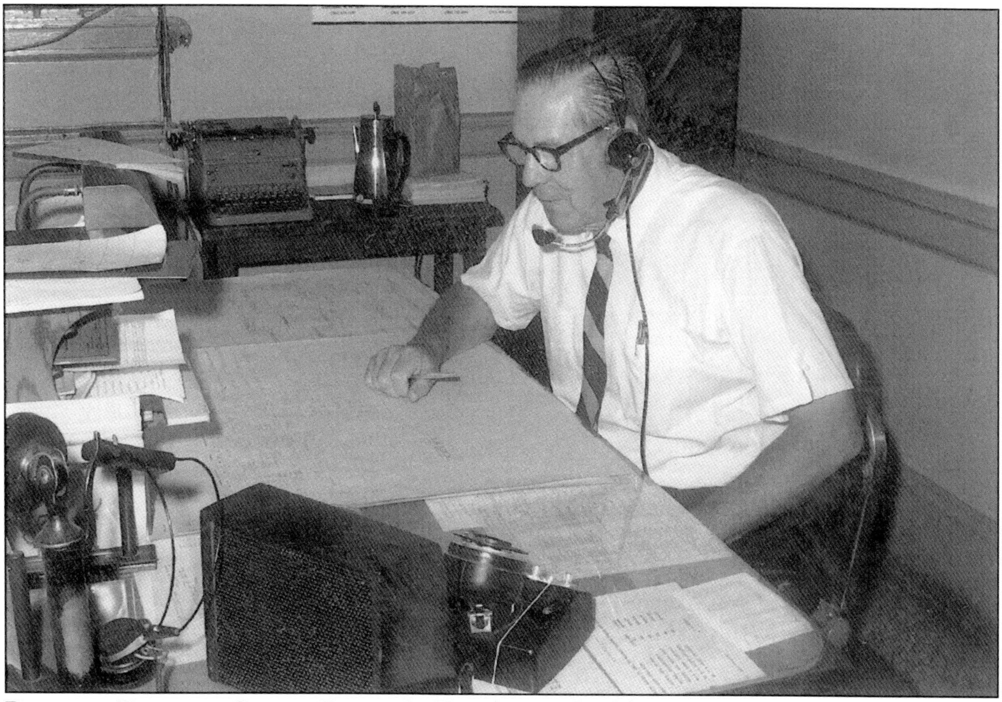

Railroad Dispatch Office. George A. Shingleton, chief dispatcher, works in the dispatcher's office at the B&O Station in the late 1950s. By the mid-1970s, the B&O had ended passenger train service through this area. In November 1976, Amtrack started an experimental two-year program of passenger service from Washington, D.C. to Cincinnati on the "Shenandoah," which went through Grafton. This effort was not successful. A second unsuccessful effort by the Shenandoah ended in 1981. (Photo courtesy of Peggy Robinson.)

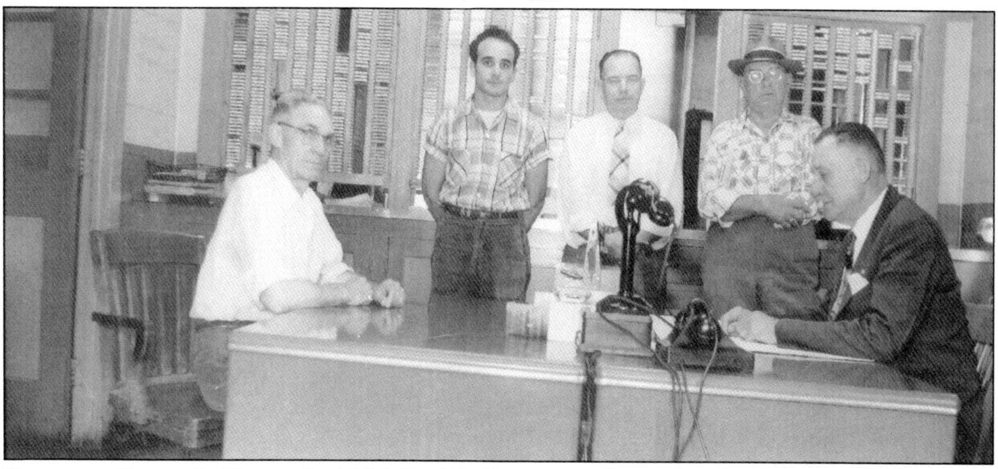

Railroad Caller's Office. In 1956, Fred E. Sapp, crew dispatcher for 51 years with the B&O Railroad, retired. From left to right are the following: (seated) field caller Carl Stutler, and Sapp; (standing) field caller Tony Cassella, W.E. (Billy) Boyles (Sapp's successor), and retired field caller Robert Rennie. The office was in the B&O Station. The duty of the callers was to call train crews to come to work as they were needed to staff various trains that arrived in the Grafton yards and were being prepared for departure to other destinations. (Photo courtesy of Wayne McDevitt.)

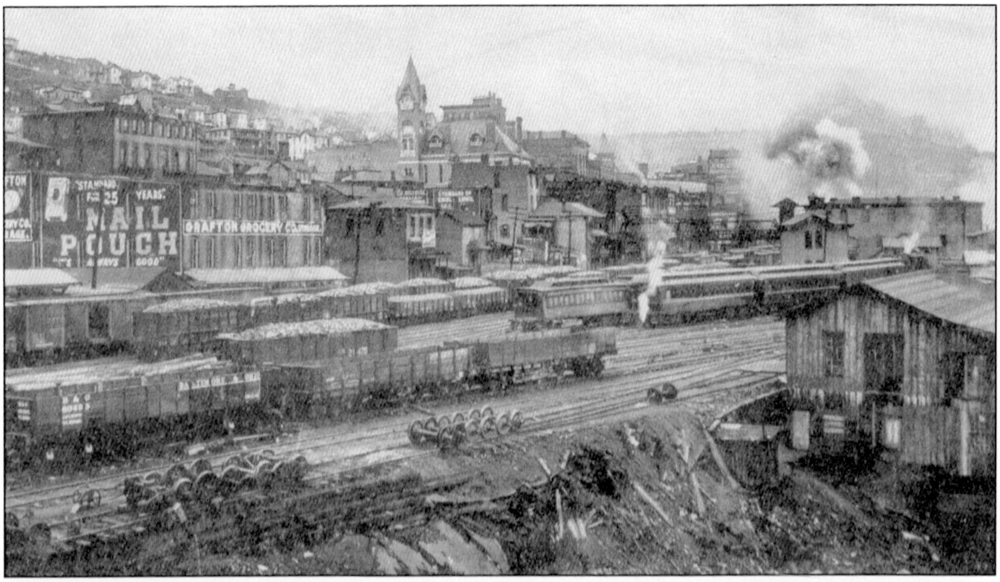

Grafton and Its Rail Heritage. This postcard view of Grafton would have been a typical view for many years to travelers who were arriving in Grafton by rail. Today the scene has changed as many of the old rail yard structures are gone. Some of the Latrobe Street buildings have been razed. Some were taken down after they were destroyed by fire. The tower roof of the county courthouse has been removed and the adjacent Jarrett building was razed to make room for a courthouse annex. (Photo courtesy of Peggy Robinson.)

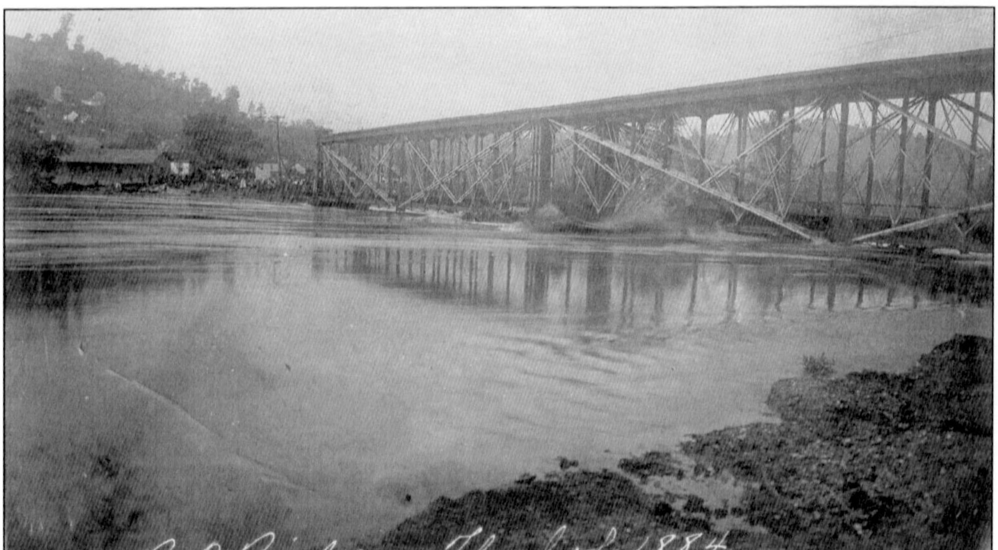

Early Flooding. The B&O Bridge across the Tygart River was damaged in the flood of 1884. Grafton has been protected from major flooding since construction of the Tygart Dam began in January 1935. Early histories record major floods on the Tygart River in 1832, 1884, 1888, and 1912. The flood of 1888 was particularly bad as the raging waters lifted the historic covered bridge at Fetterman from its piers and carried it away. Heavily loaded freight cars were pushed over the length of the B&O bridge to try and hold it in place. (Photo courtesy of James Bolliger.)

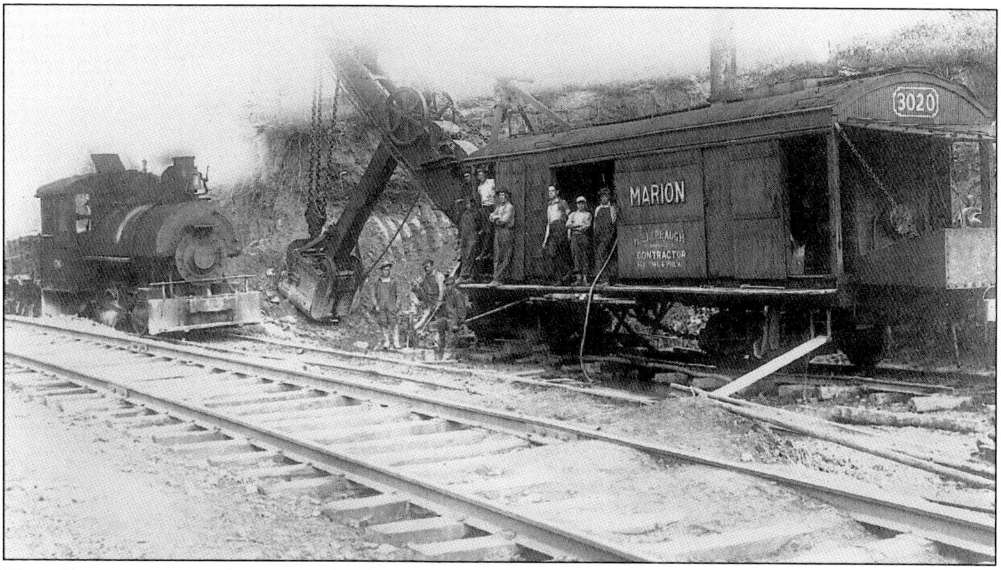

The Railroad at Simpson. Railroad workers labor on the rail tracks near the Simpson community. Simpson is located 9 miles southwest of Grafton and it is one of the oldest towns dating from when the area was part of the western section of early Virginia. Early Simpson had a bakery, operated by Harry and Dorsey Phillips; and a blacksmith shop, operated by Philip "Flip" Constable. Lee Davis ran a boardinghouse and Mini Davis operated a hotel. Both were needed as many of the early miners came here from other areas. (Photo courtesy of Geneva Phelps.)

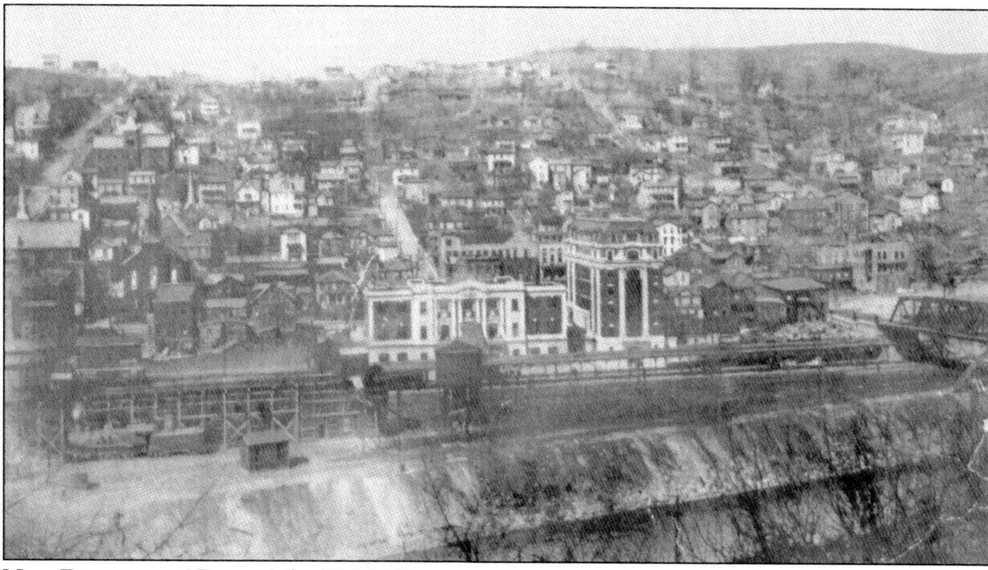

New Depot and Hotel. John T. McGraw was instrumental in getting the new B&O Passenger Station in Grafton in the early 1900s. He offered to provide the land for the station, and to build a modern hotel next to it, if the B&O would agree to build the station. With the assistance of George Whitescarver of Grafton, the deal was completed with the B&O. Today, both structures have been purchased by the Vandalia Foundation and Vandalia Redevelopment Corporation. The lobby of the station is to become a railroad museum. (Photo courtesy of Wayne McDevitt.)

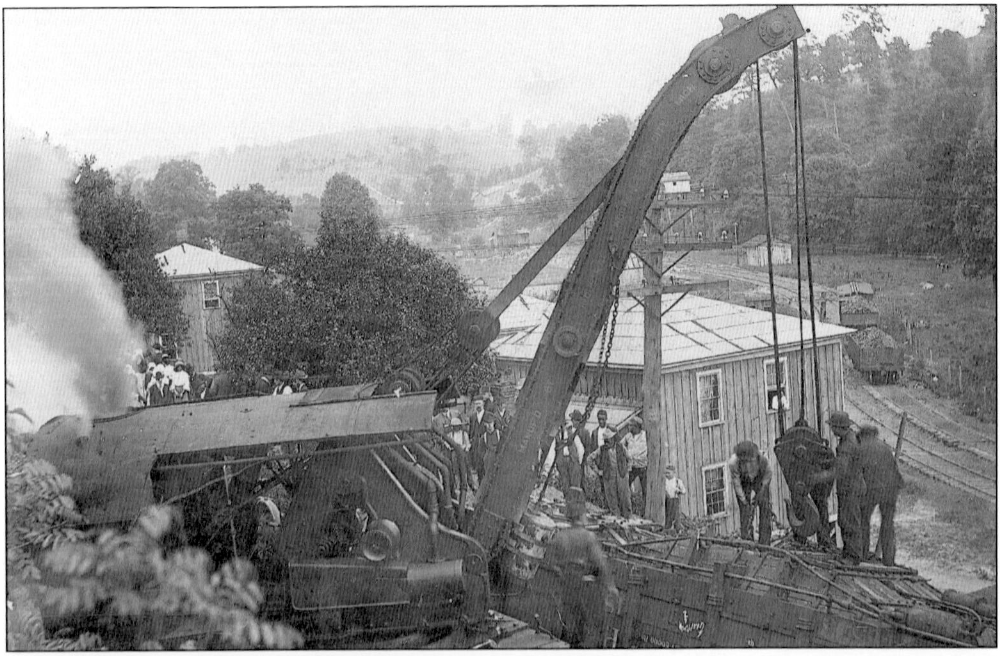

Train Wreck at Simpson. Tom Wyckoff, photographer, had a business in Simpson. Several of his photographs survive, including ones of a railroad wreck that occurred near the home of the late E. Lodge Ross. The above photo is of another train wreck at Simpson. Farming and the mining of coal were the chief means of employment in early Simpson. The New York Coal Company established the first coal mine in the area. This mine was opened and readied for operation by William Drainer, formerly of Doddridge County.

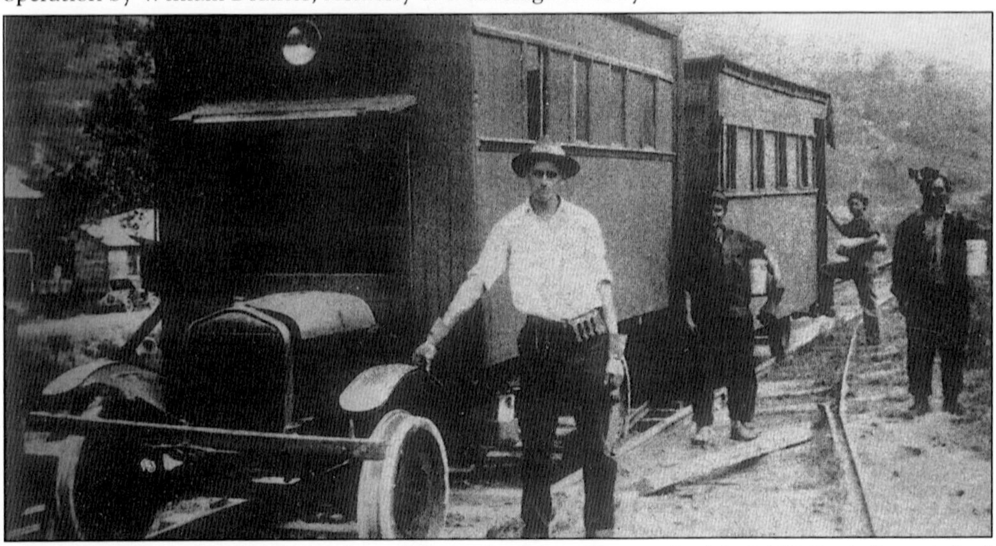

The Flemington Jitney. Constructed from the front chassis of a Model T Ford, Jitney's had wheels that fit the rail tracks and coaches with seats for passengers and space for standing. The front of the Jitney was used to haul mail, baggage, and freight. The Jitney was gasoline powered. From left to right are conductor Leslie "Ick" Haddix of Philippi, "Shorty" Perk of Belington, and Oris Cleavenger of Brownton. The name of the paperboy at the back of the Jitney is not known. The photo was taken in 1924. (Photo courtesy of Geneva Phelps.)

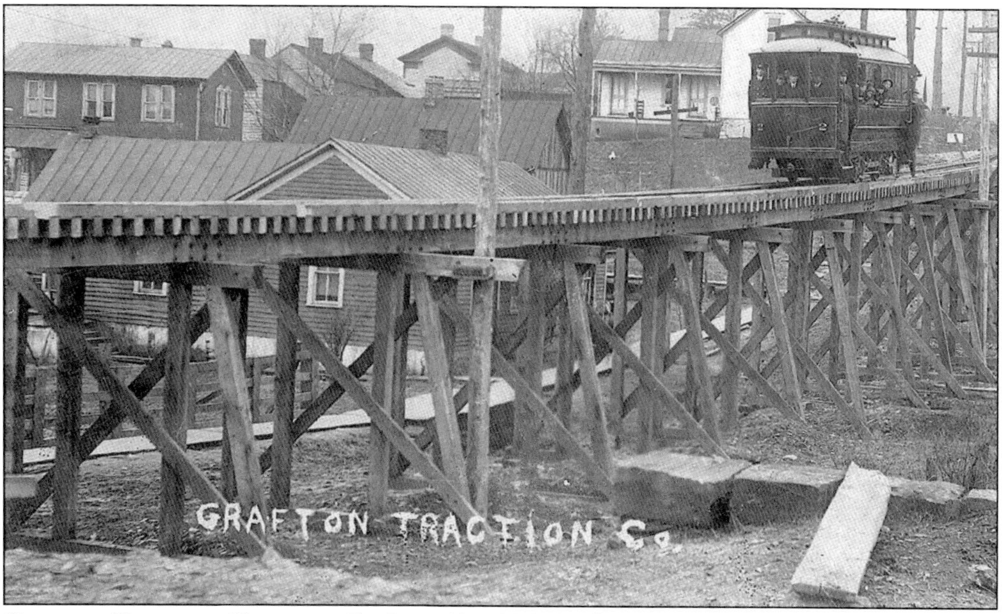

GRAFTON TRACTION COMPANY. On June 18, 1906, Grafton City Council passed an ordinance granting the "City Traction Company" the right to construct a streetcar system within the city. In a few years, the name of the company was changed to the Grafton Traction Company. The streetcars operated for many years and are a familiar sight in postcard scenes of the city from this time period. In the early 1900s, a city with a streetcar line was considered to be a truly progressive city. The system had switches and passing points. (Both photos courtesy of Peggy Robinson.)

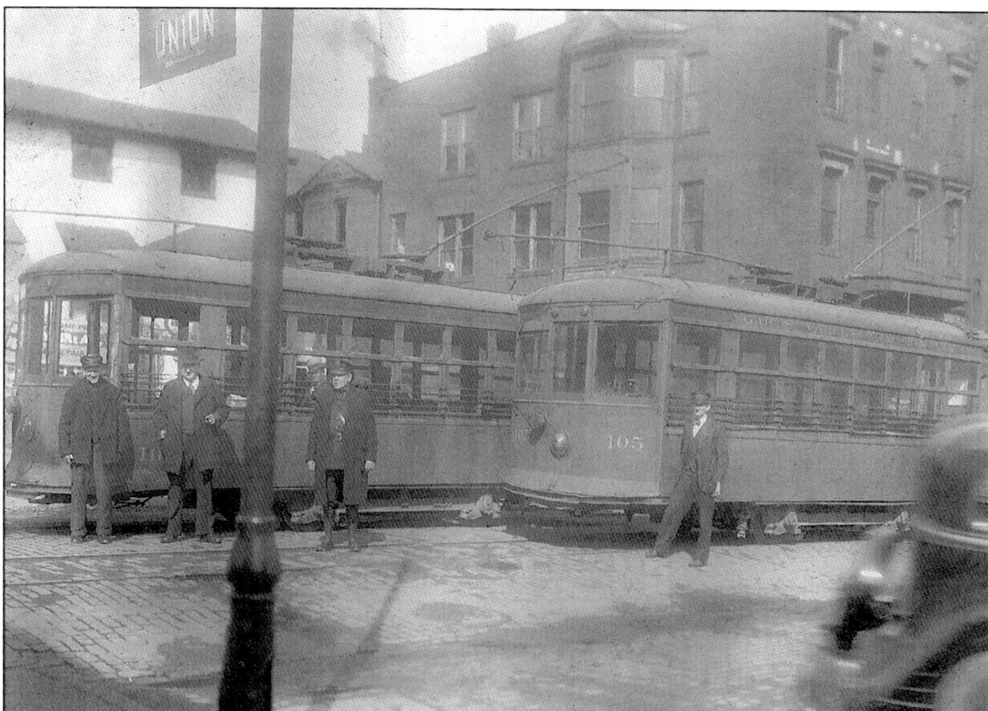

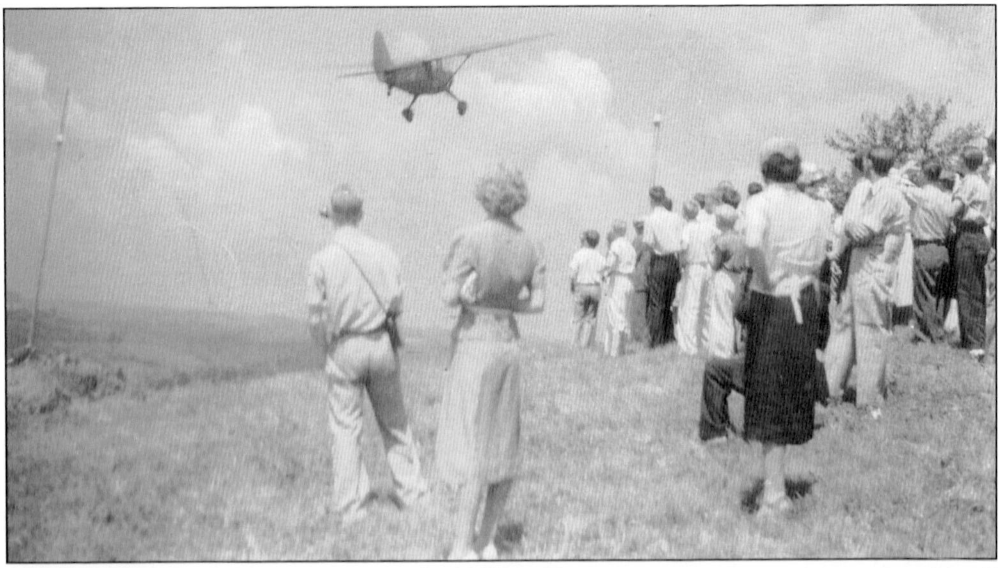

AIR MAIL SERVICE. Grafton was among the 20 West Virginia communities to inaugurate air mail service in 1939. All American Aviation of Pittsburgh flew a pick-up route that was authorized by Congress. The first official flight was June 25, 1939, and Grafton offered an official first day cover designed for stamp collectors. Air mail service ended in 1949. The pick-up and drop-off point was first at Bluemont Cemetery, but the location was later changed. This Harold Fawcett photo is courtesy of the Bluemont Cemetery Historical Collection.

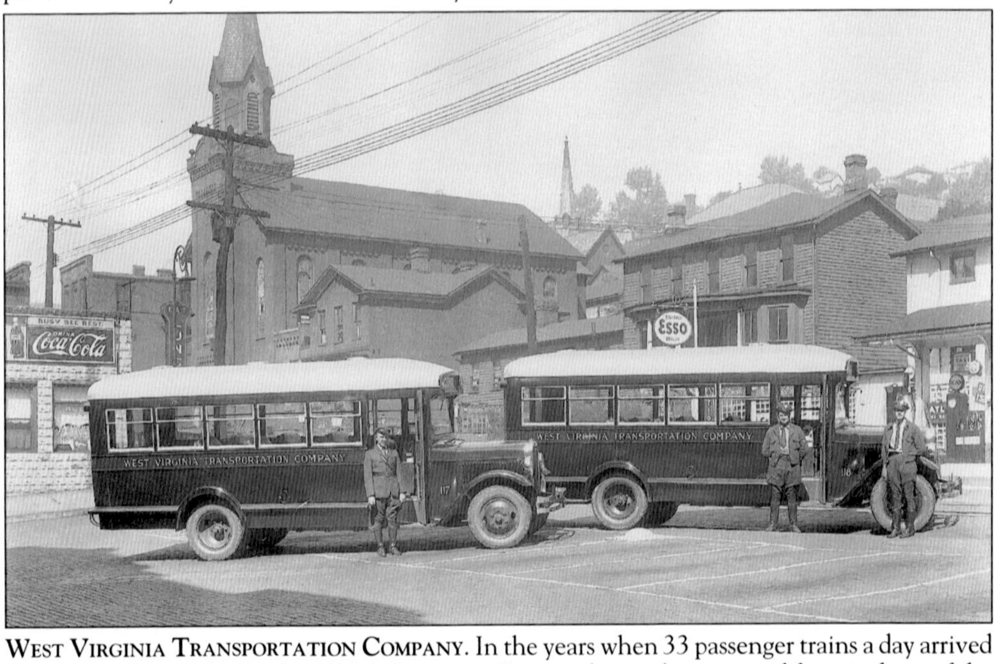

WEST VIRGINIA TRANSPORTATION COMPANY. In the years when 33 passenger trains a day arrived and departed from the Grafton B&O Passenger Station, buses also operated from in front of the station arriving and departing on a schedule complimentary to the schedule of the trains. Also note the Coca-Cola sign on the former Busy Bee Restaurant and the Esso sign of the service station across the street. All of the buildings on each side of the Mother's Day Shrine block were razed to provide space for the garden plazas of the Shrine.

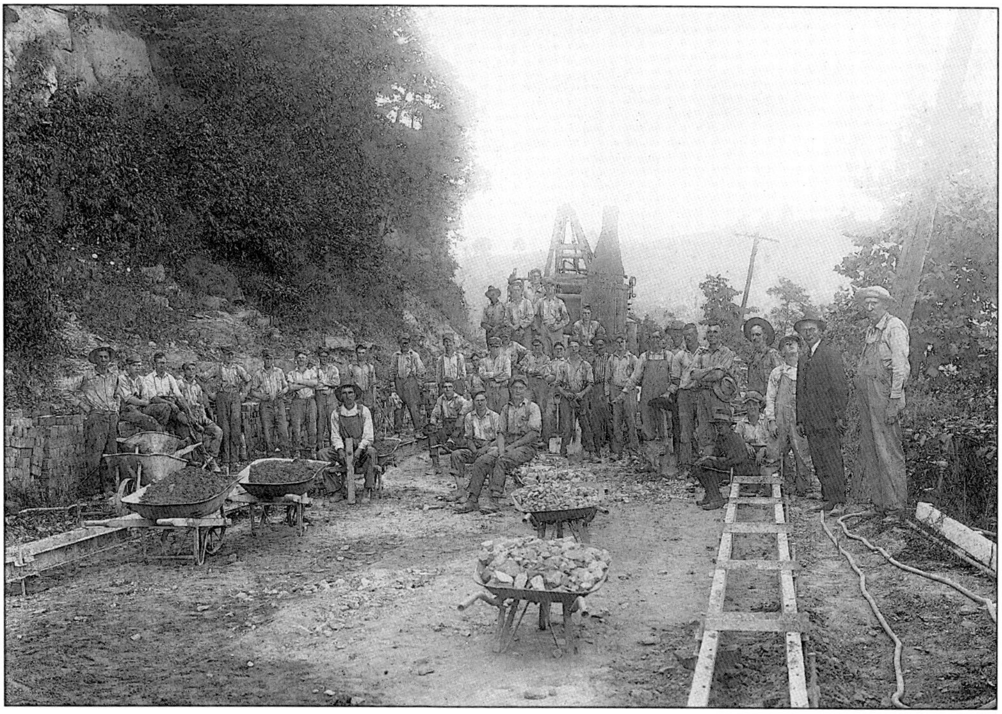

First Brick Highway. On November 25, 1919, the first brick highway between two towns in the nation was opened between Grafton and Pruntytown. It was a fine Thanksgiving Day, and many locals drove their automobiles out to try out the new road. It was built on a section of the old Northwestern Turnpike. Brinkman's History states that the county court had the road built using local labor with an engineer in charge of the work. The section to Pruntytown was completed in 1919 and in 1920 it was completed to the forks of the Clarksburg/Fairmont Pike.

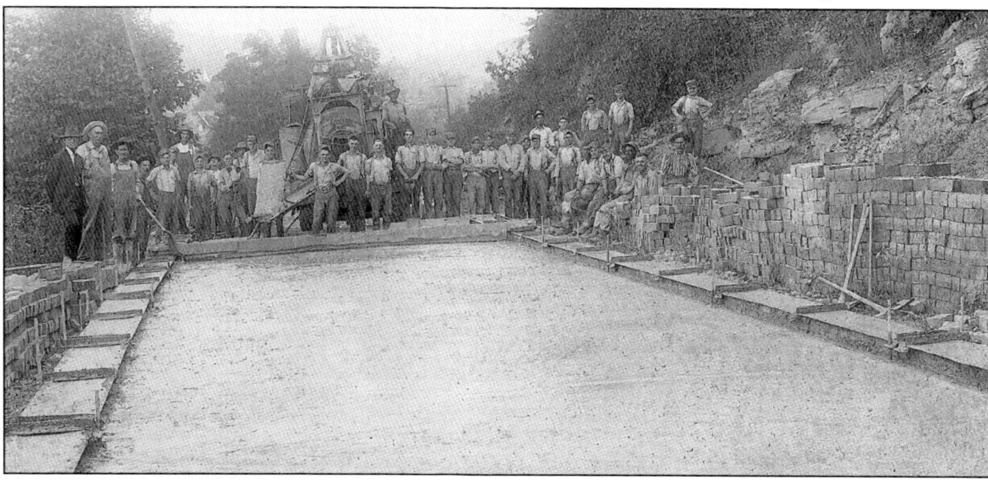

Building of U.S. Route 50. In 1919, the Taylor County Court solicited bids for completion of the brick surfacing of the Pike from Fetterman Bridge to Pruntytown. The Brinkman history states that the lowest bid to be received was $61,000. Even with a $3,000 allowance for machinery, the low bid was still at $58,000, well above the $30,000 the County Court had decided was sufficient to cover the project. In response to the high bids, the County Court rejected all the bids and opted to use local labor, instead of using a contractor.

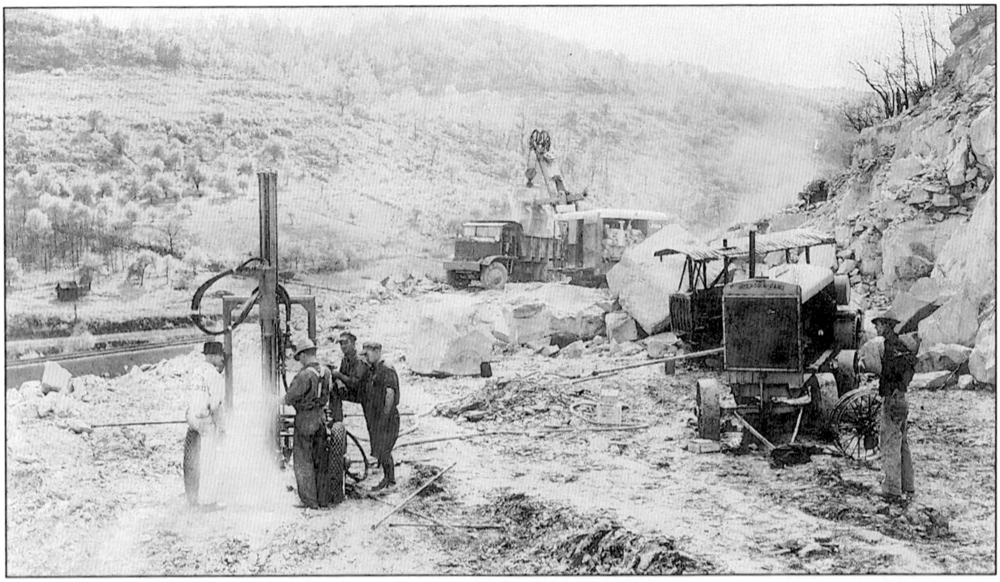

Rerouting of Route 50. Work to reroute U.S. Route 50, between Grafton and Thornton, included this section that became known as the Ivandale Straight. The original section of the highway remains in use and is known as Old Route 50. This is near a former railroad stop named Lesmalinston. Named by Dr. Ernest L. Love, the name comes from parts of his mother's maiden name, Mary Malinda Latham, combined with parts of the druggist's middle name of Livingston. (Photo courtesy of Mary Susan Shafferman.)

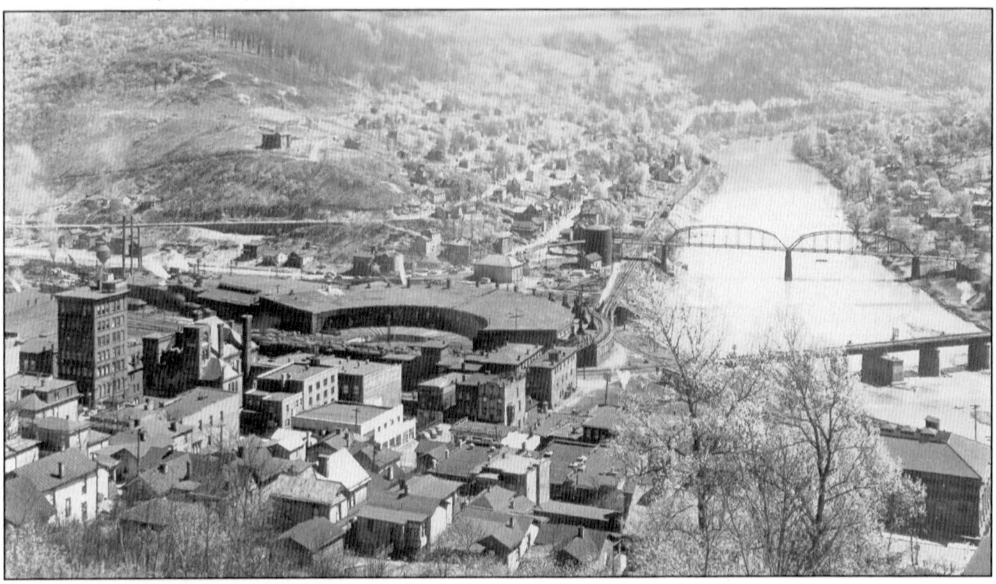

The Southside Bridge. At one time this was known as the "singing bridge" for the sound created by automobile tires moving across the open-mesh steel grating that covered the deck area of the bridge. In 1985, the bridge was replaced by a concrete structure. Since the rail lines along the east side of the Tygart River had been relocated with the construction of the Tygart Dam, the level of the new bridge was lowered on that side as there no longer was a need for the bridge to be high enough to allow trains to pass underneath. (Photo courtesy of Peggy Robinson.)

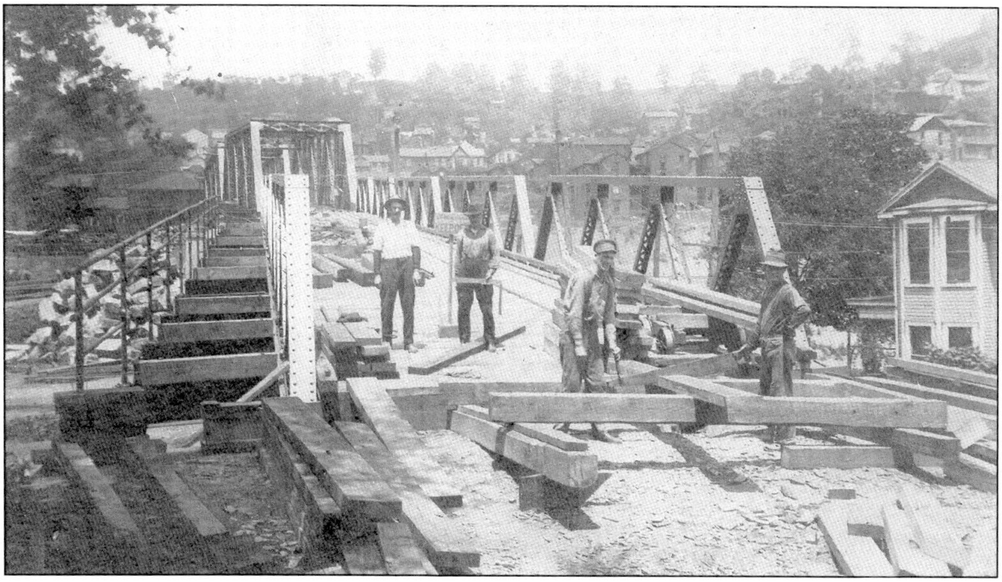

The Bridge Street Bridge. Carrying traffic from East Main to Barrett Street, the Bridge Street Bridge crosses the railroad tracks at the eastern edge of the main Grafton yards. The bridge remains a popular spot for railroad buffs to view and to photograph rail traffic moving through the Grafton yards. The bridge is near the East Main Street traffic signal and intersection that defines one end of the historic downtown business district. It is near the B&O Passenger Station and is one of the main routes to Tygart Lake State Park. (Photo courtesy of Norma Wyckoff.)

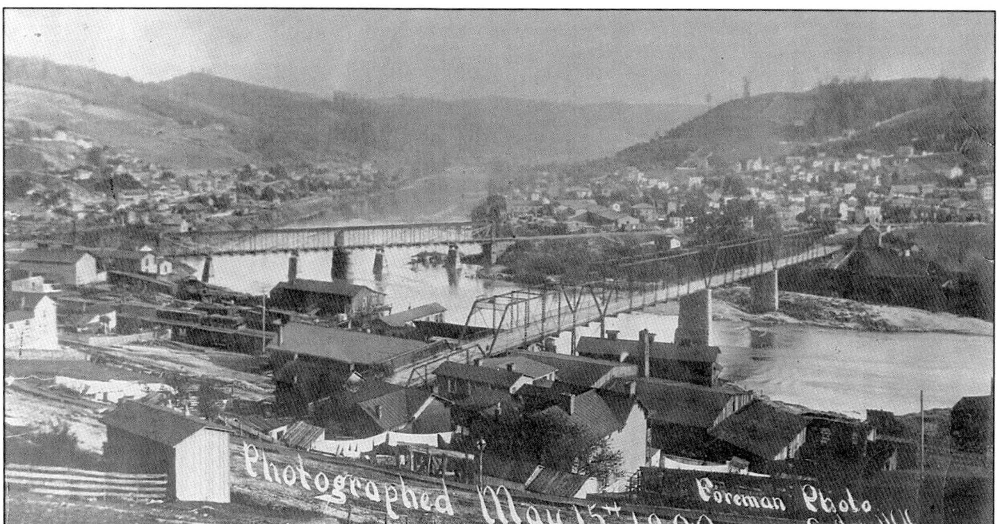

The St. Mary's Bridge. The first bridge between Grafton and West Grafton was built in 1889. Prior to this, people, horses, and wagons had to cross through the river. In the background is the B&O Railroad Bridge. One of the oldest remaining structures in the Grafton rail yards, a former freight station is located beside this bridge on the Grafton end, just across Latrobe Street from the Grafton Post Office. Across the bridge from the freight station is a large warehouse structure that is known as the Speidel/Musgrove Wholesale Grocery. (Photo courtesy of James Bolliger.)

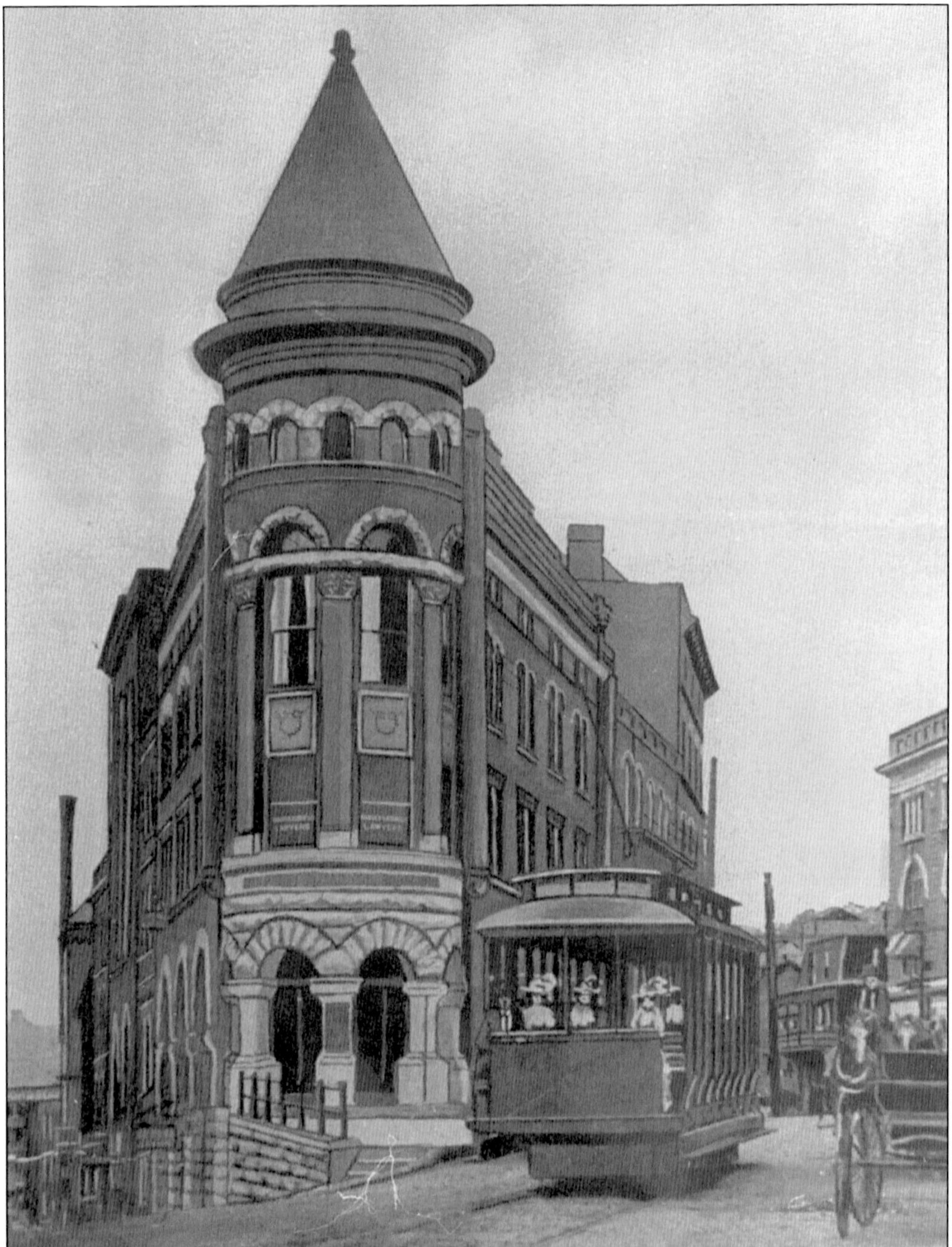

The Grafton Bank. Originally chartered in October 1873, it became the First National Bank of Grafton on December 29, 1879. It was housed in this landmark building, at the corner of Main and Latrobe Streets, from 1896 until 1966, when the building was razed and a new building constructed. The bank was listed in 1910 as #77 on an honor roll of 8,000 banks in the U.S. The new bank placed its offices below street level and the street level became parking. The First National Bank became First Community Bank on November 1, 1988. (Photo courtesy of Peggy Robinson.)

Three

Memorial Day and Military

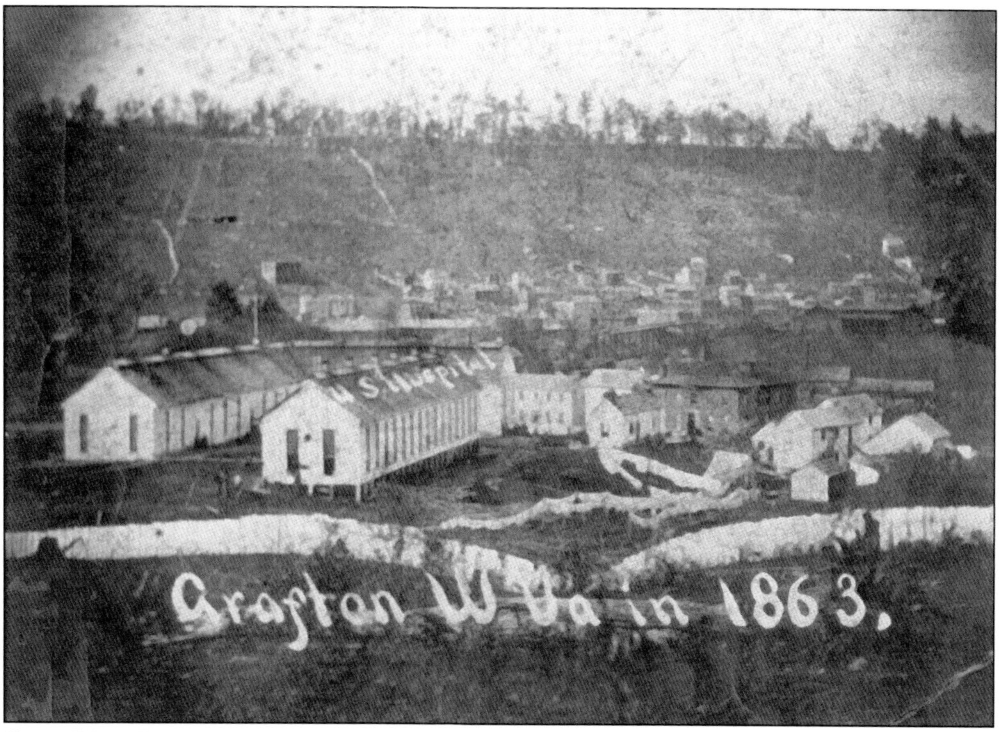

Civil War Federal Hospital. According to the Brinkman history, in April of 1862 the federal government purchased land at the northwest corner of Beech and Walnut Streets in West Grafton and had a hospital built on the site. The purpose of the new facility was to care for casualties from the Civil War. Surgeon General R.W. Haslet was placed in charge of the hospital. The government constructed a brick mansion on the opposite corner of the block from the hospital as a residence for the director, his assistants, and the staff of nurses. Brinkman says that, upon completion of the hospital, trains and Army wagons arrived daily, carrying the wounded from the war. The injured were treated and admitted to the hospital. There was a morgue along Beech Street where those who died were taken. The bodies were then taken up Maple Avenue for burial. (Photo courtesy of James Bolliger.)

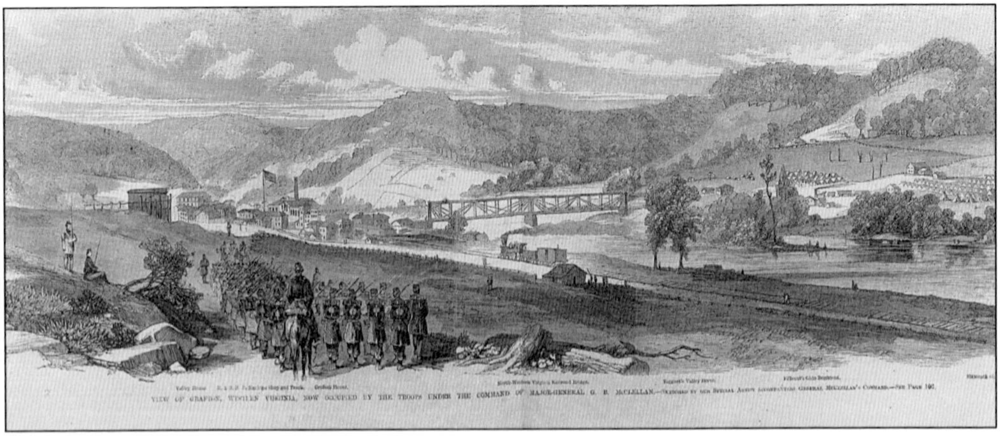

View of Grafton. While the B&O rail yards of Grafton were considered a key strategic holding of the Civil War period, no real battles occurred in Taylor County. Grafton and Taylor County sent delegates to the May 13, 1861 Wheeling convention that was debating a move by the western section of Virginia to reorganize the state government of Virginia after the official government had succeeded from the Union. Both Union and Confederate forces sought to mobilize the area. (Photo courtesy of Peggy Robinson.)

A Patriotic Envelope, Postmarked July 1861, Grafton, VA. "Liberty and Union Now and Forever" is proclaimed on this envelope that was typical of patriotic envelopes circulated during the Civil War years. These patriotic envelopes were very popular among those who wanted to show their support for the Union cause. The cancellation date isn't real clear, but is believed to read "Cancelled at Grafton, VA., July 1861?," which was prior to West Virginia gaining statehood. Collectors still count such envelopes as a prize find. (Photo courtesy of Wayne McDevitt.)

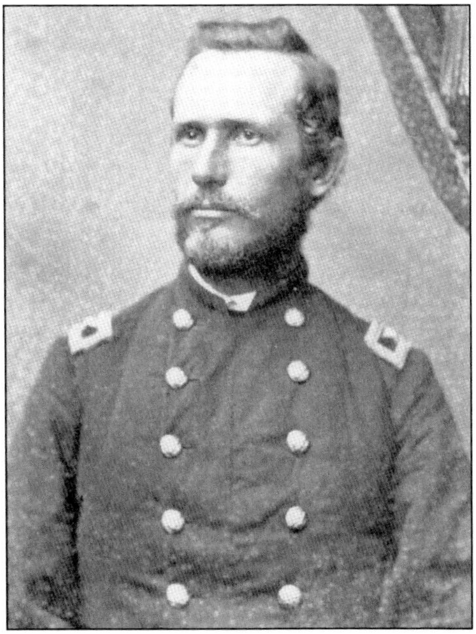

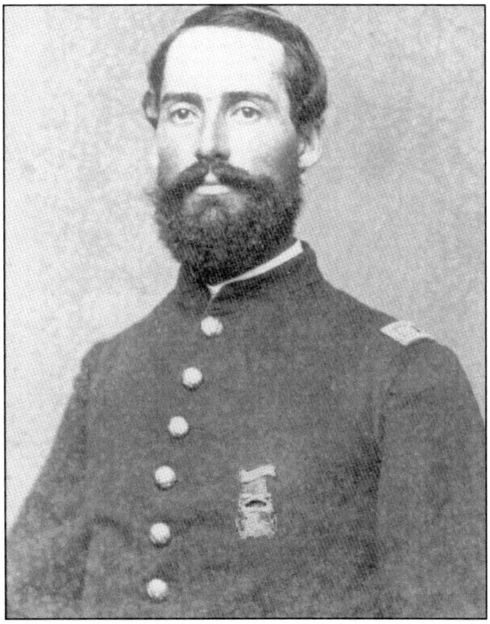

LEFT: COL. GEORGE R. LATHAM (US). He organized the "Grafton Guards" in 1861, which later became Co. B, 2nd VA Infantry. He left the service as a brevet brigadier general.
RIGHT: FIRST LT. FABRICIUS A. CATHER (US). A member of Co. B, 2nd VA Infantry, he resided at Flemington, VA.

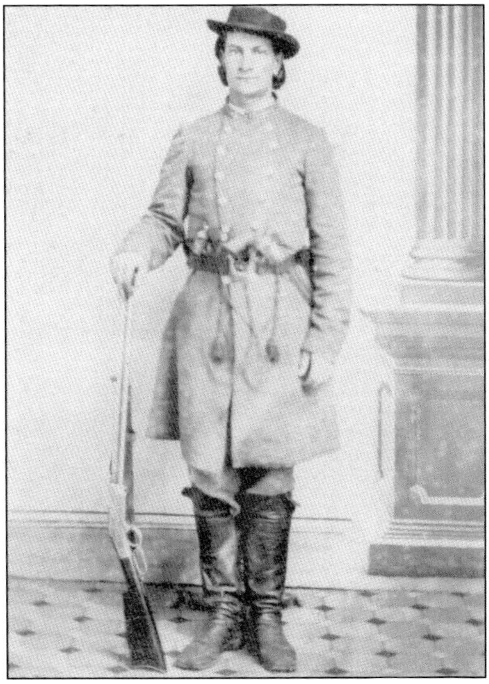

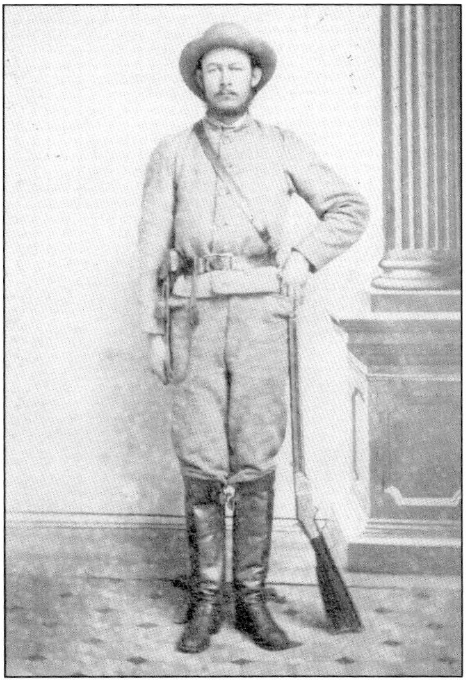

LEFT: PVT. WILL SHIRLEY (US), CO. H, 2ND VA INFANTRY. He is shown here dressed in a Confederate "Scout" uniform.
RIGHT: PVT. JOHN W. WILLHIDE (US), CO. B, 2ND VA INFANTRY. He is also shown dressed in a Confederate "Scout" uniform. He resided at Webster, VA.

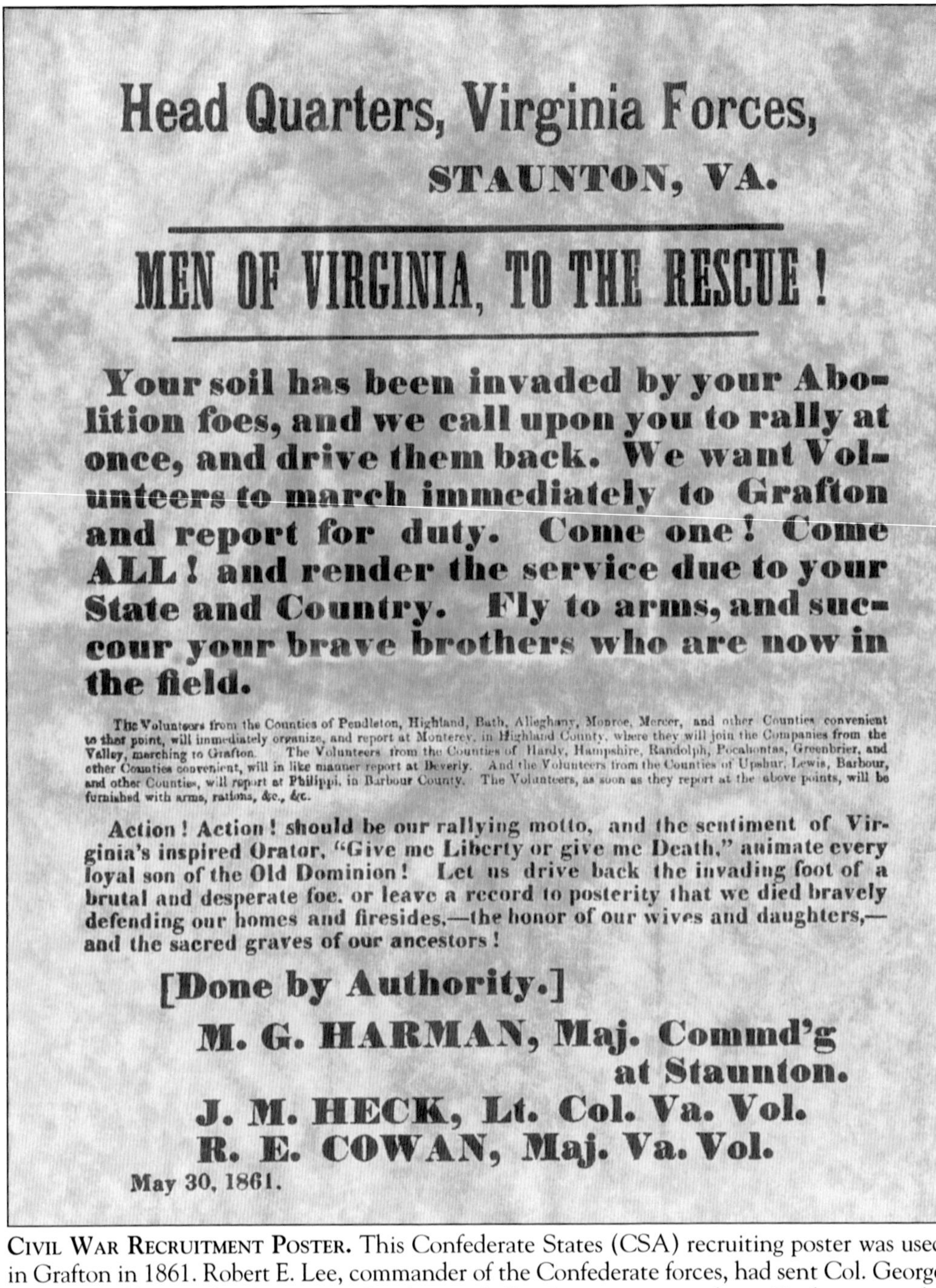

Head Quarters, Virginia Forces,

STAUNTON, VA.

MEN OF VIRGINIA, TO THE RESCUE!

Your soil has been invaded by your Abolition foes, and we call upon you to rally at once, and drive them back. We want Volunteers to march immediately to Grafton and report for duty. Come one! Come ALL! and render the service due to your State and Country. Fly to arms, and succour your brave brothers who are now in the field.

The Volunteers from the Counties of Pendleton, Highland, Bath, Alleghany, Monroe, Mercer, and other Counties convenient to that point, will immediately organize, and report at Monterey, in Highland County, where they will join the Companies from the Valley, marching to Grafton. The Volunteers from the Counties of Hardy, Hampshire, Randolph, Pocahontas, Greenbrier, and other Counties convenient, will in like manner report at Beverly. And the Volunteers from the Counties of Upshur, Lewis, Barbour, and other Counties, will report at Philippi, in Barbour County. The Volunteers, as soon as they report at the above points, will be furnished with arms, rations, &c., &c.

Action! Action! should be our rallying motto, and the sentiment of Virginia's inspired Orator, "Give me Liberty or give me Death," animate every loyal son of the Old Dominion! Let us drive back the invading foot of a brutal and desperate foe, or leave a record to posterity that we died bravely defending our homes and firesides,—the honor of our wives and daughters,—and the sacred graves of our ancestors!

[Done by Authority.]

M. G. HARMAN, Maj. Commd'g at Staunton.

J. M. HECK, Lt. Col. Va. Vol.

R. E. COWAN, Maj. Va. Vol.

May 30, 1861.

Civil War Recruitment Poster. This Confederate States (CSA) recruiting poster was used in Grafton in 1861. Robert E. Lee, commander of the Confederate forces, had sent Col. George A. Porterfield to Taylor County to take charge of all military operations here. Grafton was to be one of the assembly sites for Confederate volunteers. Porterfield complained that the area had well-armed federals and that citizens were afraid to join the Confederate cause. (Photo courtesy of Rick Reese.)

EARLY MEMORIAL DAY PROGRAM. This is a May 30, 1901 Decoration Day program of the Union veterans organization the Grand Army of the Republic. On May 27, 1866, a parade and cemetery decoration program was initiated in Waterloo, NY, that is recognized today as the birth of Memorial Day. Work on the Grafton National Cemetery started in 1867. A May 30, 1868 observance was planned, but postponed until June 14, because of the weather. Decorating the graves with flowers began in 1869. (Photo copy courtesy of Darlene Ford.)

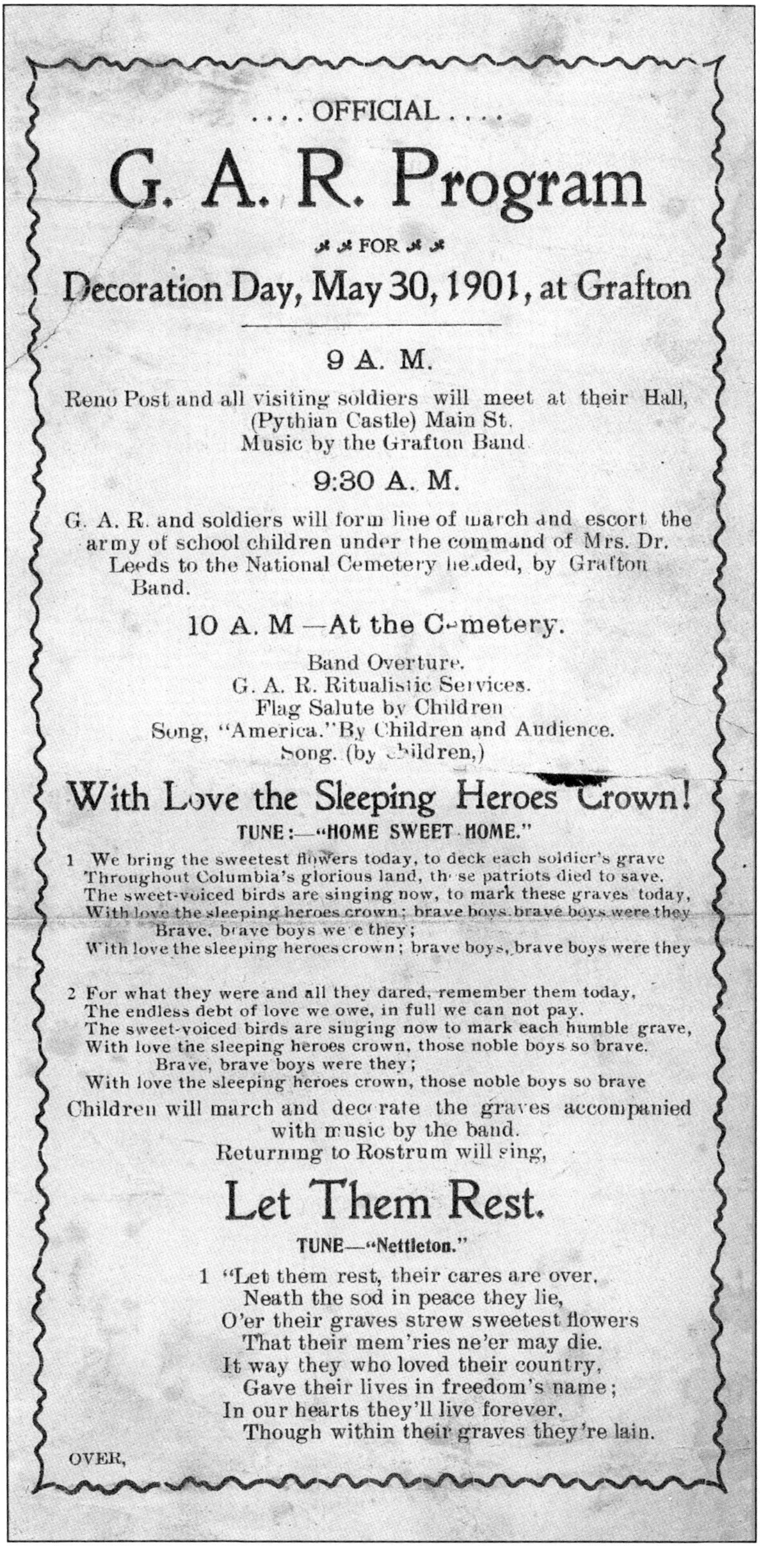

. . . . OFFICIAL . . . .

G. A. R. Program

FOR

Decoration Day, May 30, 1901, at Grafton

9 A. M.

Reno Post and all visiting soldiers will meet at their Hall, (Pythian Castle) Main St.
Music by the Grafton Band.

9:30 A. M.

G. A. R. and soldiers will form line of march and escort the army of school children under the command of Mrs. Dr. Leeds to the National Cemetery headed, by Grafton Band.

10 A. M—At the Cemetery.

Band Overture.
G. A. R. Ritualistic Services.
Flag Salute by Children
Song, "America." By Children and Audience.
Song. (by children,)

With Love the Sleeping Heroes Crown!

TUNE:—"HOME SWEET HOME."

1 We bring the sweetest flowers today, to deck each soldier's grave
Throughout Columbia's glorious land, those patriots died to save.
The sweet-voiced birds are singing now, to mark these graves today,
With love the sleeping heroes crown; brave boys, brave boys were they
Brave, brave boys were they;
With love the sleeping heroes crown; brave boys, brave boys were they

2 For what they were and all they dared, remember them today,
The endless debt of love we owe, in full we can not pay.
The sweet-voiced birds are singing now to mark each humble grave,
With love the sleeping heroes crown, those noble boys so brave.
Brave, brave boys were they;
With love the sleeping heroes crown, those noble boys so brave

Children will march and decorate the graves accompanied with music by the band.
Returning to Rostrum will sing,

Let Them Rest.

TUNE—"Nettleton."

1 "Let them rest, their cares are over,
Neath the sod in peace they lie,
O'er their graves strew sweetest flowers
That their mem'ries ne'er may die.
It way they who loved their country,
Gave their lives in freedom's name;
In our hearts they'll live forever,
Though within their graves they're lain.

OVER,

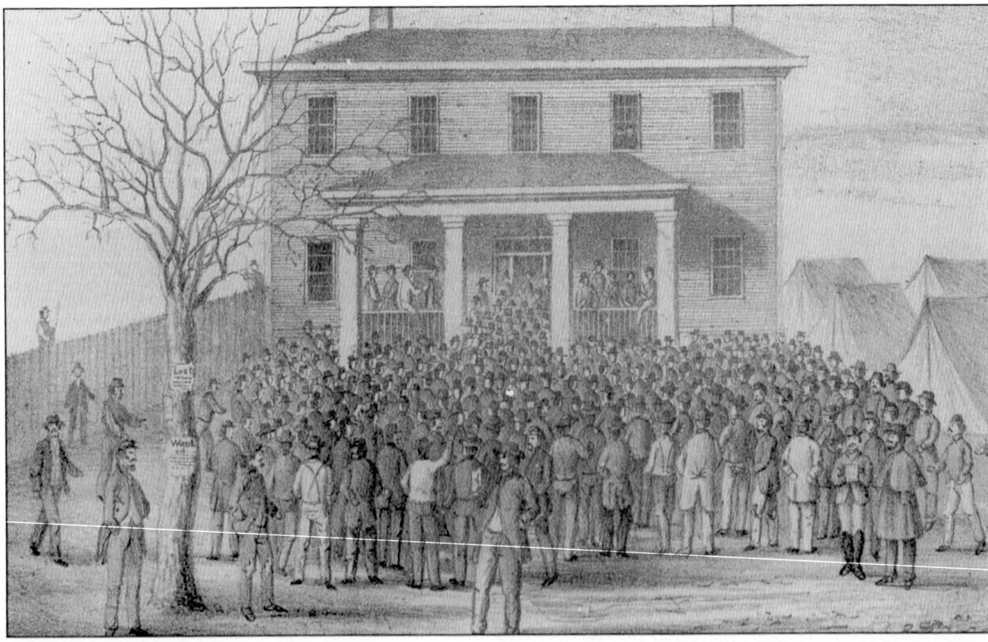

The Jarvis Birthplace. This federal mail call at the Jarvis home in Webster is from 1861. During this time period, Gen. George B. McClellan used a room on the first floor, to the right of the entrance, as his office. Webster was a supply depot and nearby Grafton was of significance because it was a hub of the B&O Railroad. Troops camped near the Jarvis home. Today, an area across from the Jarvis home has been developed into the Ocean Pearl Felton Historical Park. (Photo courtesy of the Department of the Army, Carlisle Barracks, PA.)

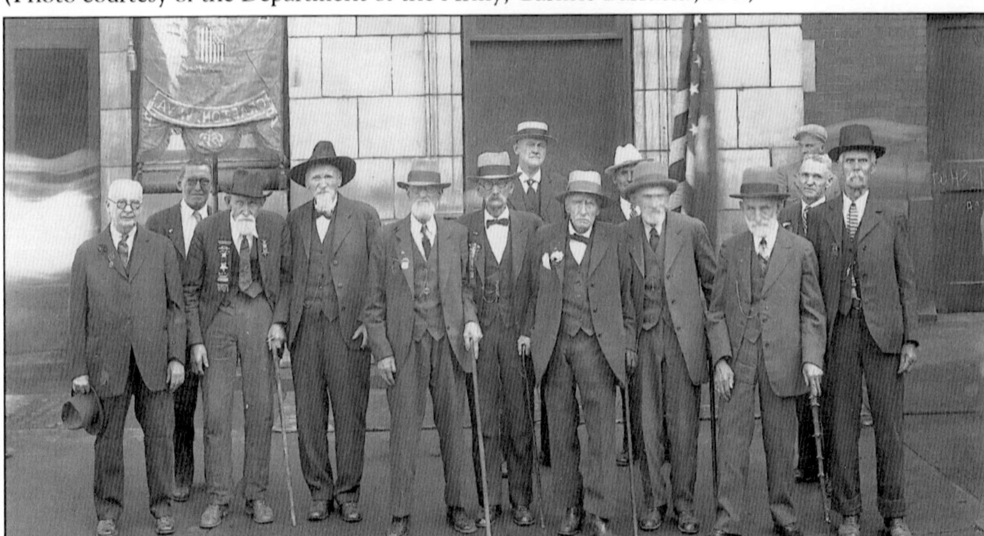

Civil War Veterans. This group of Taylor County Civil War veterans gathered in the 1920s for a photo in front of the B&O Passenger Station along East Main Street in downtown Grafton. Most of the names of the individuals have been lost over time, but two of the men were Robert L. Tallman and John I. Hoffman, both of Barbour County. Hoffman later lived in Taylor County. West Virginia has routinely posted the highest per capita enlistment of its young men as the call to duty was issued.

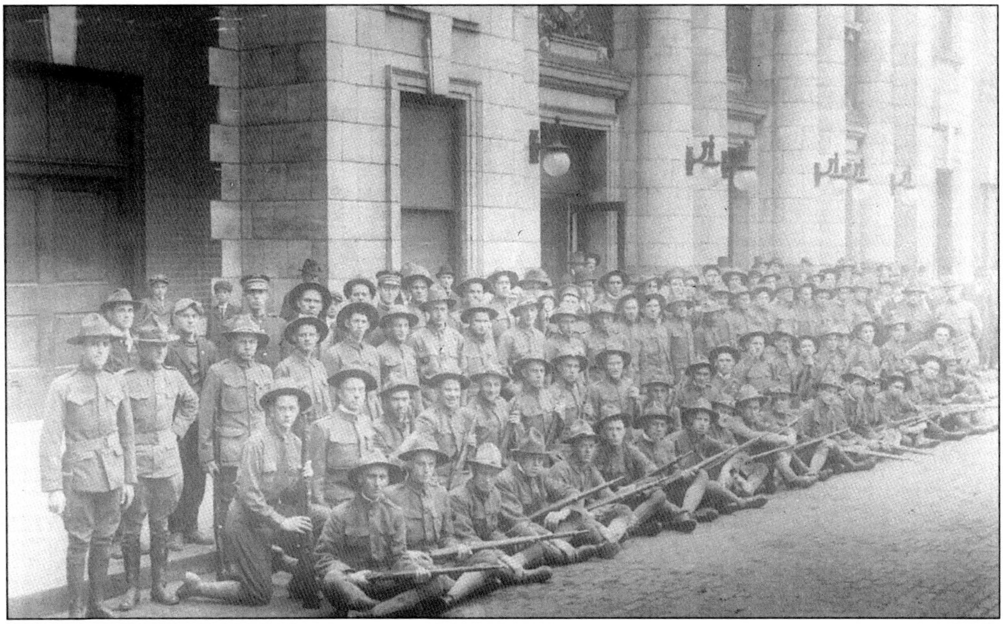

World War I Veterans. Veterans of Co. E, 1st West Virginia, from Grafton and Taylor County pose for a photo in front of the Grafton B&O Passenger Station on April 1, 1917. The young men and women of Grafton and Taylor County always have marched off to war when the call came. The community still has active veterans' organizations and is home to the 363rd Military Police Company of the U.S. Army Reserves. The 363rd is housed at the T. Bailey Brown Armory, just off of Riverside Drive.

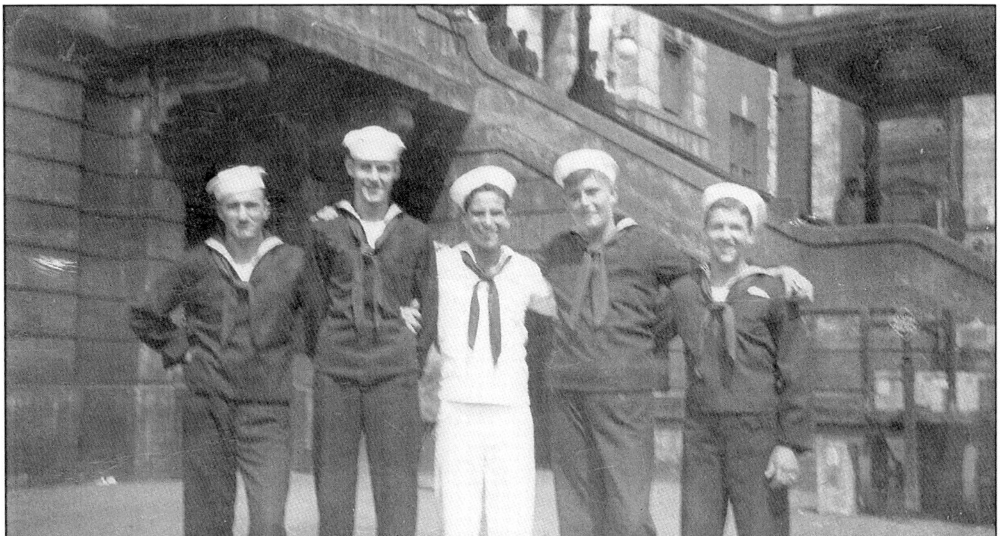

U.S. Navy Sailors. These Grafton and Taylor County U.S. Navy sailors from World War II pose for a photo as they prepare to leave for active duty. The men had been home on leave after completing Boot Camp training. Shown are Charles T. McGee, John Flanagan, Richard H. Robinson, Howard Cross, and Russell Isner. This photo was taken in July 1943 outside the B&O Passenger Station in downtown Grafton. The historic train station was the site for arrival and departure of many of the war veterans. (Photo courtesy of Peggy Robinson.)

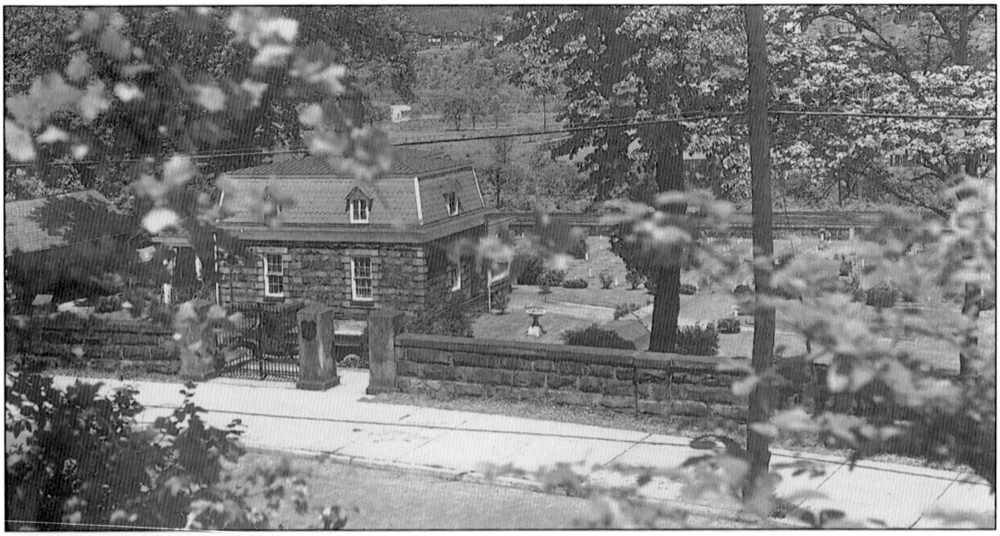

Grafton National Cemetery. West Virginia's two National Cemeteries are located in Grafton and Taylor County. The historic Grafton National Cemetery includes the grave of T. Bailey Brown, listed as the first Union soldier to die in a face-to-face struggle in the early days leading up to the Civil War. In 1868, flower strewing days started and youth would march to the National Cemetery and decorate the graves of fallen soldiers. This observance grew into today's annual Memorial Day parade and National Cemetery observances.

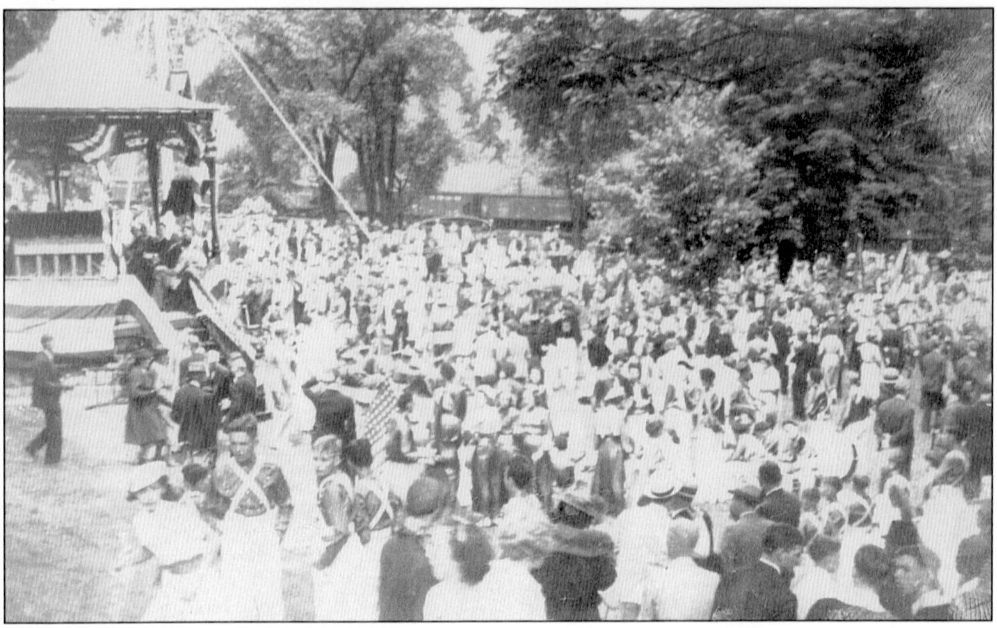

Grafton National Cemetery. Shown is a Memorial Day observance at the Grafton National Cemetery from the 1930s. The Brinkman history says Mayor William Mallonee issued a proclamation asking all citizens to lay aside their tasks at bench, forge, and shop and join Civil War veterans in observance of Flower Strewing Day on Monday, May 30, 1869. In 1912, Grafton held its first homecoming week in conjunction with Memorial Day exercises. Annual Memorial Day and Homecoming activities continue today. (Photo courtesy of Norma Wyckoff.)

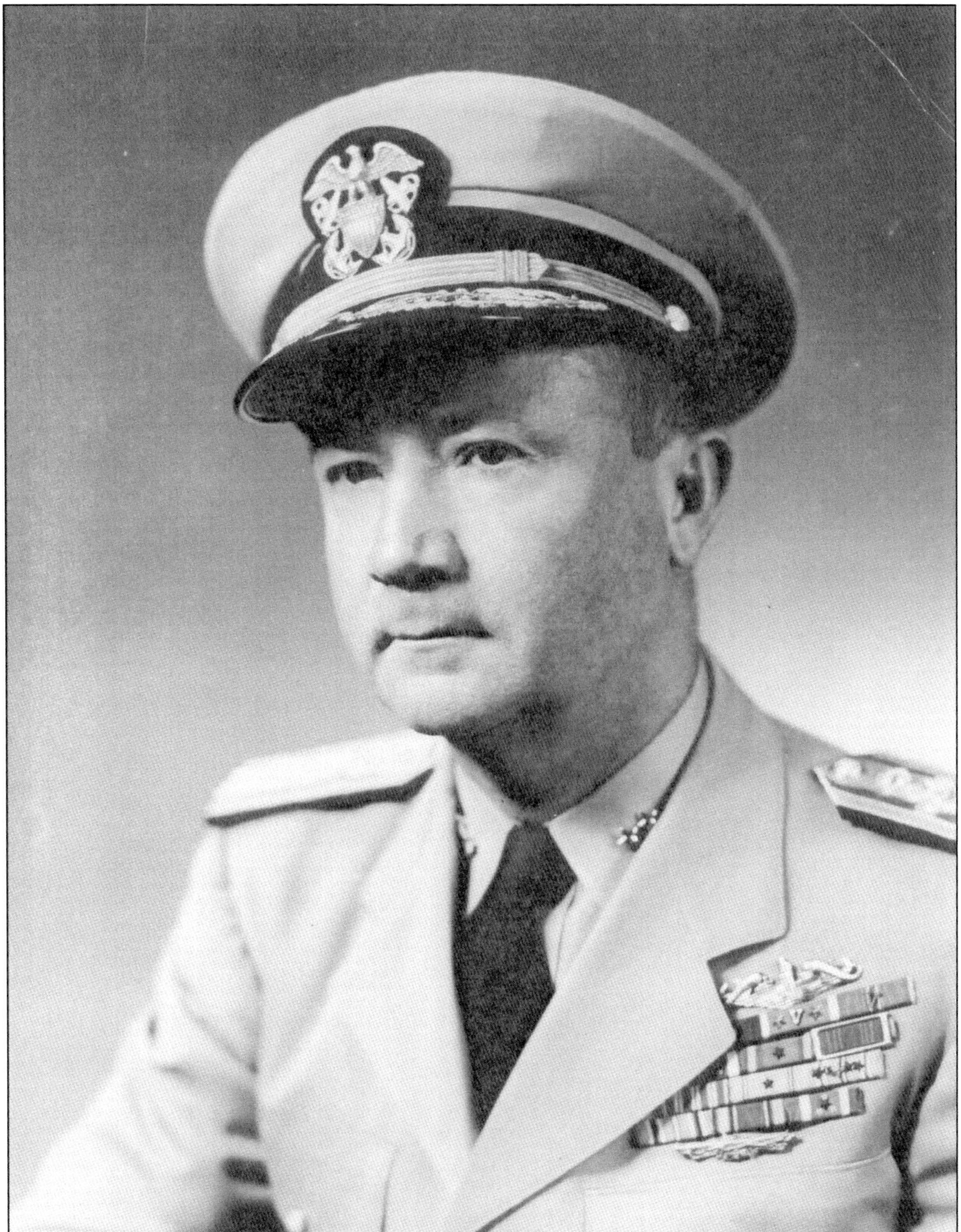

FREDERICK BURDETT WARDER (1904–2000). Warder, often called "Fearless Freddy," was raised in Grafton and had an illustrious naval career dating from his graduation from the U.S. Naval Academy in 1925 to his retirement in 1962. He reached the rank of rear admiral. Naval historians credit Warder and his contemporaries with forming the pattern of underseas sub warfare that hastened the defeat of Japan during World War II. His heroism as commander of the submarine *Seawolf* brought him fame and later a book, based on his leadership in the South Pacific area, was published. In 1942, Taylor County honored him with a Frederick B. Warder Day. (Photo courtesy of G. Thomas Bartlett III.)

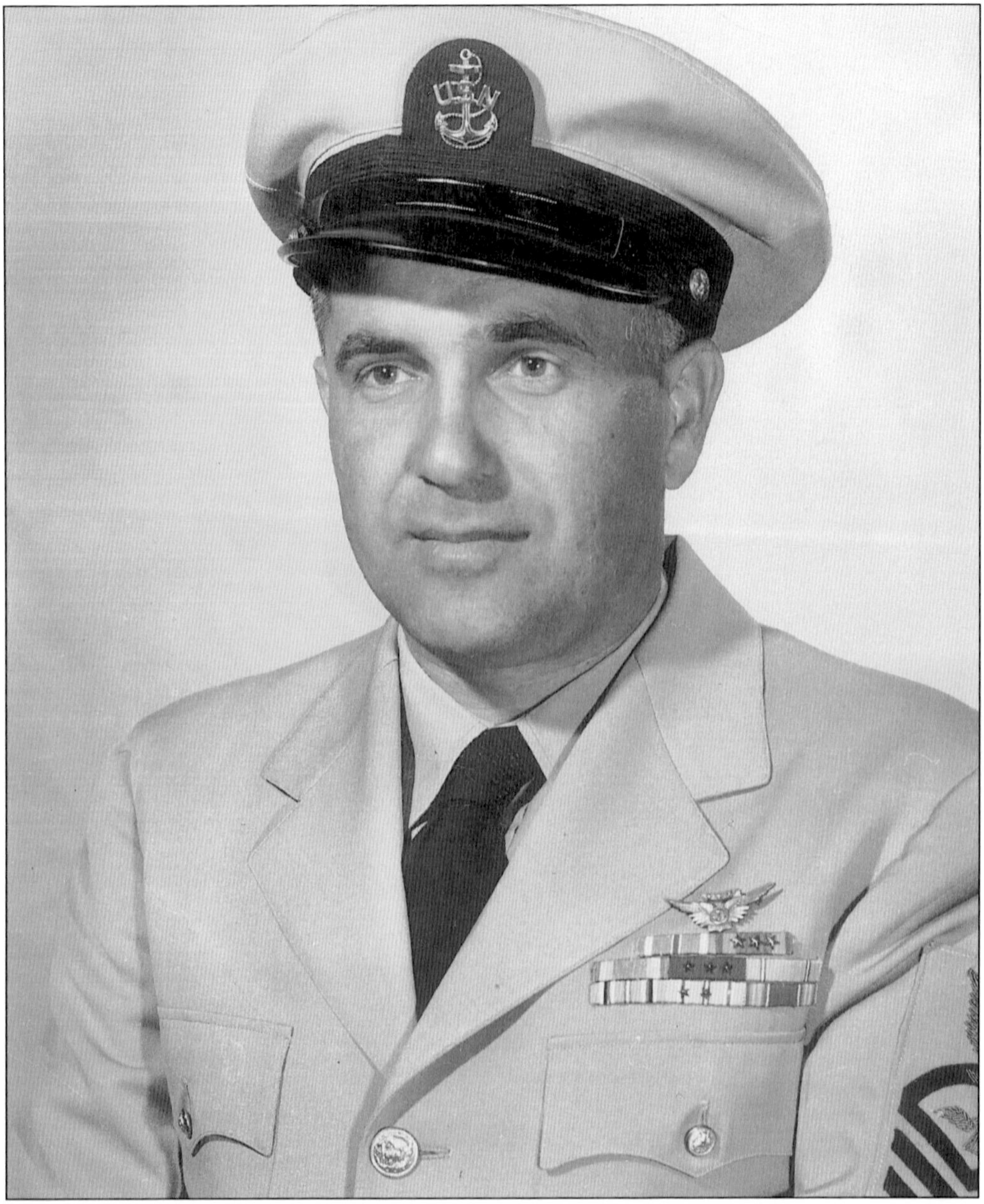

HAROLD S. "JABO" FAWCETT. Fawcett, a World War II U.S. Navy photographer from Taylor County, photographed the December 7, 1941 Japanese attack on Pearl Harbor. Some of the photographs he took that day are world famous. Unfortunately, the photographs were frequently published without being identified as his. He spent the rest of World War II in the South Pacific. Flying home in December 1943, his transport sea plane made an emergency landing at sea, and six days passed before the crew was rescued. In 1946, he photographed the atomic test explosions at Bikini Atoll. For years, Fawcett participated in Memorial Day and other veterans ceremonies as a Pearl Harbor survivor. He was a 1935 GHS graduate, enlisted in the Navy in 1936, and retired in 1955 as a chief photographers mate. Returning to Taylor County in 1973, he presented programs about his military experiences to schoolchildren. He died in 1999. (Photo courtesy of Norma Fawcett.)

Four

Tygart Dam

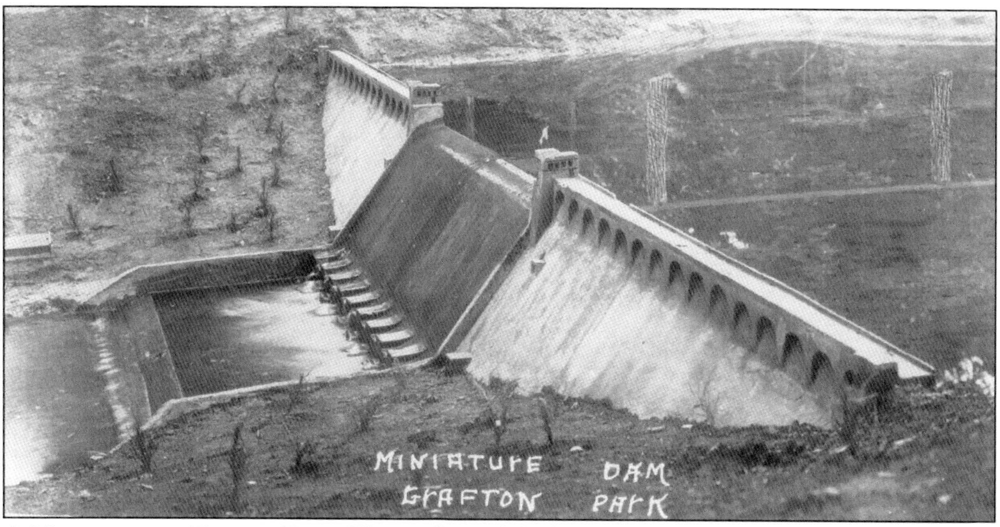

A Miniature of Tygart Dam. This scale model of the Tygart Dam was built around 1934 at Grafton City Park. The model still exists within the park and is located on acreage at the foot of Tygart Dam. The need for a constant supply of water to the Monongahela River was finally addressed in the early 1930s, following a record drought that halted navigation on the river. By August 2, 1934, L.G. Warren was named general superintendent of the Frederick Snare Corps Tygart Dam force. Work began on the Tygart Valley River Dam in January 1935. In March, the first fatality occurred when Charles Leary fell 30 feet and drowned. Records from May 9, indicate that more than 700 were working on the dam; this number had grown to 2,744 by October 1936. The pouring of cement started on May 28, 1935, and the last bucket was poured on September 19, 1937. This marked the ending of construction of the dam, although clean-up projects continued until February 1938. While 25,766 people visited the dam in November 1937, the official dedication day in October 1938 drew only a few workmen and tourists. At the time of its construction, Tygart Dam was the largest pure concrete structure east of the Mississippi River, containing more than 1.25 million cubic yards of concrete. It is 1,921 feet long, 207 feet wide at the base, and 230 feet high. A U.S. Army Corps of Engineers report in 1959 listed the total cost of the project at $18,432,000. Flood waters have come close, but have not yet reached a height sufficient to flow down the dam's spillway. When maintenance work is not under way, summer tours are offered at 12:45 p.m. on Wednesday's down through the interior of Tygart Dam by the U.S. Army Corps of Engineers. (Photo courtesy of Rick Reese.)

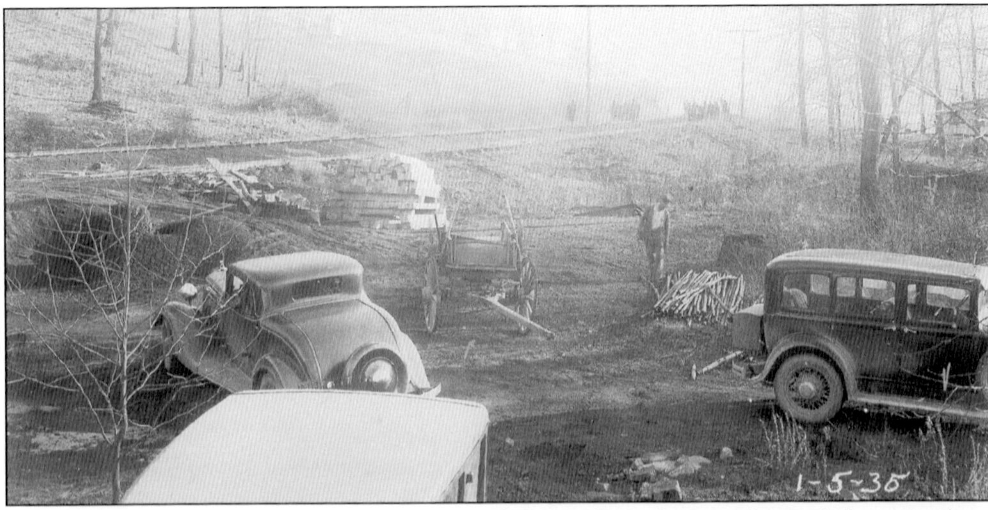

Tygart Dam Work Starts. Construction of Tygart Dam forever changed the area above and below the massive concrete structure. What had been residential and farm land is now covered by a 10-mile recreation lake that is more than 100 feet deep in spots. A former rail line between Grafton and Philippi was relocated. With construction in the mid-1930s, during the Great Depression, and a priority status given to local workers, this provided much needed employment opportunities. (Photo courtesy of Rick Reese.)

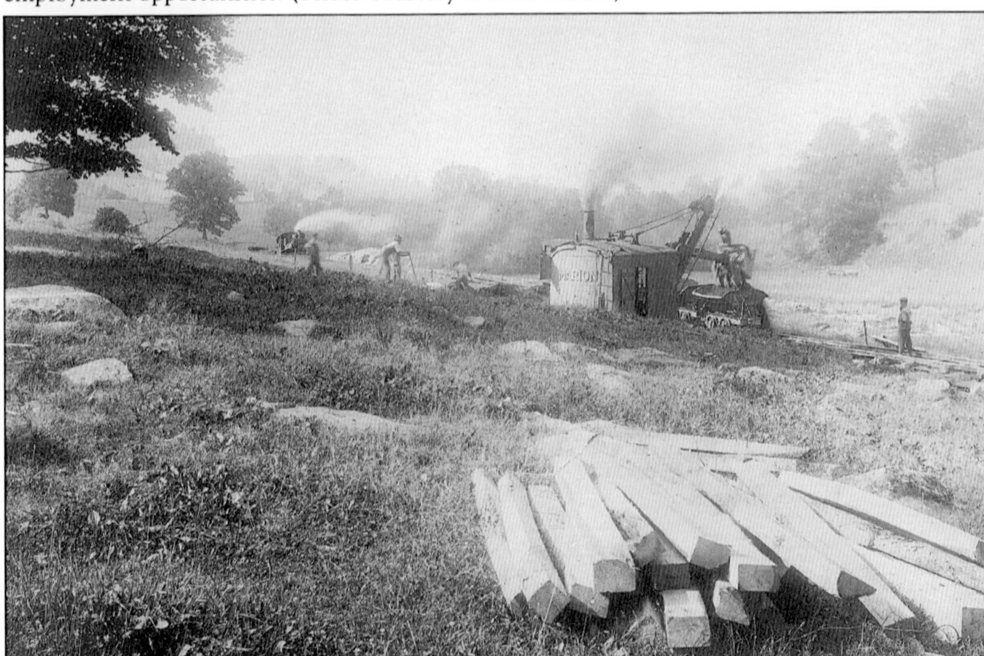

Taking Up the Rails. Initial preparation for construction of Tygart Dam included clearing land and relocating a former rail line between Grafton and Philippi. Some families, homes, and cemeteries also had to be relocated. Some of these properties were damaged by flooding in November 1935, as the construction had blocked the normal flow and the river backed up. The flood control function of the dam is credited with having saved millions of dollars in damages over the years.

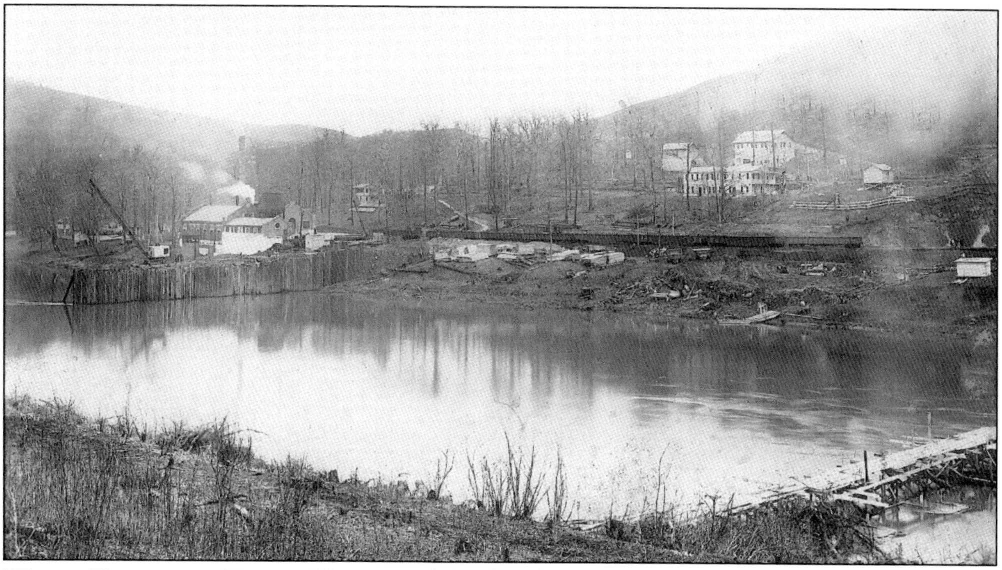

Water Filtration Plant. The city of Grafton boasts that it has some of the best tasting municipal water in the country. The city's water intake lines for the municipal water filtration plant travel through the base of Tygart Dam and the large lake provides a bountiful supply of water, even through dry seasons. After a new plant was built in the 1980s, operation was turned over to the Taylor County Public Service District. Today, water is pumped to most sections of the county, as well as to some areas in adjoining counties.

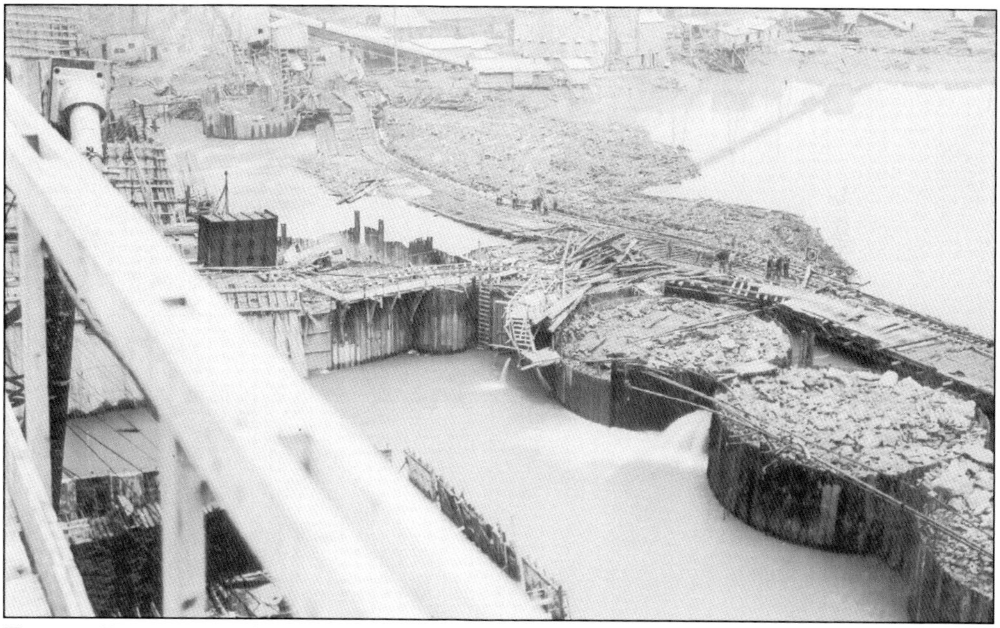

Tygart Dam under Construction. It is somewhat hard to look at the finished Tygart Dam and imagine how the area looked prior to and during the early stages of construction, such as in the scene shown above. Constructed between 1935 and 1938, the dam was the largest pure concrete structure east of the Mississippi. At least 10 workers died during the construction. Construction started in January 1935 and ceased in September 1937. (Photo courtesy of Rick Reese.)

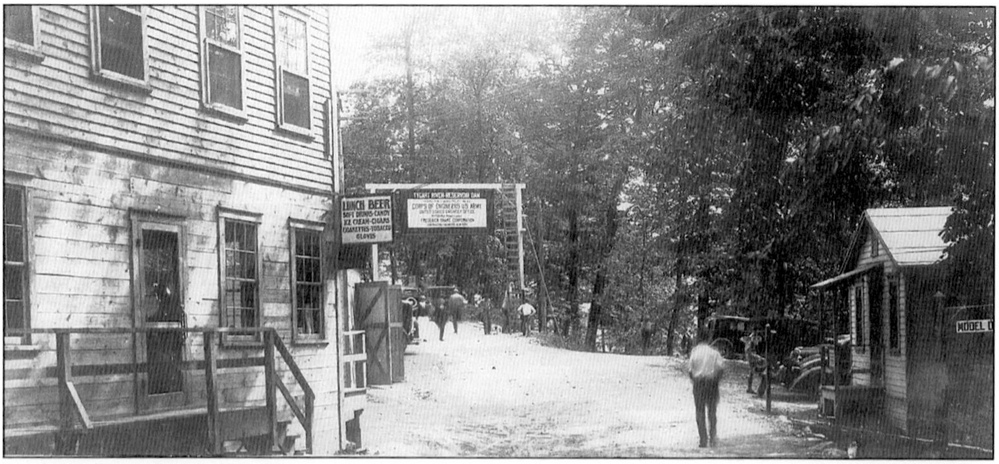

TYGART DAM PROJECT OFFICE. Grafton City Park became home to the project office for the massive construction project that created the Tygart Dam. The land that makes up the city park was donated to the city of Grafton in 1885 by Francis Durbin. Grafton built a water pumping station here in 1913. A Consolidated Manufactures Company plant was built in 1914. In 1916, it was sold and later became the Carr China Company. The Park View Community began to grow once the china plant began operations. (Photo courtesy of Rick Reese.)

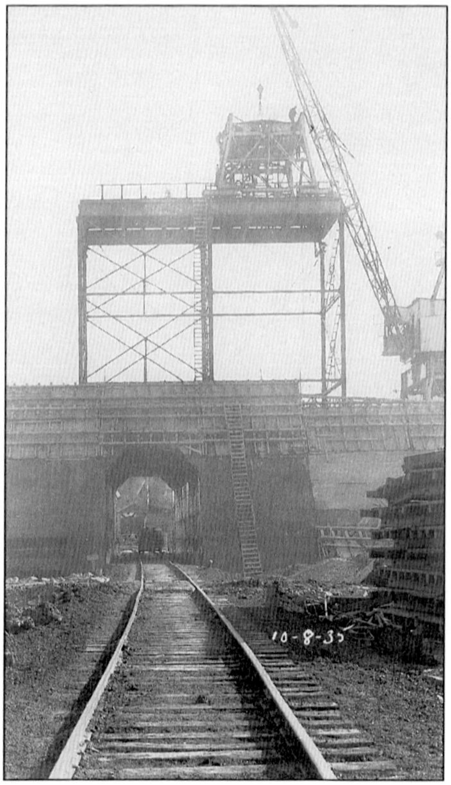

TUNNEL TRACKS. During the early period of the construction of Tygart Dam, the Grafton-Philippi tracks continued to operate. However, the rail line had to be taken up as the lake created by the dam construction eventually covered the site of the former tracks. (Photo courtesy of Rick Reese.)

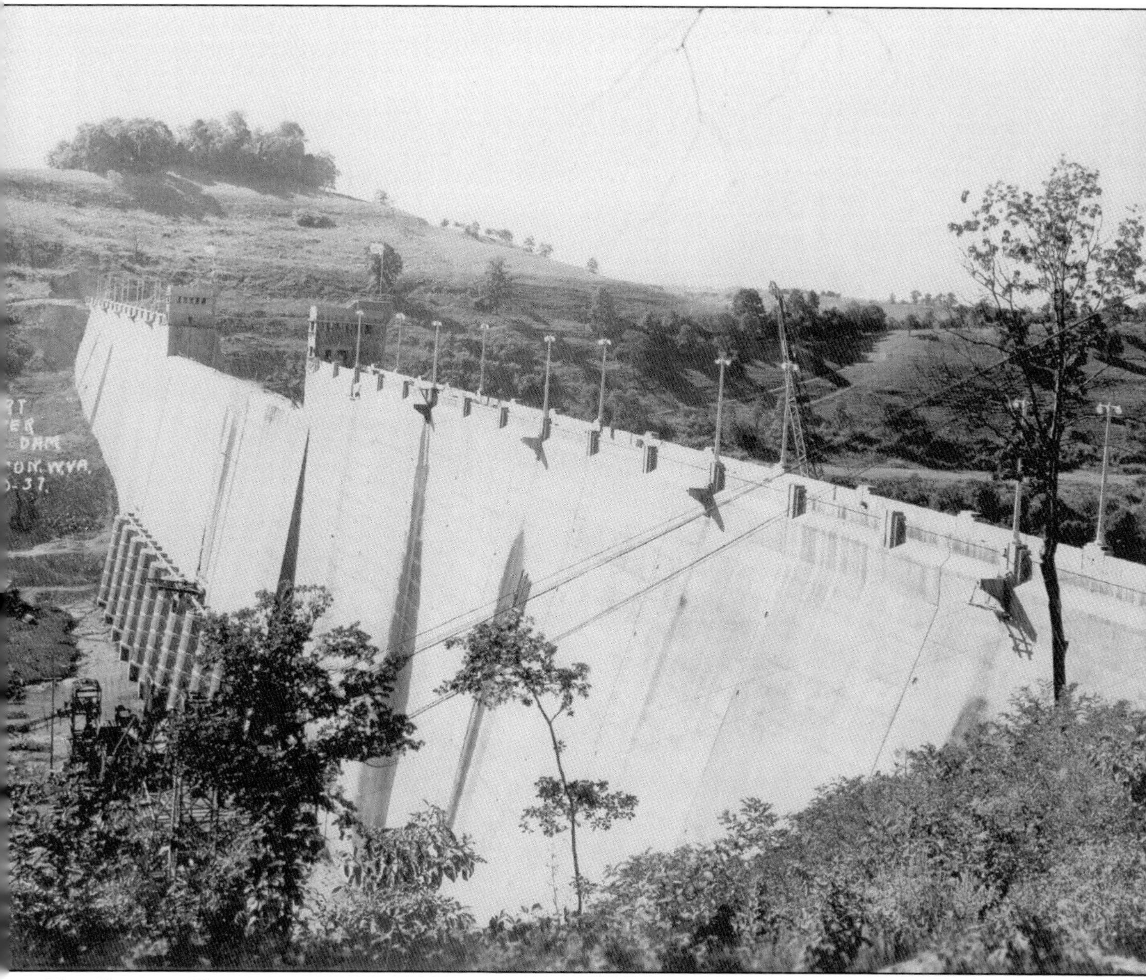

The Finished Product. Tygart Dam is operated by the U.S. Army Corps of Engineers as a flood control facility, providing protection along the Tygart and Monongahela Rivers to Pittsburgh. The dam was designed to hold spring runoff for release during the dry summer months and this assists with navigation. The recreational uses of the lake are an indirect benefit of the dam. Tygart Lake State Park has been developed around the lake and offers a marina, lodge, restaurant, cabins, picnic areas, and more. (Photo courtesy of James Bolliger.)

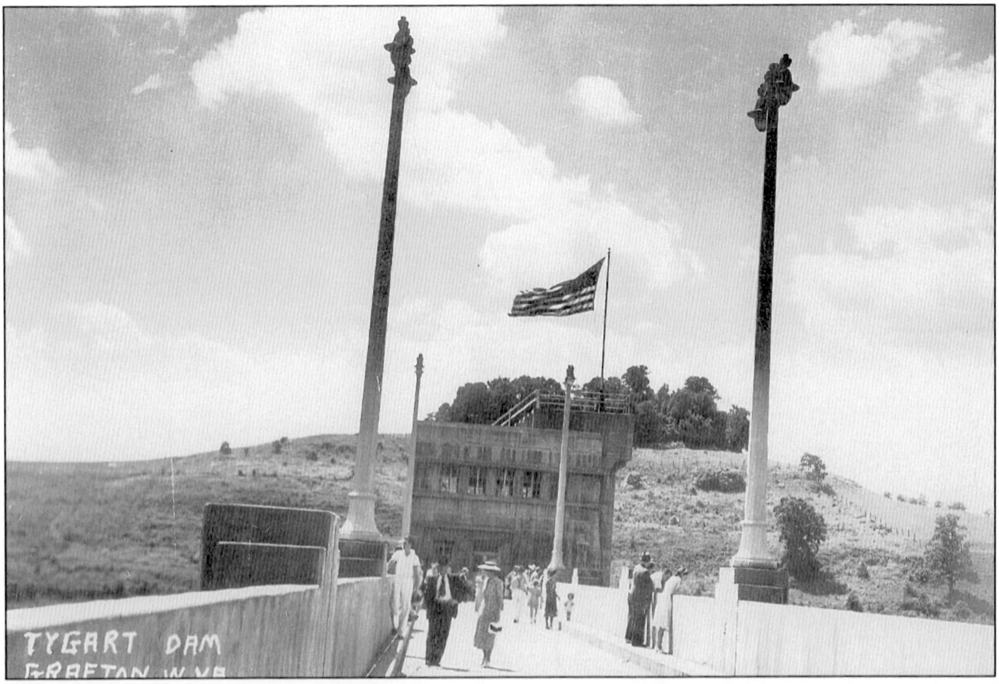

View from the Top. Since its completion, the U.S. Army Corps of Engineers have operated and maintained Tygart Dam. The flood control facility became a popular tourists attraction. Many visitors simply enjoy a walk out across the top of the dam to about the mid-point, from where they can see Grafton City Park, the Taylor County Public Service District's water filtration plant, and part of Tygart Lake. Tours also are offered through the dam's interior. (Photo courtesy of Wayne McDevitt.)

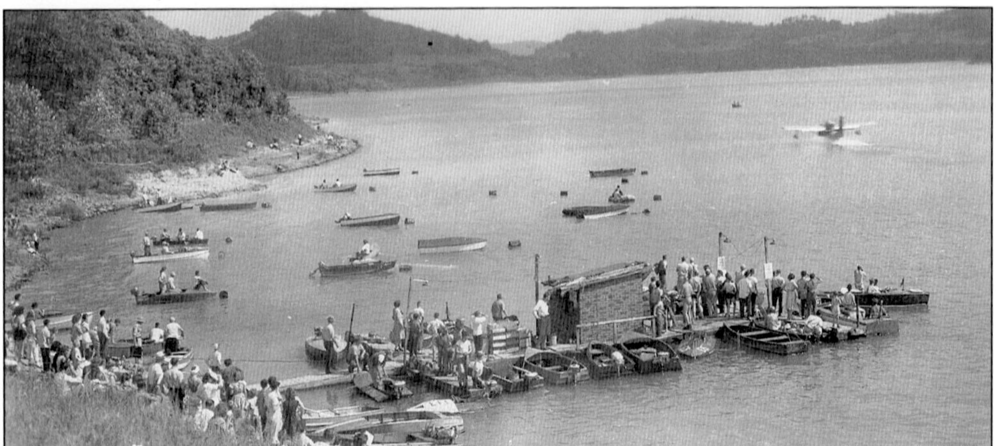

The Tygart Lake Marina. This view is believed to be from the 1950s. Construction of Tygart Dam created a beautiful large lake with some 10 miles of shoreline. Boating, water skiing, the use of jet skies and other recreational activities have made Tygart Lake a popular destination for Grafton and Taylor County residents and visitors, many who return each year, from West Virginia and neighboring states. Each year Tygart Lake State Park is visited by travelers from all over the U.S. and from around the world. (Photo courtesy of Wayne McDevitt.)

Five

BUSINESS AND INDUSTRY

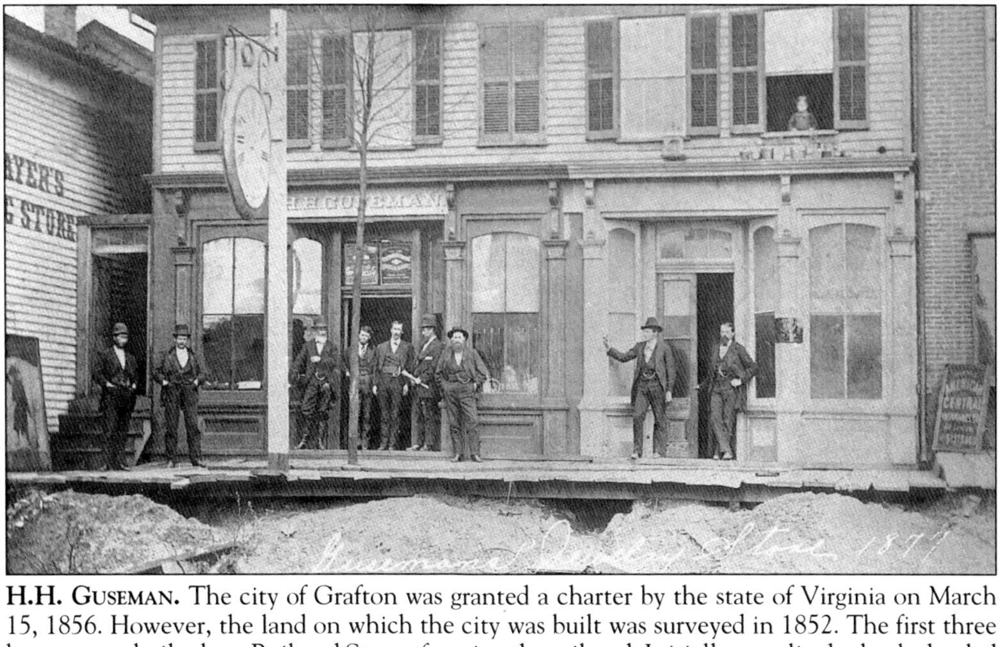

H.H. GUSEMAN. The city of Grafton was granted a charter by the state of Virginia on March 15, 1856. However, the land on which the city was built was surveyed in 1852. The first three houses were built along Railroad Street, fronting the railroad. Initially, supplies had to be hauled through the woods from Fetterman. Thomas McGraw, one of Grafton's first settlers, came with the first construction train of the B&O. He opened the first store along Railroad Street on May 1, 1852. In 1853, several houses and stores were built. George R. Latham opened the first school in Grafton the following year. The H.H. Guseman Store, shown here, is believed to have been one of the early Grafton Stores built along Railroad Street, fronting the railroad. Notice the board sidewalks that were common during this time period. (Photo courtesy of Marvin Gelhausen.)

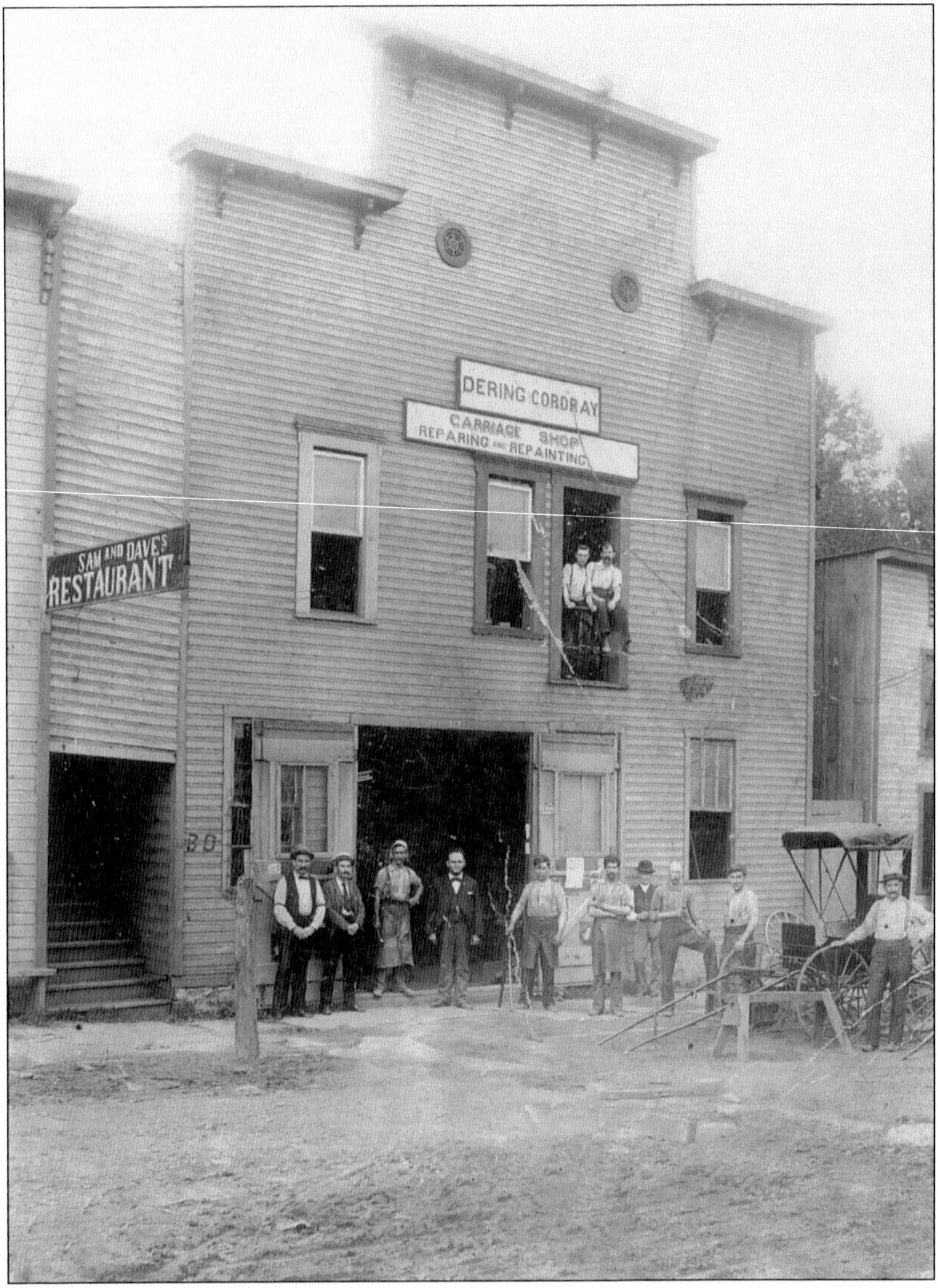

The Carriage Shop. The Dering Cordray Carriage Shop did repairing and repainting work. Also shown is a sign for Sam and Dave's Restaurant, located either in the adjacent building or up the stairs between the two buildings. Notice the blacksmith-style aprons that several of the carriage shop workers are wearing. Also note the dirt street, which was common in the early days of the horse-drawn carriages. While this was a carriage shop, Grafton was also known to have several livery stables to care for horses. (Photo courtesy of Peggy Robinson.)

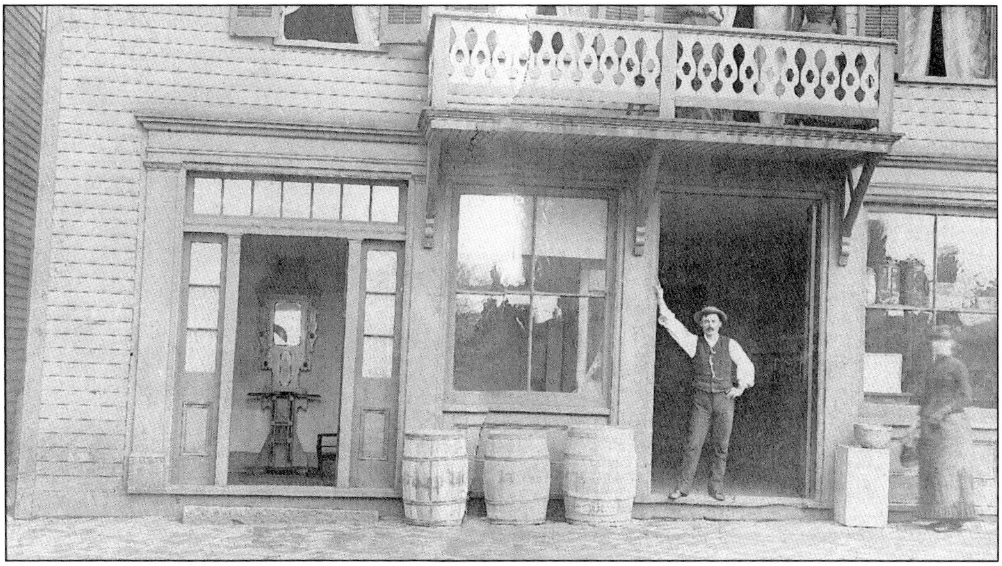

THE KERNAN BAKERY. Edward Kernan established a bakery along Latrobe Street in 1865. As his business became established and increased, he bought lot 207 along West Main Street and built a two-story frame business and dwelling, moving his family to the second floor of the property. He operated his bakery for at least the next 25 years, enjoying a nice business operation. The practice of operating a Main Street business and living above it was typical of a number of the early Grafton business operations. (Photo courtesy of Rita Jean Robinson.)

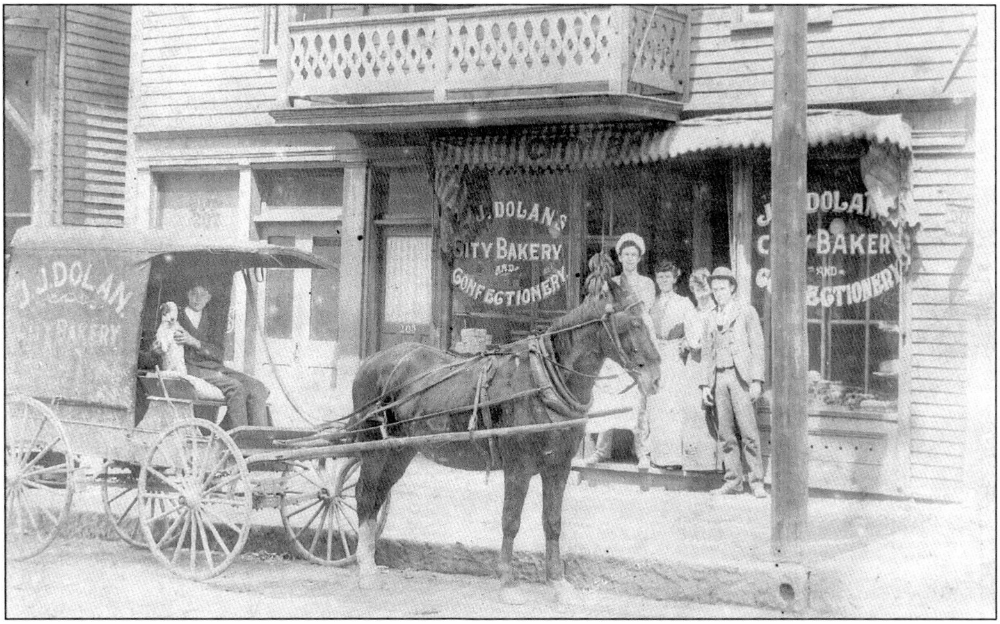

J.J. DOLANS CITY BAKERY AND CONFECTIONERY. This business was located at 205 West Main Street in 1902. While still in the horse and buggy days, note the improvements that have come to the city of Grafton. Cut stone runs along the street edge of the sidewalk, which appears to be made of poured concrete. Gone are the old boardwalk sidewalks. Notice the youth in the carriage holding up a dog. The bakery also has some type of canopy overhang to decorate and shelter its main business entry.

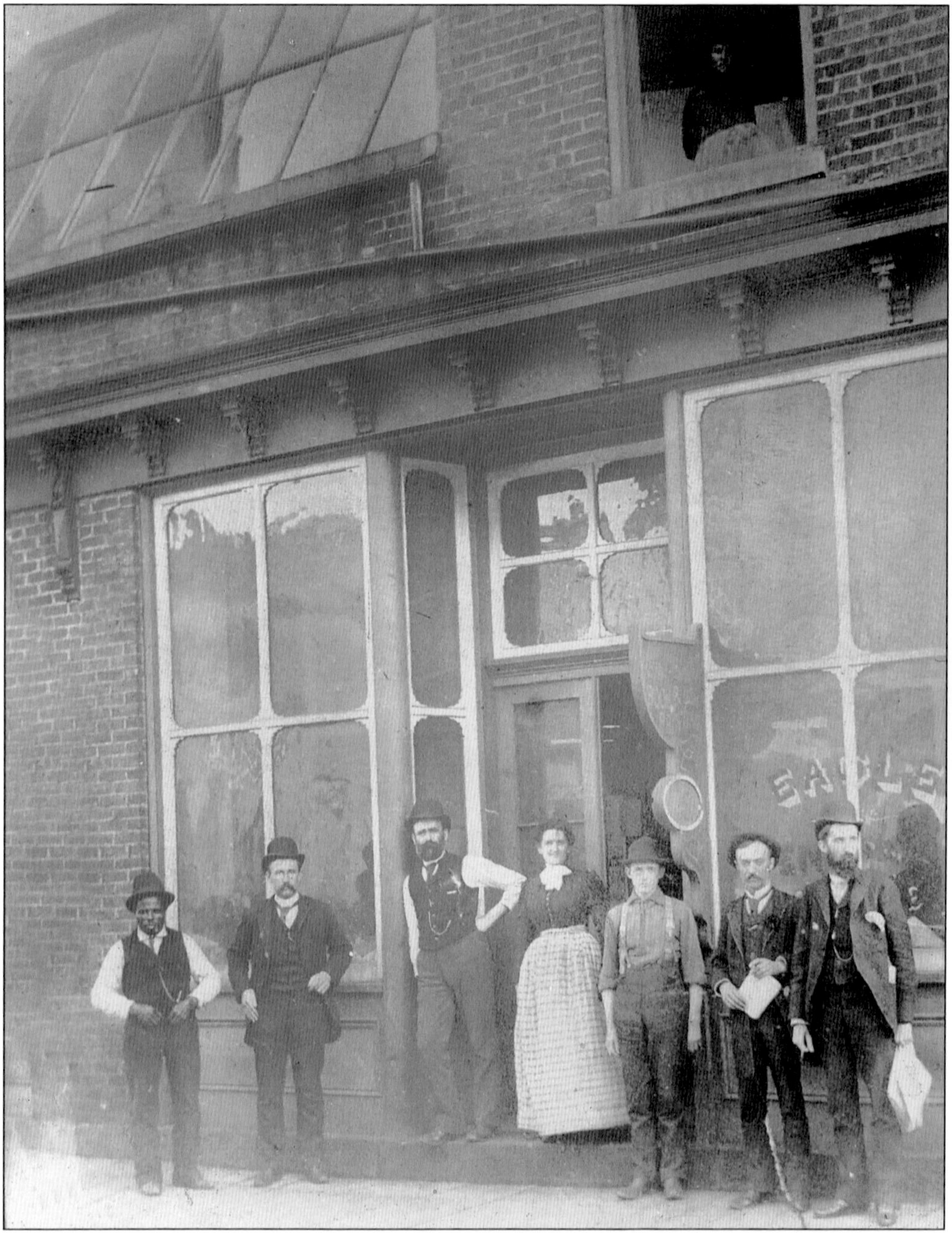

The *Eagle*. One of Grafton's early newspaper ventures was the *Grafton Eagle*. The first edition was printed on Friday, May 16, 1878. In Howard H. Holt's January 1926 history of Taylor County for the *West Virginia Review*, he lists the starting date of the *Eagle* as questionable, but has it publishing to 1885. Then he has the *Grafton Eagle-Sentinel* publishing from 1885 to 1888. A July 8, 1887 *Grafton Eagle* and November 9, 1888 (Vol. 11, No. 26) issue of the *Grafton Eagle-Sentinel* survive.

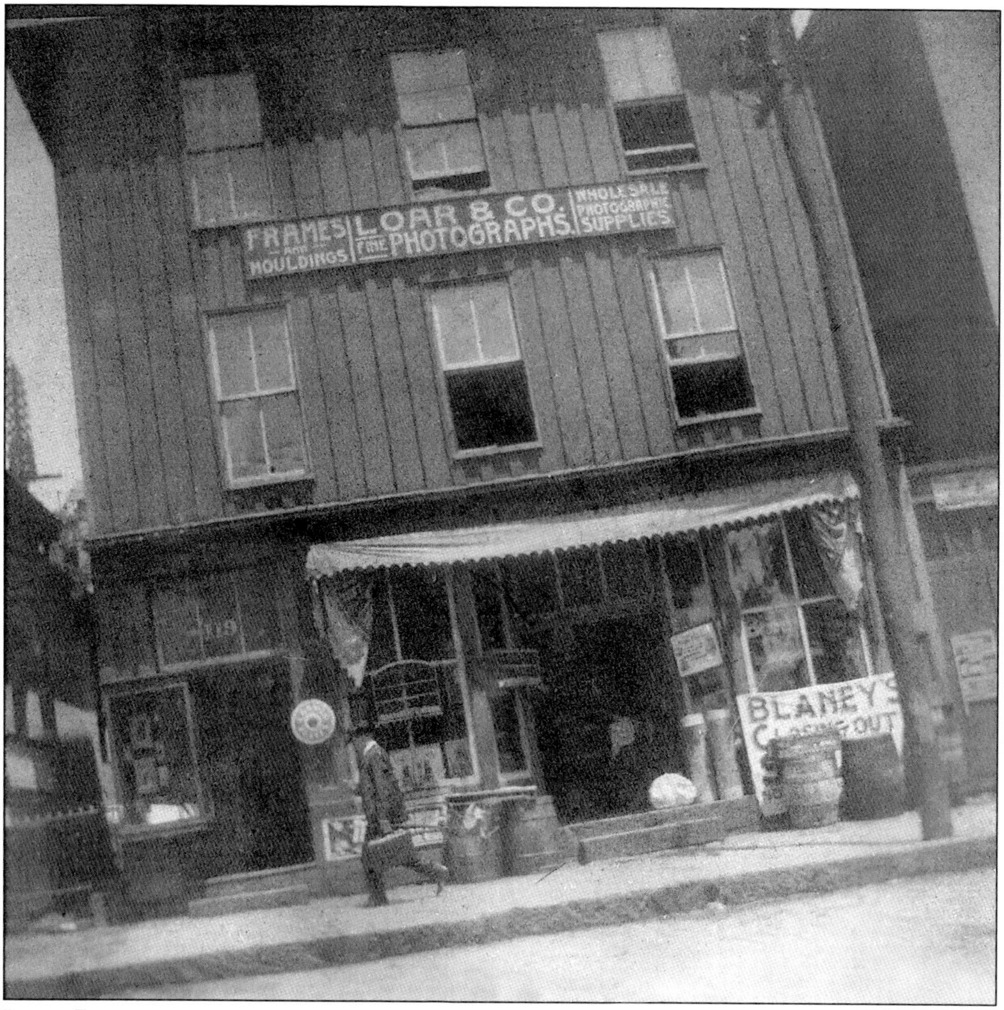

Loar Photography. Loar and Company Fine Photographs for many years photographed Grafton and Taylor County families and events. Much of the Loar collection of photographs was donated to the West Virginia Collection at West Virginia University some years after the Loar and Co. went out of business. Their business sign in the above photo notes that they carry wholesale photographic supplies, frames, and moldings. Also note the street level sign behind the barrels that notes Blaney's Closing Out Sale.

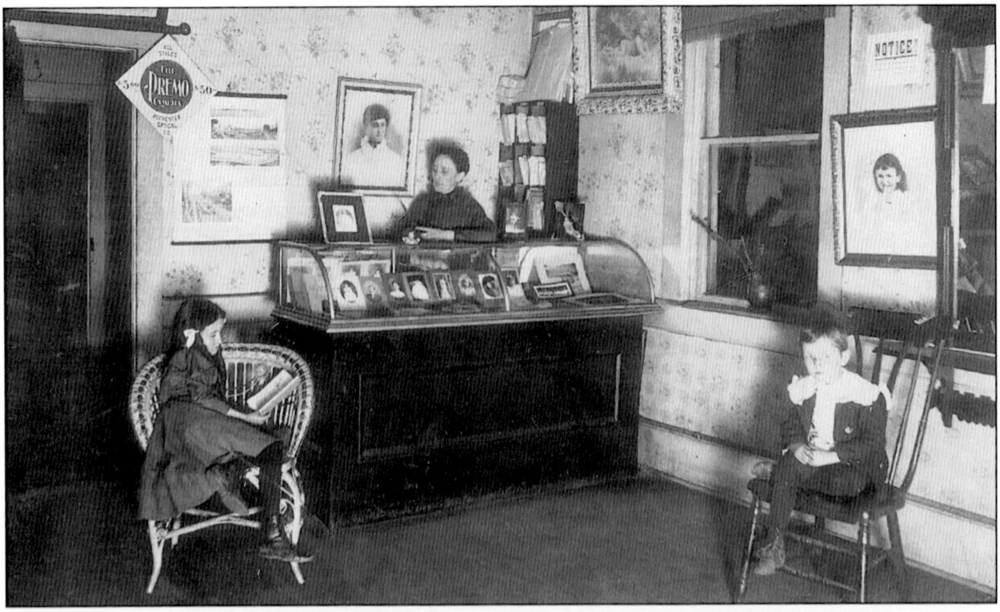

INSIDE OF LOAR'S PHOTOGRAPHY. W.R. Loar was a dealer in picture frames, pictures, and art goods, and a maker of the finest photographs, according to the label on the back of the original of this photograph. The shop was located at 119 West Main Street. The Loar family owned and operated a photography business in Grafton for many years. Notice the attire of the two youths apparently waiting to be photographed and the display of photos at the counter and on the walls.

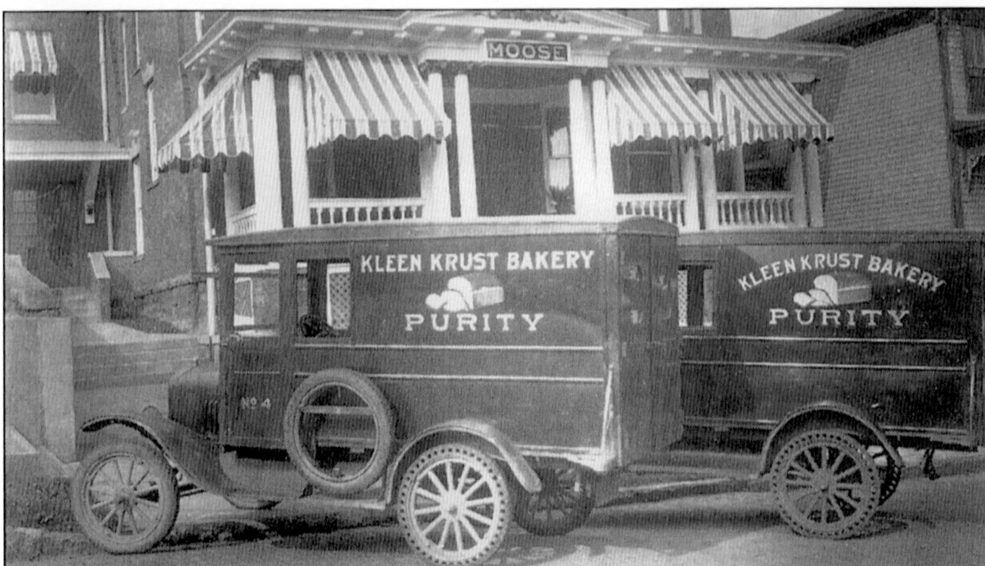

THE KLEEN KRUST BAKERY. Apparently Grafton had several bakeries over the years. Notice the wheels on these Kleen Krust Bakery delivery trucks and the brick paving of West Washington Street. In the background is the former location of the Grafton Moose Club. This West Washington Street structure was previously the home of the L.L. Loar family. An addition was added at the rear after the Moose Club began operating from the building. This structure now stands vacant and the structure that was to the right of the house has been razed.

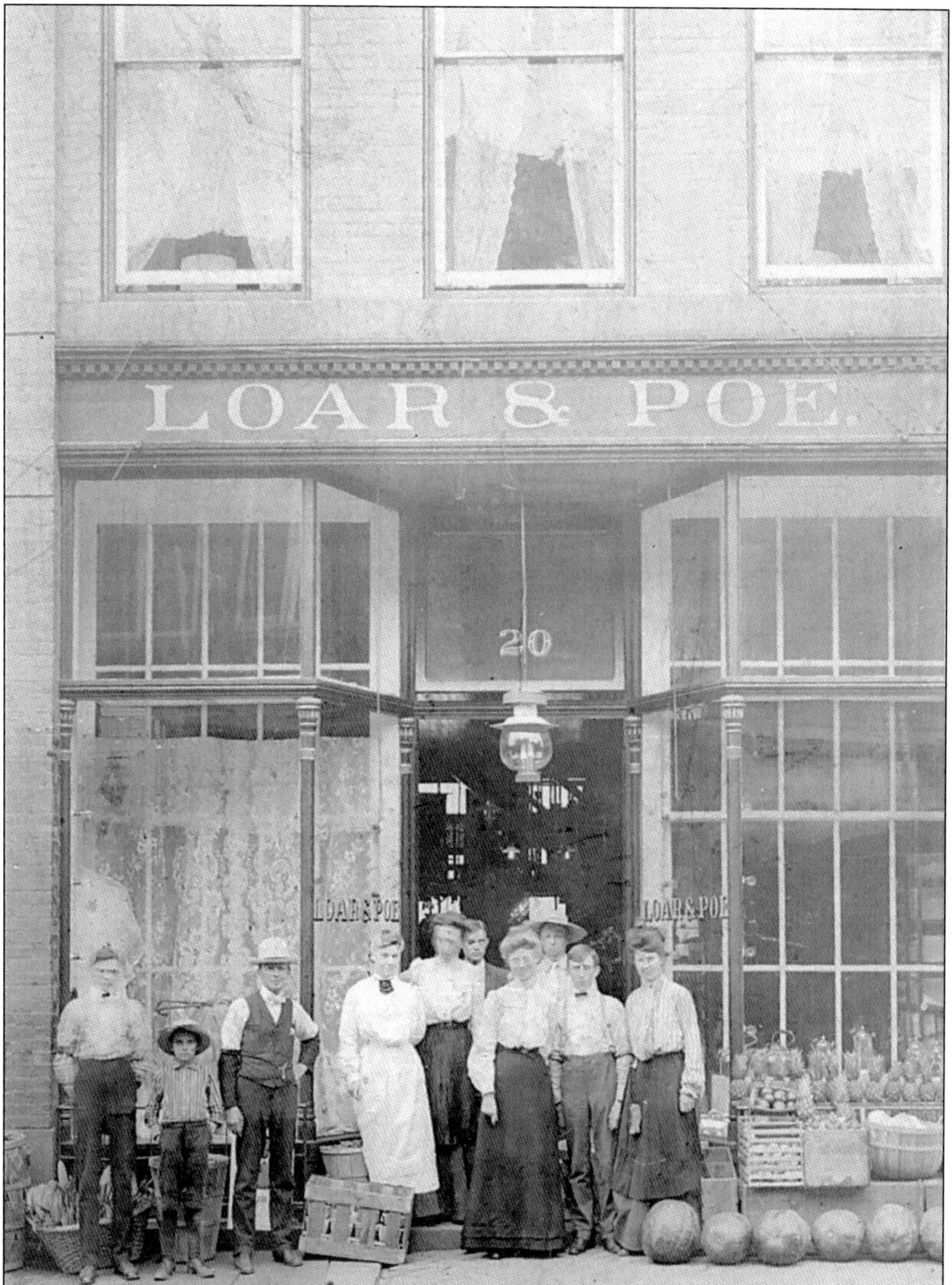

LOAR & POE. Owned and operated by L.L. Loar and B.F. Poe, the Loar and Poe store at 20 West Main Street sold groceries, boots and shoes, carpet, curtains, made-to-order clothing, and gentlemen's clothing. Notice the light that hangs above the entrance to the store and the watermelons lined up just below a row of baskets and crates containing vegetables. The street is brick with a cut stone curb and concrete sidewalk. The store is located in an impressive brick structure with decorative corner posts in the front windows.

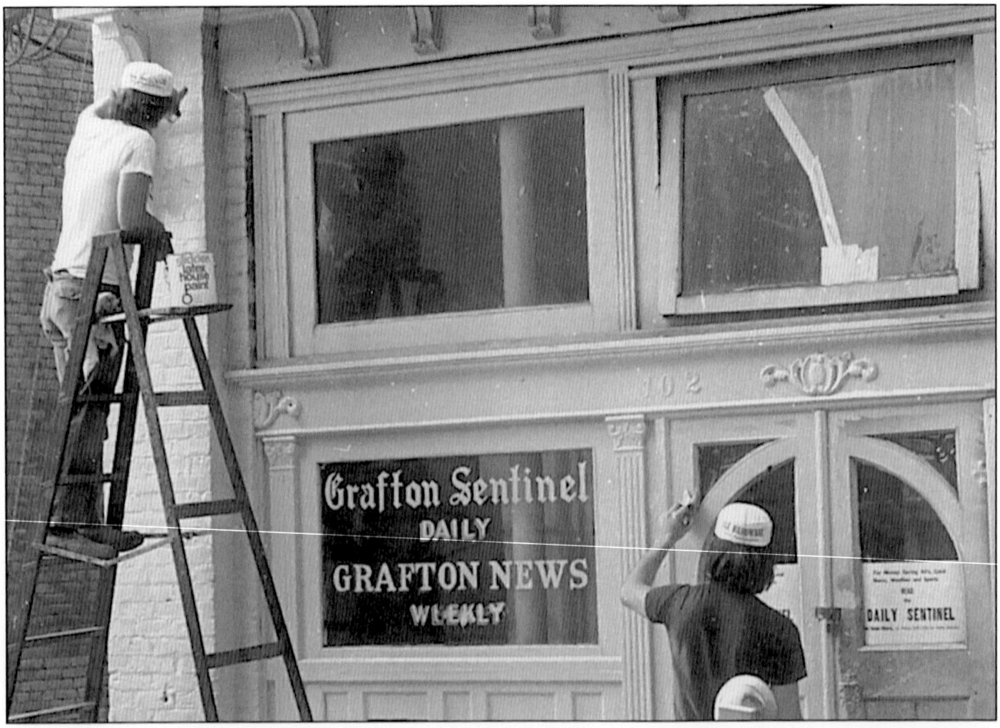

The Grafton Sentinel. Grafton's primary newspaper for generations, the *Grafton Daily Sentinel* was located in an old hotel building at 102 Latrobe Street. It operated during the years when lead type was set by hand. The city's current newspaper, the *Mountain Statesman* states that it is successor to the *Daily Sentinel*, founded in 1870. On September 11, 1975, the *Mountain Statesman* stopped publication as a daily newspaper and went to a three-times-per-week publication schedule. (Photo courtesy of Marvin Gelhausen.)

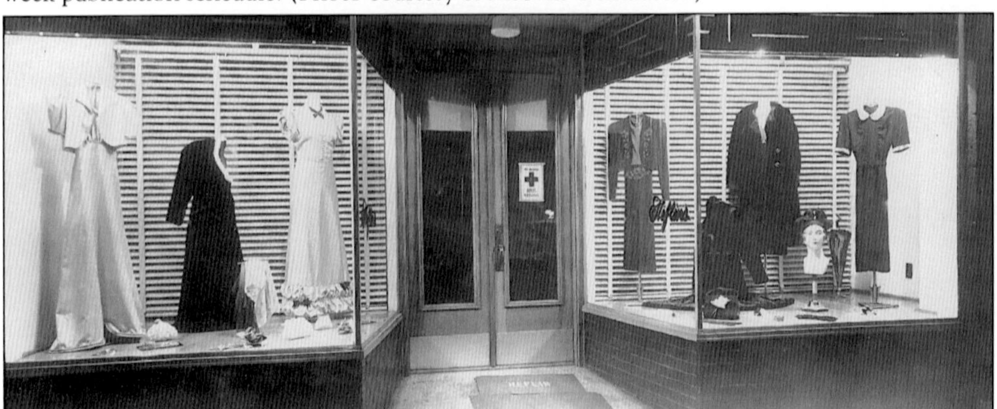

Heflin's Store. The midst of a depression may seem an odd time to start a new business, but two residents of Grafton did just that in 1932. Anna M. Heflin and her daughter Genevieve, wife of Fred Jackson, opened Heflin's Style Shop, a ladies ready-to-wear store along West Main Street. It operated for 34 years and was located at three different locations, 72, 115, and 68 West Main Street. For health reasons, Anna left the store in 1945 and Fred C. Jr. took over management and later the ownership of the store. He continued the operation until February 1966.

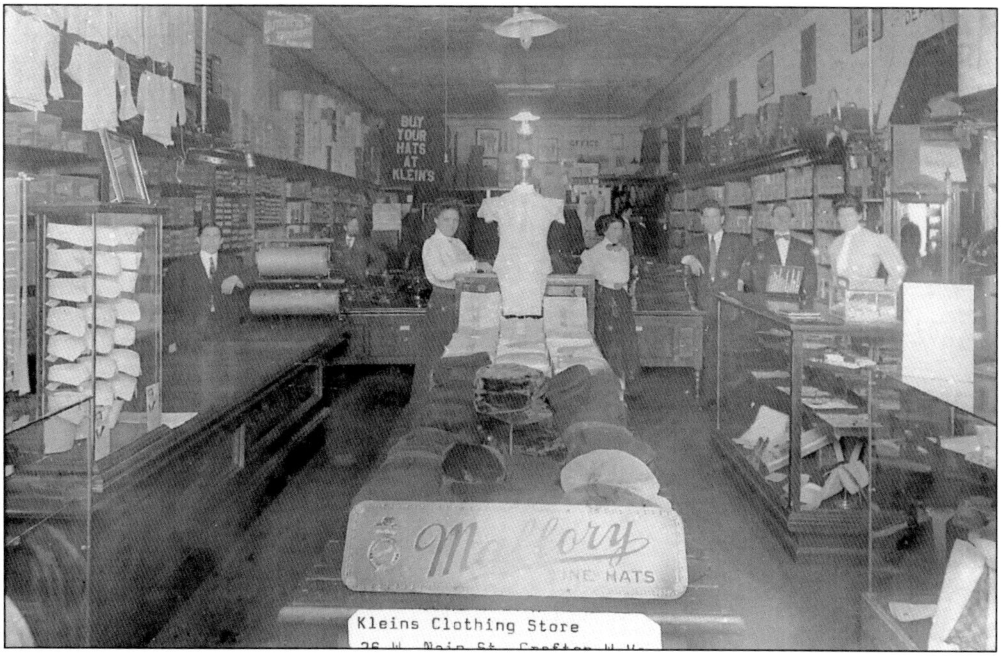

KLEINS CLOTHING STORE. This business was located at 26 West Main Street. Little additional information is available, but it was a business typical of the era when Grafton was an up and coming city. With the B&O Railroad as the main employer, the city was attracting business and industrial plants. Many entrepreneurs opened a wide range of business ventures that served citizens and those just passing through. Most clothing stores offered tailored, made-to-fit selections, unlike today's general one-size fits all options.

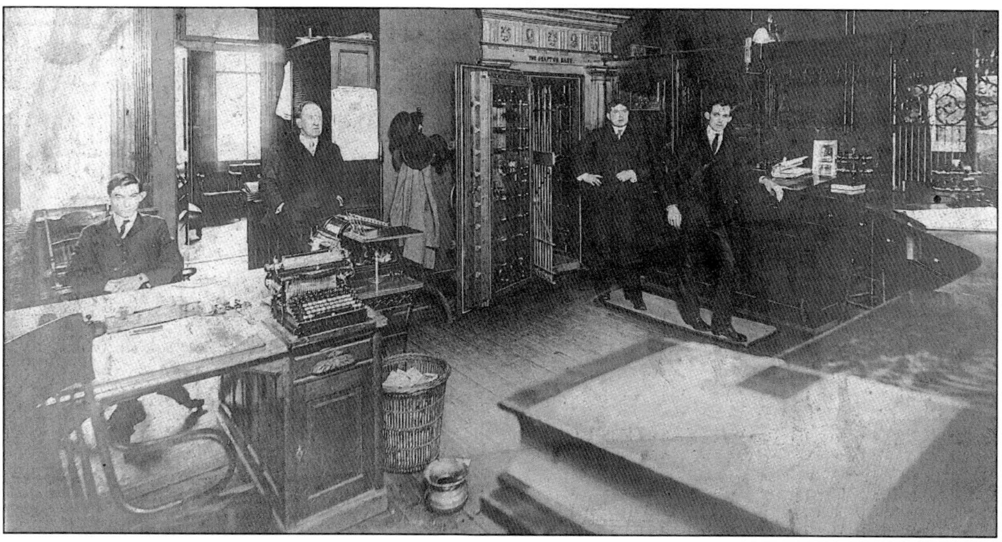

THE GRAFTON BANK. One of several banking facilities that served Grafton and Taylor County in prior years, the Grafton was chartered in July 1897, making it the first bank in Taylor County. John T. McGraw purchased a building formerly used by the First National Bank and completely remodeled it as the site for his new bank. Ironically, his sister Mary married Charles R. Durbin, son of Francis Marion Durbin (1837–1894); it was Charles who organized the Grafton Bank. In 1880 the Grafton became First National Bank. It failed in January 1915.

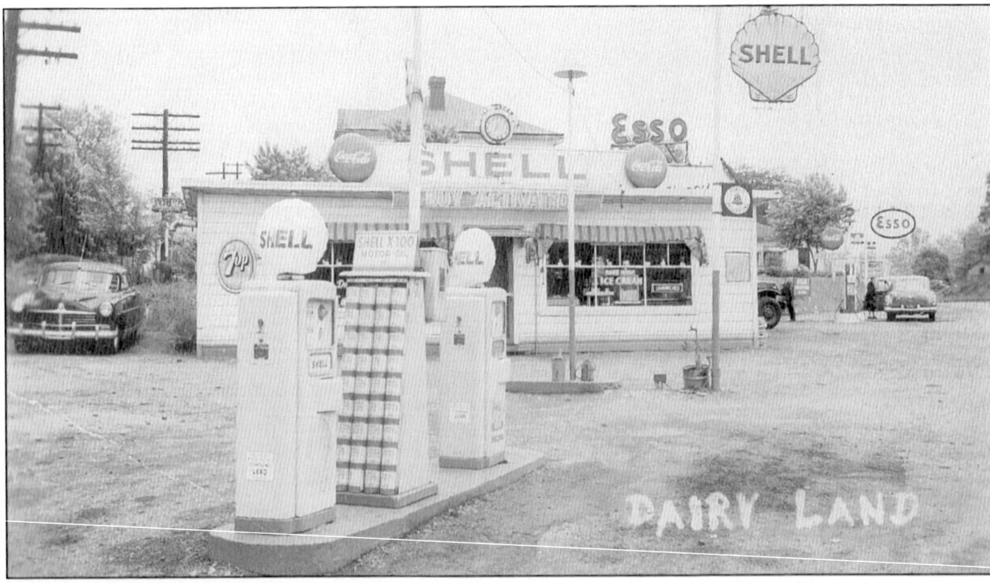

DAIRY LAND, JUNCTION OF ROUTE 50 AND OLD ROUTE 50. (Photo courtesy of Wayne McDevitt.)

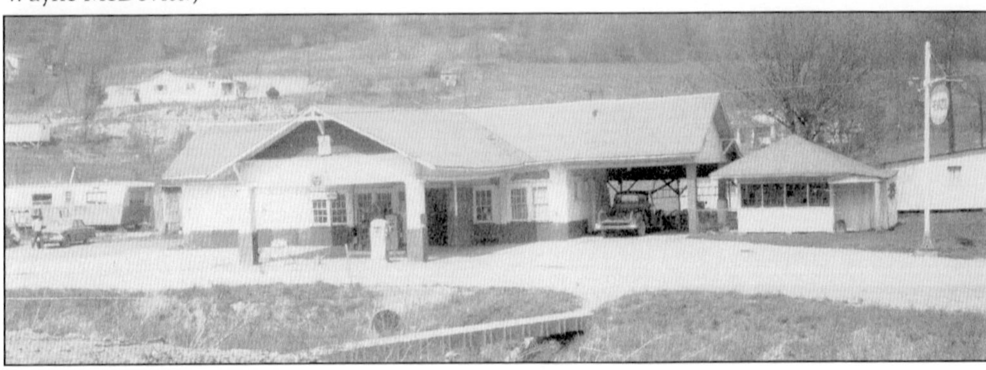

KELLEY FILLING STATION, IN THE WOODFORD ADDITION. (Photo courtesy of Norma Wyckoff.)

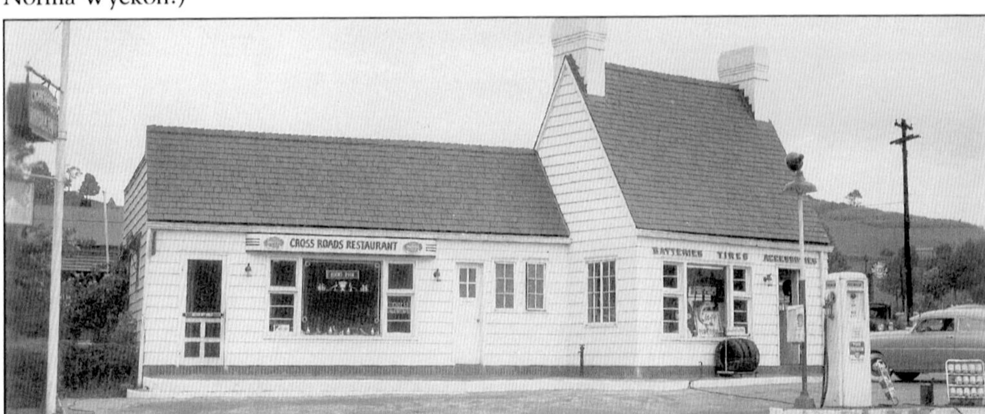

THE CROSS ROADS RESTAURANT, AT THE BLUEVILLE INTERSECTION. (Photo courtesy of Rick Reese.)

The J.V. Skelley Decorative Shop. Mr. Skelley was a well-known painter and decorator in Grafton. Shown is one of several Grafton locations where Skelley located his business over the years. In 1940, Skelley lived at 34 West Washington Street. (Photo courtesy of Wayne McDevitt.)

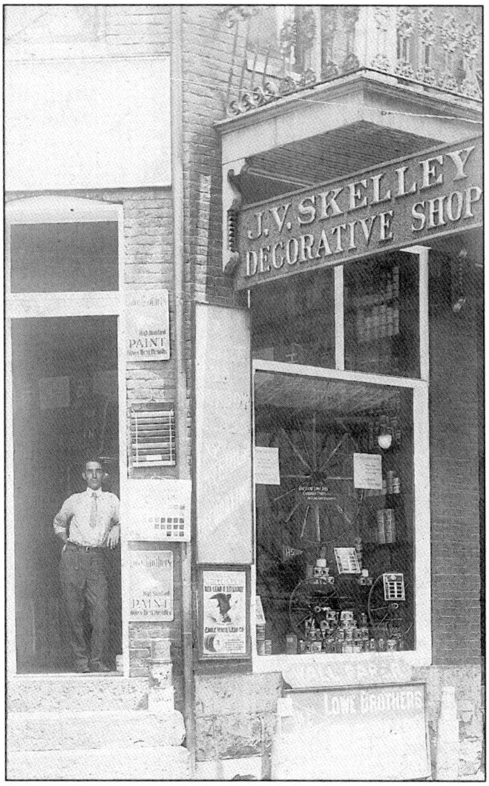

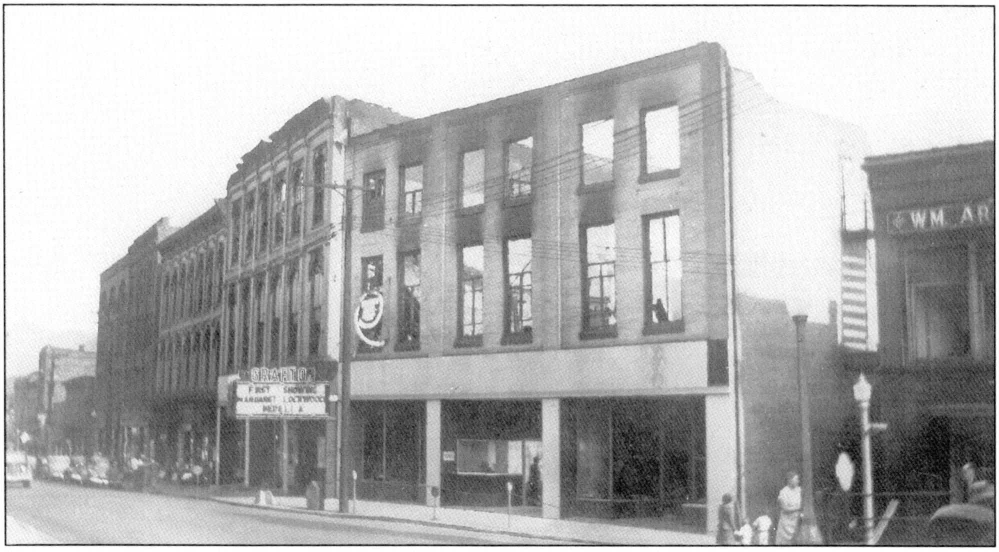

The Brinkman Opera House. The opera house was one of three buildings that made up the Brinkman Block, constructed on the south side of Main Street by John George Brinkman. The street level had seven store rooms. Brinkman used two rooms for a grocery and dry goods store, and rented the other five. The second and third floors held the Opera House Theater, a meeting hall, and the Brinkman's apartments for his wife and 11 children. Under the buildings he had a bakery and saloon. In May of 1947, fire destroyed part of the block. (Photo courtesy of Lois Heflin.)

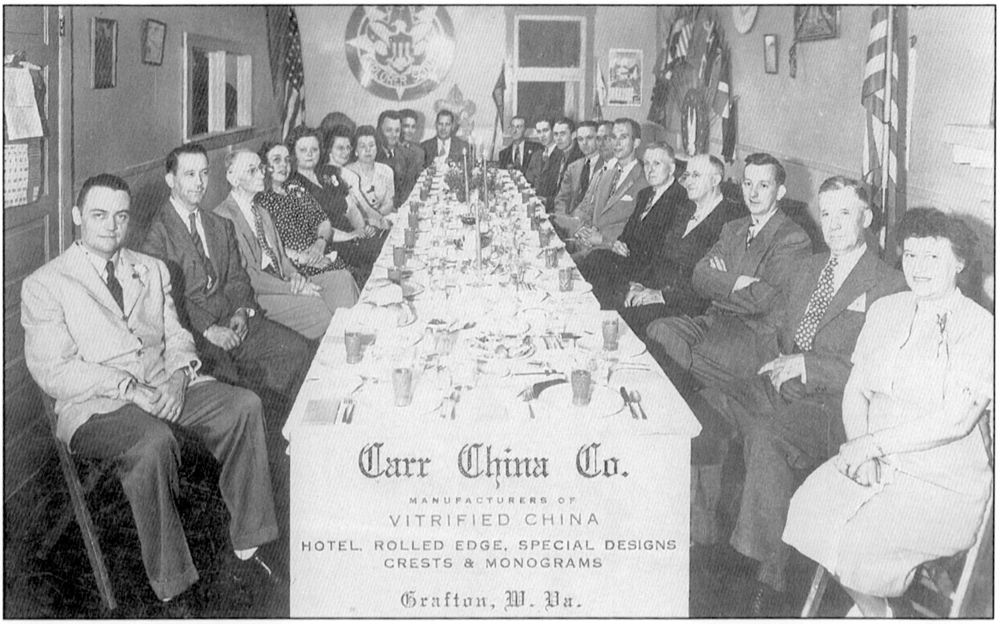

CARR CHINA COMPANY OFFICERS. Shown at a staff dinner on June 24, 1947, are the following: (on the left) Wheeler C. Bachman, James Barcus, R.W. Hilkey, Lucille Deck, Bernice Gregory, Kathleen Watkins, Mary J. Kirkpatrick, R.C. Anderson, John Kirkpatrick, L. Brimlow, unidentified, and L.J. Frey; (on the right) Edith Carr Bachman, O.E. Wyckoff, Richard Dean, C.P. Staton, Fred Henderson, George Walls, Merrett Feather, Edward Moore, Don Shaffer, and Gerald Duff. Carr China has become a popular collector item. (Photo courtesy of Wayne McDevitt.)

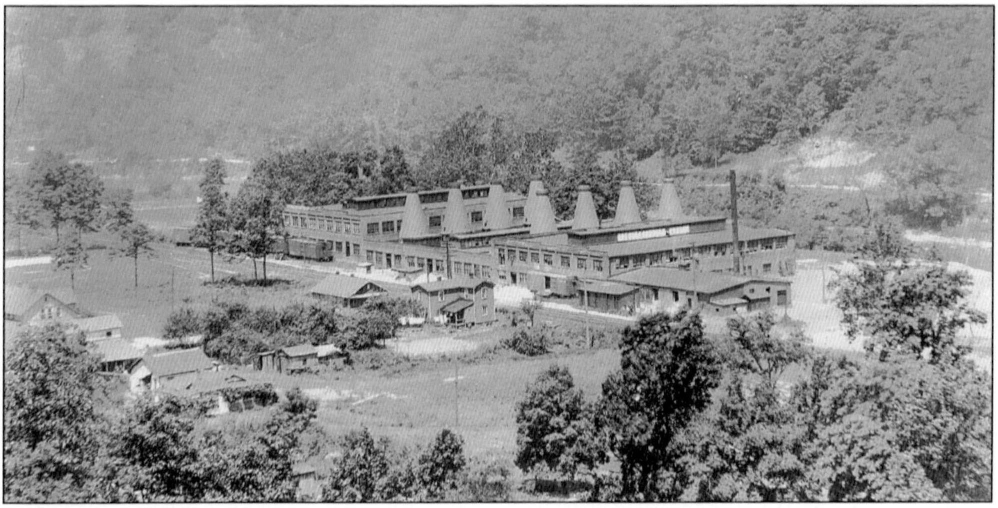

GRAFTON'S CARR CHINA PLANT. On June 1, 1916, Carr China Company received its certification of incorporation for the purposes of owning, manufacturing, buying, and selling chinaware, ironstone china, porcelain ware, semi-porcelain ware, and all other kinds of china, crockery, and sanitary ware. After World War II, plastic ware gained popularity in markets previously served by Carr China. Efforts to diversify failed and the pottery closed on July 16, 1952. Several efforts were made to reopen it, until the plant was destroyed by fire on July 16–17, 1966.

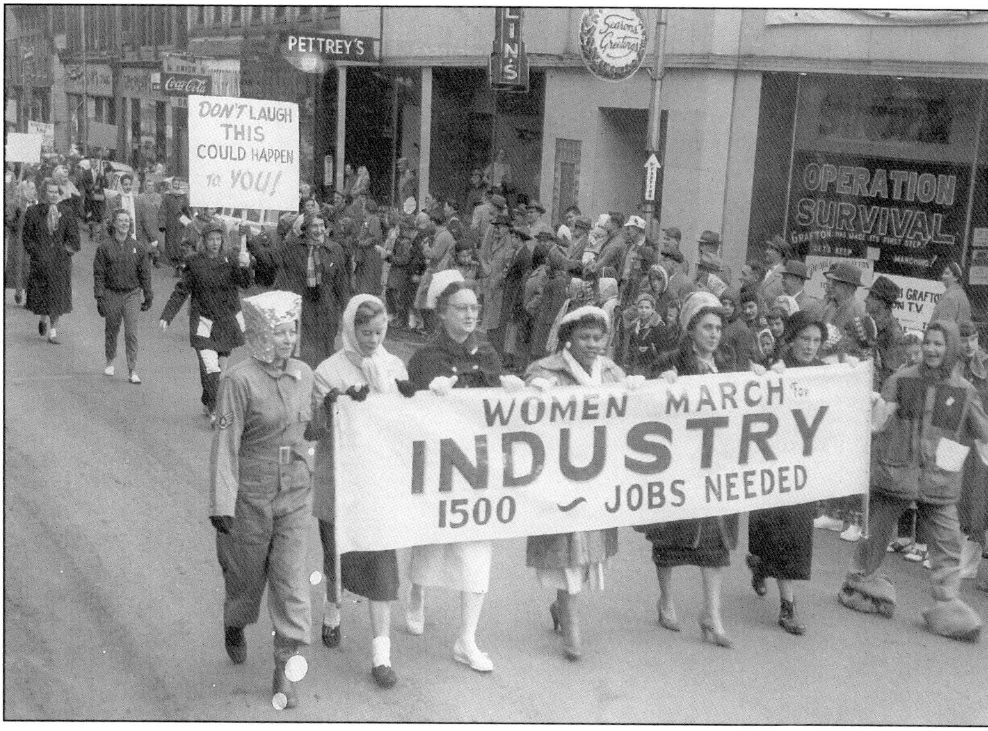

OPERATION SURVIVAL. In the late 1950s the business and industrial base of Grafton took a downward turn. The Hazel-Atlas Glass Plant was closing, and other businesses and plants had either closed or were struggling to stay in business. The women of the community organized and Operation Survival was created. As part of the effort, the women got together and marched through the downtown carrying a banner proclaiming, "Women March for Industry, 1,500 jobs needed." The efforts worked and Grafton was named an All American City in 1963.

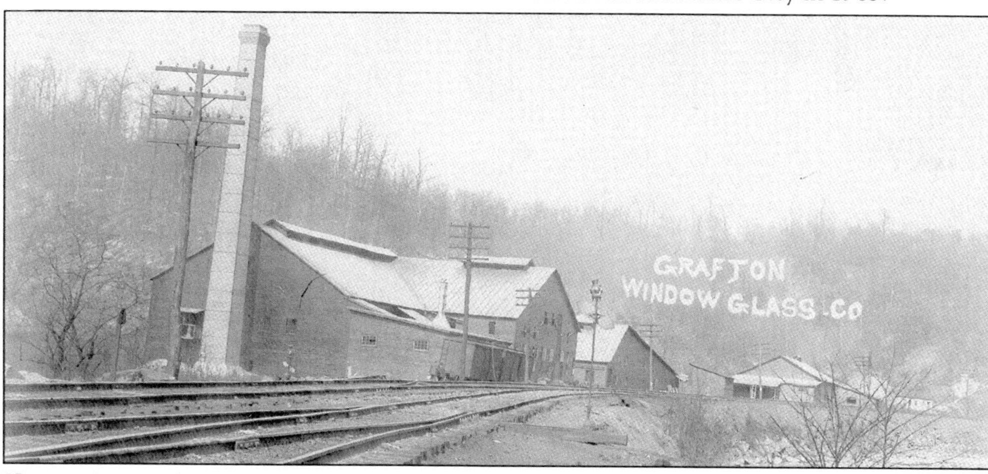

HAZEL ATLAS GLASS. In 1915, the Hazel Atlas Corporation acquired the Columbia Tile Company. William A. Beavers was trustee of the bondholders for Columbia Tile and he transferred the Fetterman Plant to Hazel Atlas on March 5, 1915. Hazel Atlas closed its doors in 1959. One of the successes of Grafton's Operation Survival and the March for Industry was that part of the Hazel Atlas plant became the West Virginia Plastics/Baby World plant and the box plant reopened. Baby World is now closed, but the box plant remains.

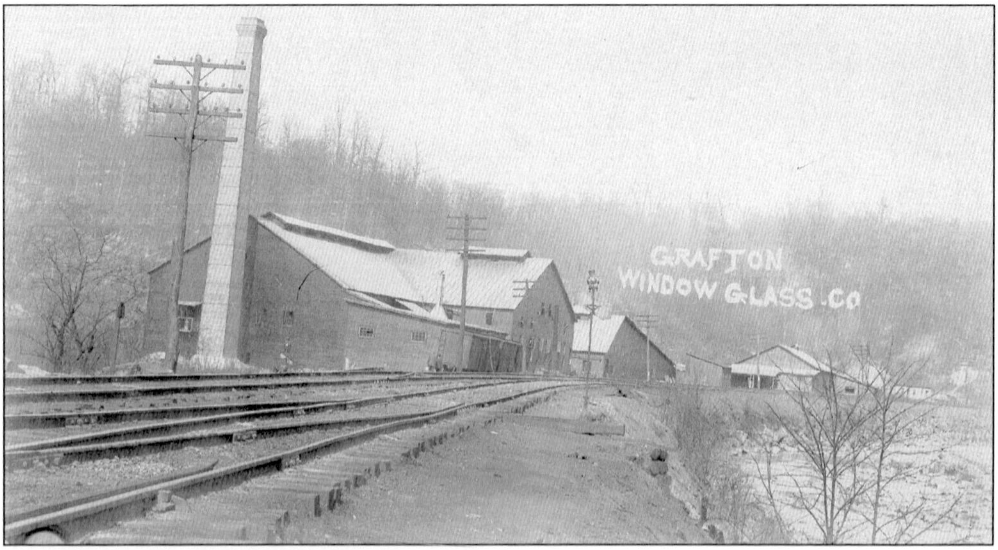

ROYAL GLASS PLANT. Originally this was the Grafton Window Glass Company. The plant was located in the East End area of Grafton. In 1913, it became the Royal Window Glass Company. Later, a group headed by Dr. O.S. Campbell operated the plant as the Campbell Glass Company. A large brick chimney is all that remains today of the structure. The site is located in a valley and is relatively flat. It is adjacent to the East End rail yard. A proposal was made to develop the land into a park, but it was eventually dropped. (Photo courtesy of Wayne McDevitt.)

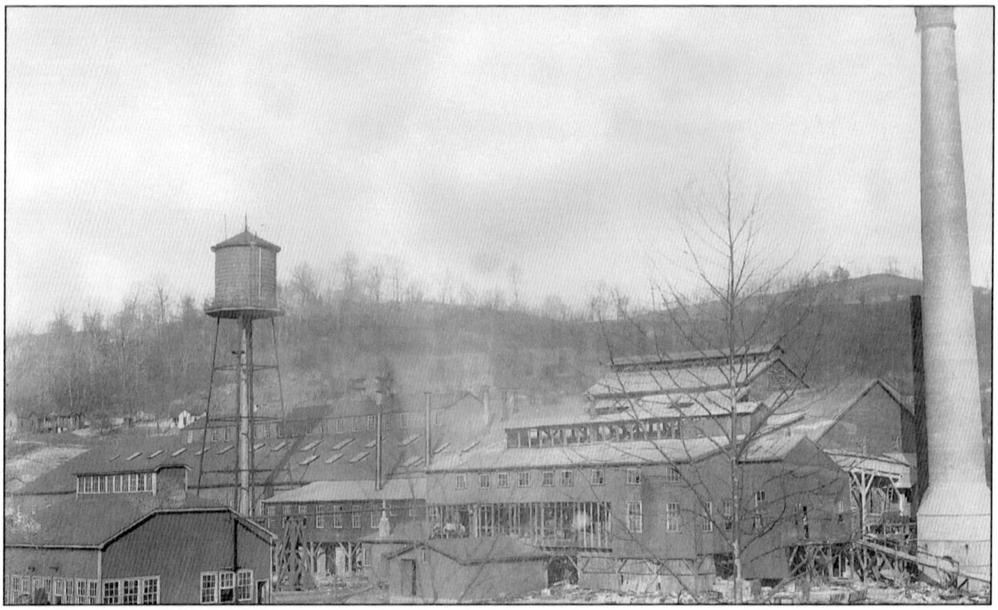

TYGART VALLEY GLASS PLANT. Originally, this was the Beaumont Glass Company, but on July 9, 1906, it became the Tygart Valley Glass Plant. In 1910, this plant was producing pressed glass tableware. It is interesting to note the number of plants that Grafton and Taylor County once had operating within its borders. During the years when most shipment was by railroad, Grafton was in an ideal location. However, this changed when trucks took over as the preferred mode of shipment and Grafton was bypassed by the interstate.

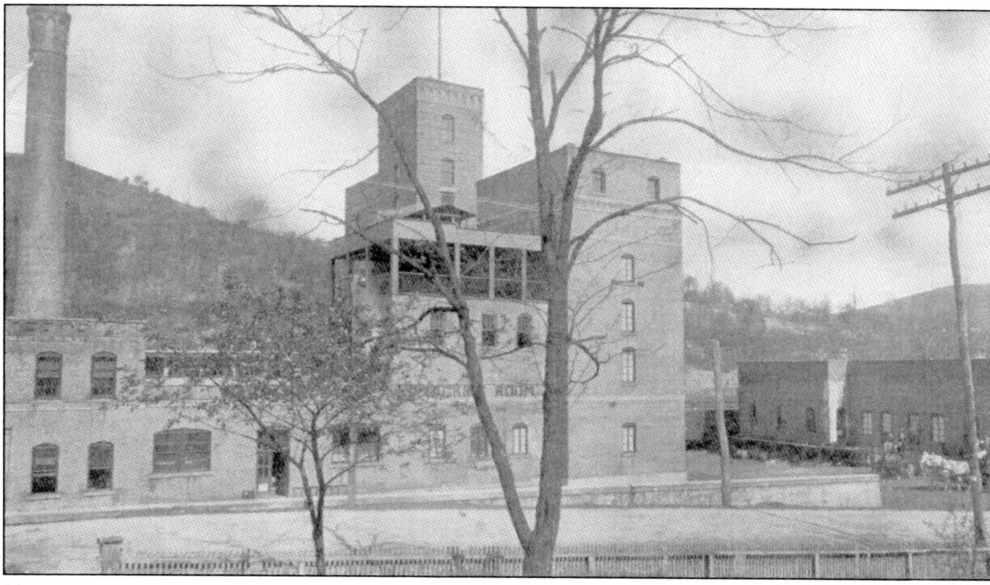

The Tygart Valley Brewing Company. Incorporated in 1905 to manufacture products associated with the brewing process, manufacture of ice, and construction of water works to furnish water to others. Prominent Grafton businessman John T. McGraw, owned one of the five common shares of stock in the company. The West Main Street Grafton location, in the Fetterman section, was later used by the W.A. Woodyard Lumber Company. The building was razed and the Grafton Manor was built on this property. (Photo courtesy of Wayne McDevitt)

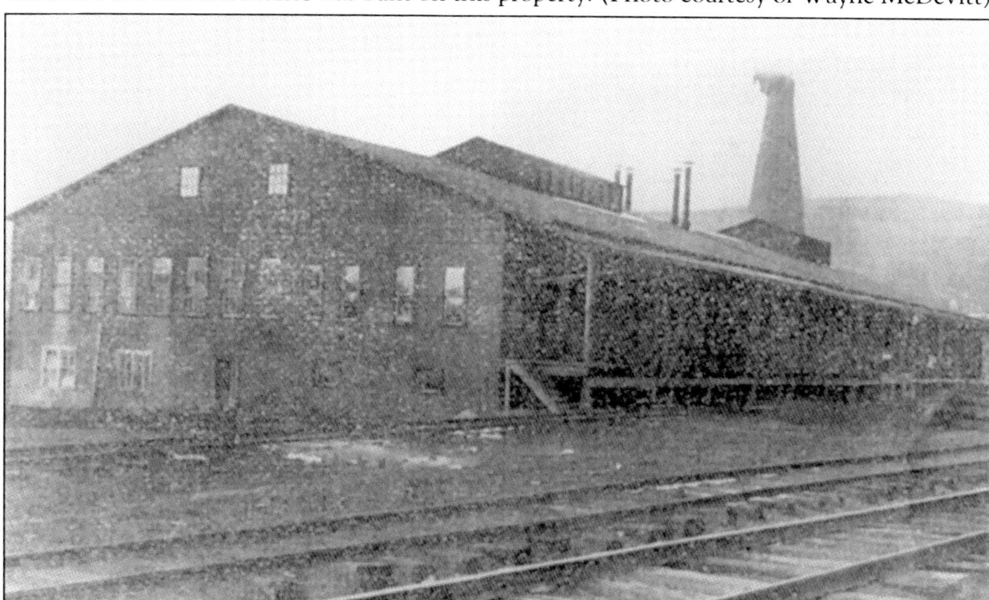

Empress Glass Plant. This business was incorporated September 2, 1905. On June 21, 1911, the Columbia Tile Company took over the old Empress Glass plant in the city's First Ward. Some of the tile used in Grafton's B&O Passenger Station came from the plant. One of the main Columbia Tile products at that time was a white tile with a dull finish that closely resembled marble. Many Grafton homes used Columbia Tile around fireplaces and in other applications. (Photo courtesy of Marvin Gelhausen.)

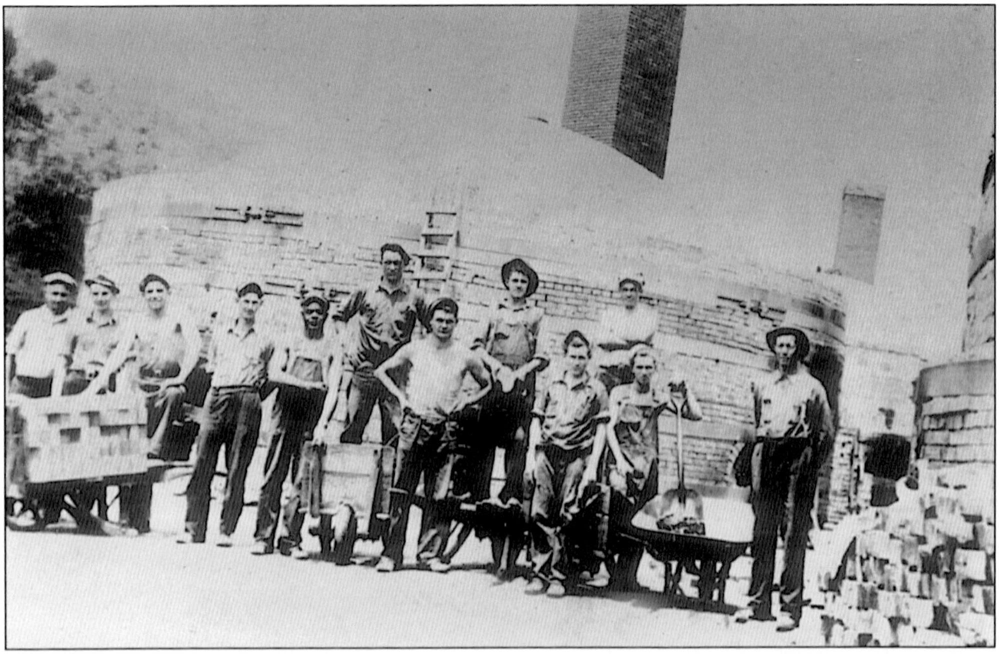

Thornton Brick Yard Employees. Travelers passing through the small community of Thornton, and other similar small communities in Taylor County, are amazed by the stories of old-timers who can recall the locations of a number of businesses, stores, mines, stone quaries, sand plants, and other means of employment in Taylor County and in nearby sections of Preston County. In the early days of these businesses, the main means of getting raw material in or products out was by shipment via the B&O Railroad. (Photo courtesy of Paul Shaffer.)

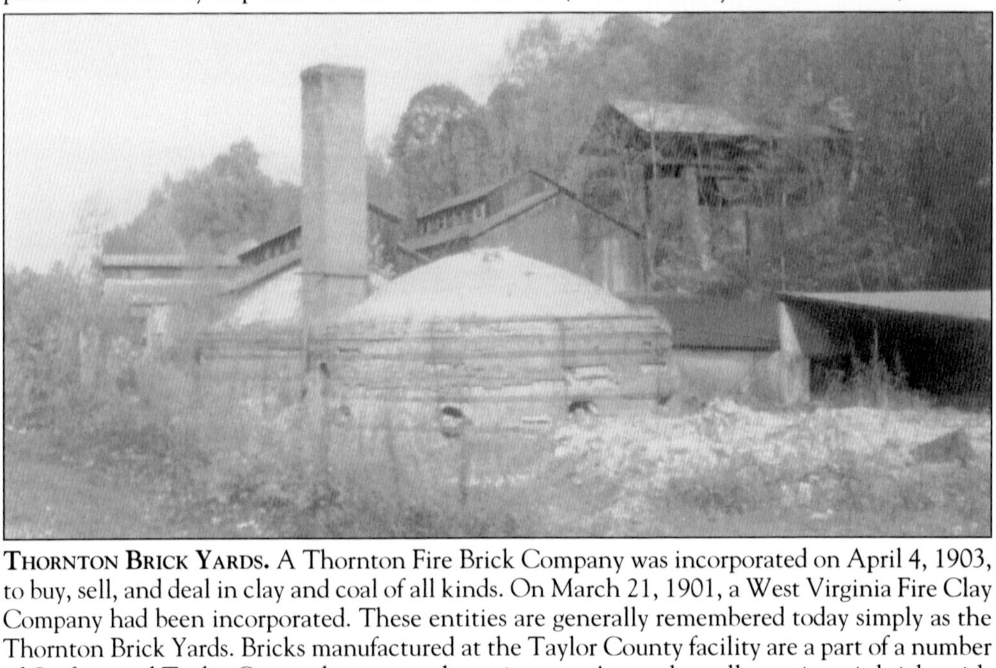

Thornton Brick Yards. A Thornton Fire Brick Company was incorporated on April 4, 1903, to buy, sell, and deal in clay and coal of all kinds. On March 21, 1901, a West Virginia Fire Clay Company had been incorporated. These entities are generally remembered today simply as the Thornton Brick Yards. Bricks manufactured at the Taylor County facility are a part of a number of Grafton and Taylor County homes, roads, patios, etc. A popular collector item is bricks with the name of the city on them. (Photo courtesy of Mary Susan Shafferman.)

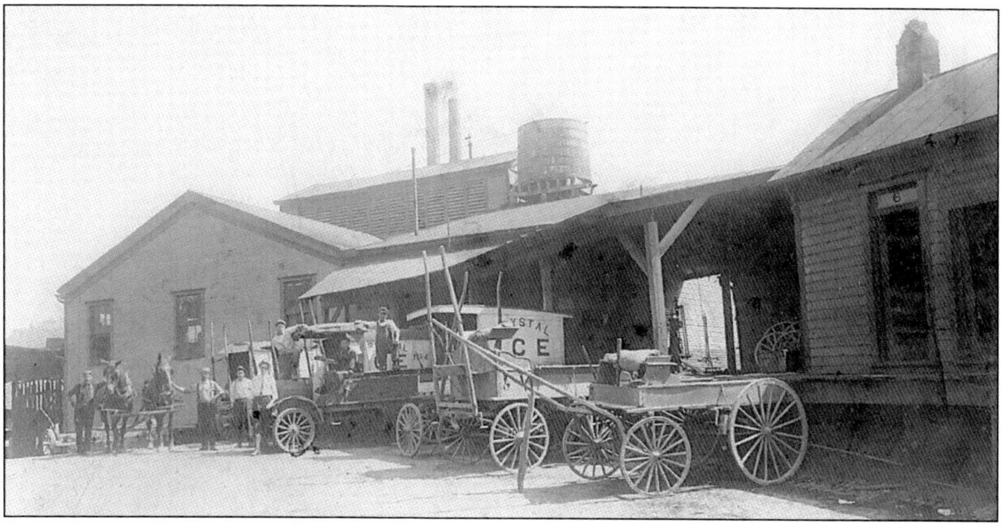

CRYSTAL ICE COMPANY. This former business establishment was located at 11 Beech Street (also listed as Jed Street). An advertisement in the 1902 Grafton City Directory states that the Crystal Ice Company created pure, artificial ice and that the shipment of their ice in boxes to nearby towns was a specialty of the company. It is difficult for today's microwave generation to even imagine living in the days before electricity and refrigeration became part of everyday life. However, there was a time when companies like Crystal Ice were a necessity.

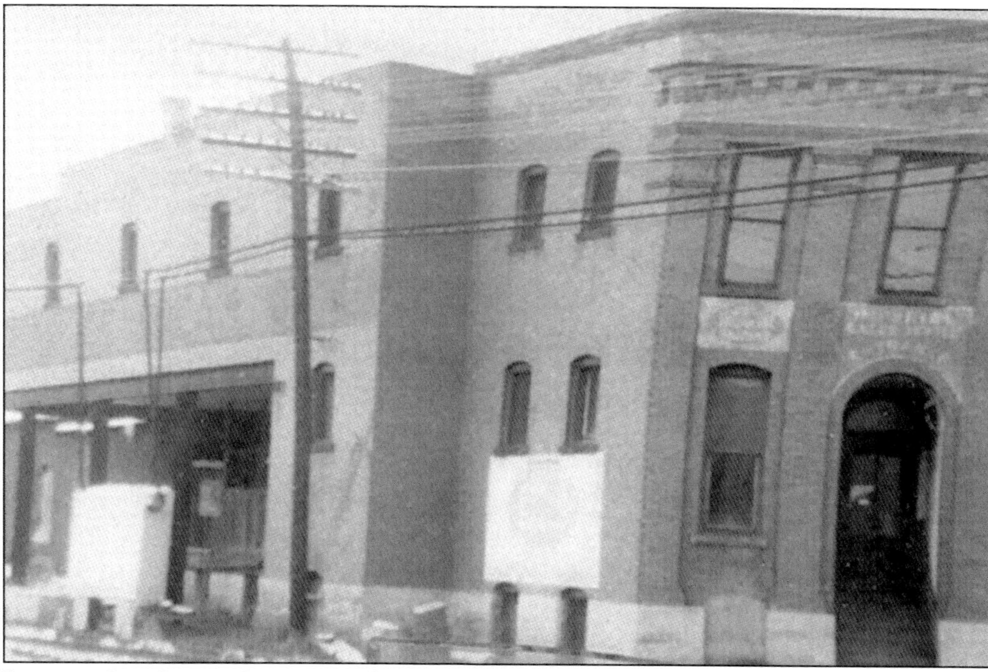

IMPERIAL ICE CREAM COMPANY. This business was located near the Beech Street crossing of the B&O Railroad. The structure was razed when U.S. Route 119 South was relocated. As the company name indicates, it manufactured the always popular product of ice cream. The company motto was, "Eat a Plate of Ice Cream Everyday." Plants were located in Grafton, Clarksburg, Fairmont, Parkersburg, Wheeling, and in Cumberland, MD. The company ran ads inviting the public to visit one of their plants anytime.

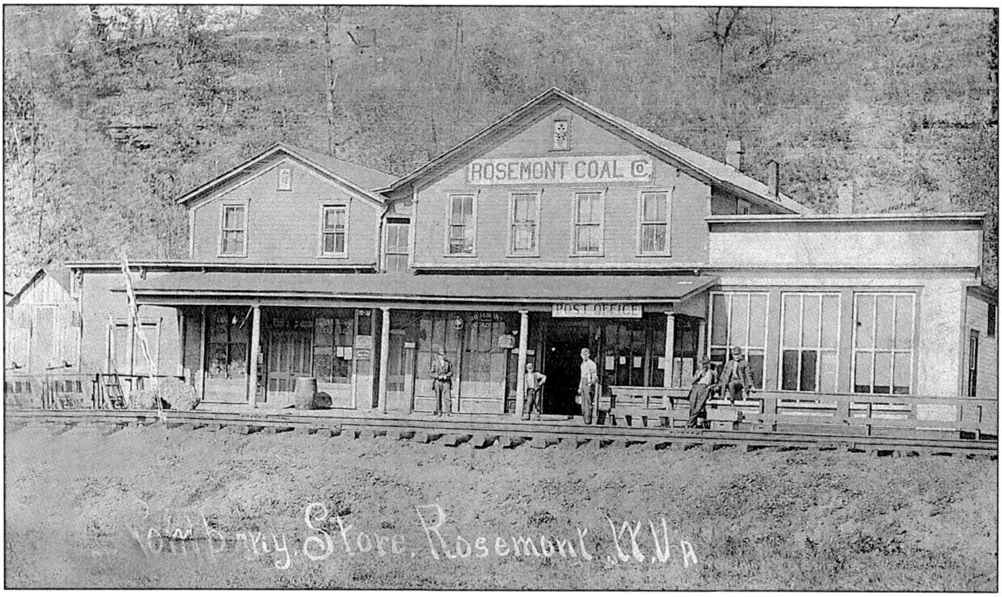

ROSEMONT COAL COMPANY STORE AND POST OFFICE. In her district history of Flemington, WV, titled *We Were We Are*, Geneva Phelps states that a number of mining operations were under way in the Flemington area in the early 1900s. Phelps says each mine built homes for their workers and located company stores nearby. The county produced 541,769 tons of coal in 1924. Coal mining provided employment in Taylor County and across West Virginia for many years. (Photo courtesy of Geneva Phelps.)

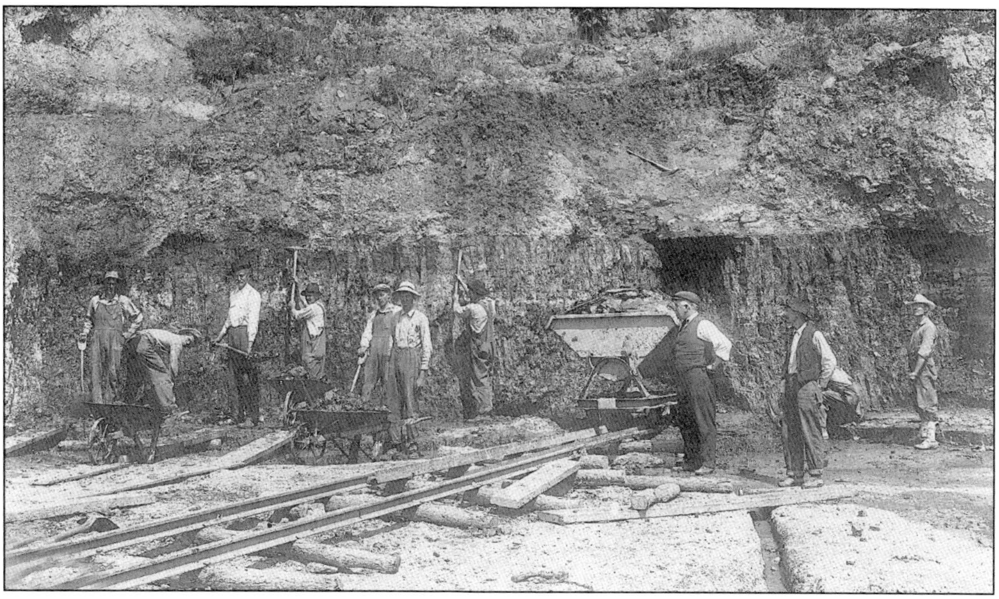

NEW YORK MINE AT SIMPSON. In the late 1800 and early 1900s there were coal mines in the Flemington, Simpson, Rosemont, Wendel, Bear Mountain, Brownton, and Galloway areas. In *We Were We Are*, Geneva Phelps says the nationalities of the miners were recorded in the early mine records. Americans were not designated, but a 1924 record lists 957 miners working inside the mines and 132 outside. Foreigners are listed at 92, with a notation of 116 Slavok and 19 black miners.

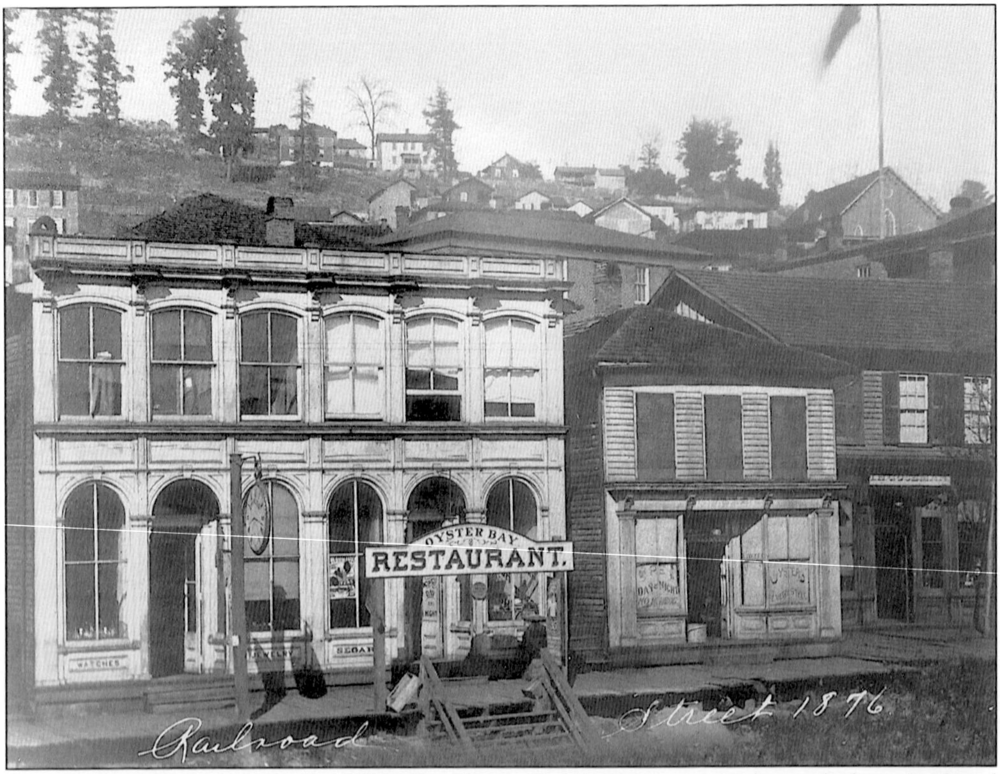

Oyster Bay Restaurant. In 1876, the Oyster Bay Restaurant was located along Railroad Street. This street was beside the B&O Railroad tracks and was the main business street in the early years of the city. Grafton's first B&O Passenger Station also was in this area. Many of these early buildings were destroyed in what has become known as the Great Fire of 1887. Over the years, fires—and before construction of Tygart Dam, floods—resulted in the loss of a number of Grafton businesses. (Photo courtesy of Marvin Gelhausen.)

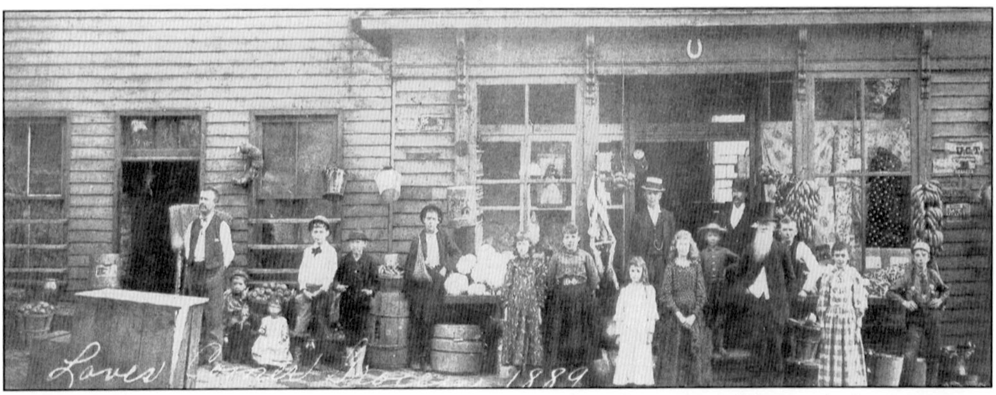

Loves Corner Grocery. Loves Corner Grocery is listed as one of the early businesses in Grafton. One copy of this frequently published historical photo has some of the people identified. From left to right are Clay Love, ? Lippencot, ? Lippencot, George Gilbert, William S. Wren, Jerry Basford, ? Hough, Eva Long, Pansy Zeck, ? Lough, Clarence Poe, James Love (owner of the store, the father of Clay, and the grandfather of Eva), Ben Poe, Annie Barron, and Ed Wren. Ed and William Wren were sons of Mary Haslup Wren. (Photo courtesy of James Bolliger.)

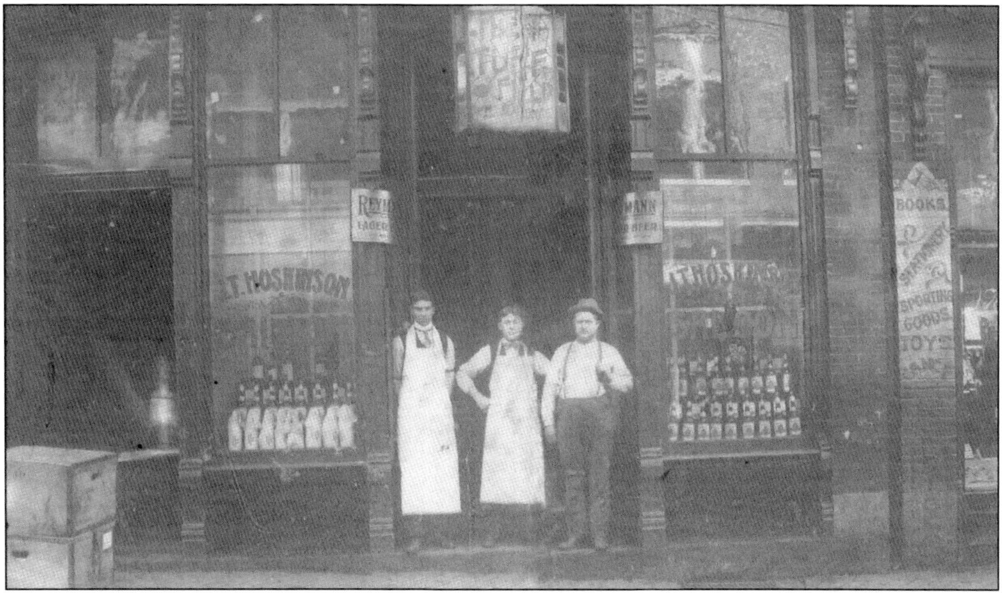

I.T. HOSKINSON. This Grafton business carried books, stationery, sporting goods, and toys. In 1910, a Grafton Board of Trade publication stated that, "It is not now, nor never has been, a boom town in any sense of the word. But Grafton is looked upon, and has long been looked upon, as one of the best regular towns in central West Virginia. Here a number of merchants have located, the oldest and most successful of whom will tell you that as a business town, the city has no peer its size in the state, or in surrounding states." (Photo courtesy of Norma Wyckoff.)

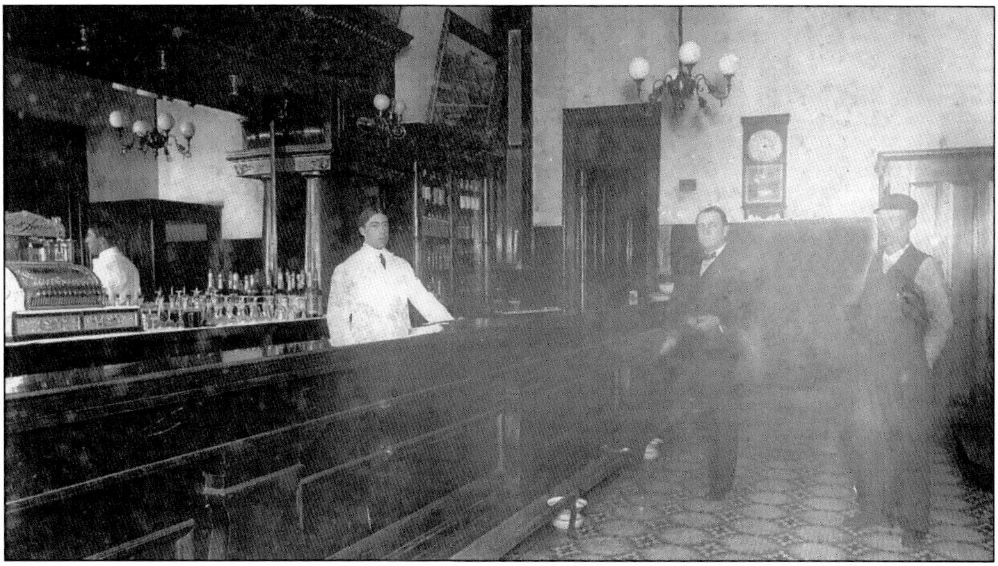

EARLY CLUB. The early days of Grafton were during a time period when saloons were popular. These were followed by fancier clubs and restaurants. Several of these types of early businesses were located along Latrobe Street. Although the location is not identified, some believe this photo may be an early look at the interior of what is today the 120 Club. If not, the appearance is typical of several buildings that once lined Latrobe Street. Notice the decorative floor tiles. They were most likely made in Grafton.

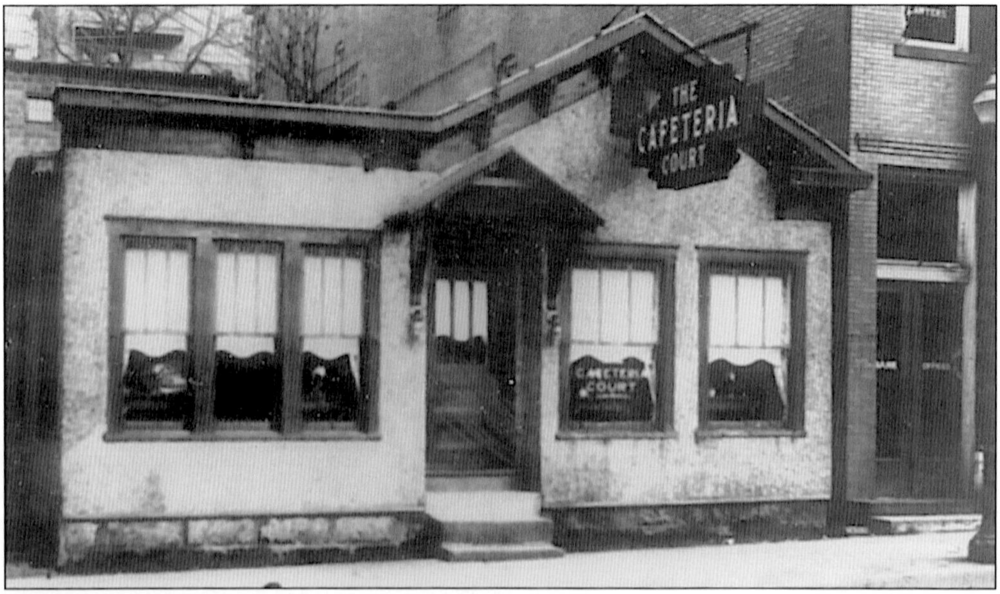

CAFETERIA COURT. Incorporated September 20, 1935, to conduct, operate, and maintain restaurants, hotels, refreshment stands, etc., Cafeteria Court was incorporated by Anna M. Heflin and Genevieve H. Jackson, both of Grafton, and Frances H. Dunham of Fairmont. It was located along West Main Street on the site currently housing the Parrish Agency, beside the VFW Memorial City Post 3081 and across the street from the Taylor County Courthouse. The Cafeteria Court building was eventually razed.

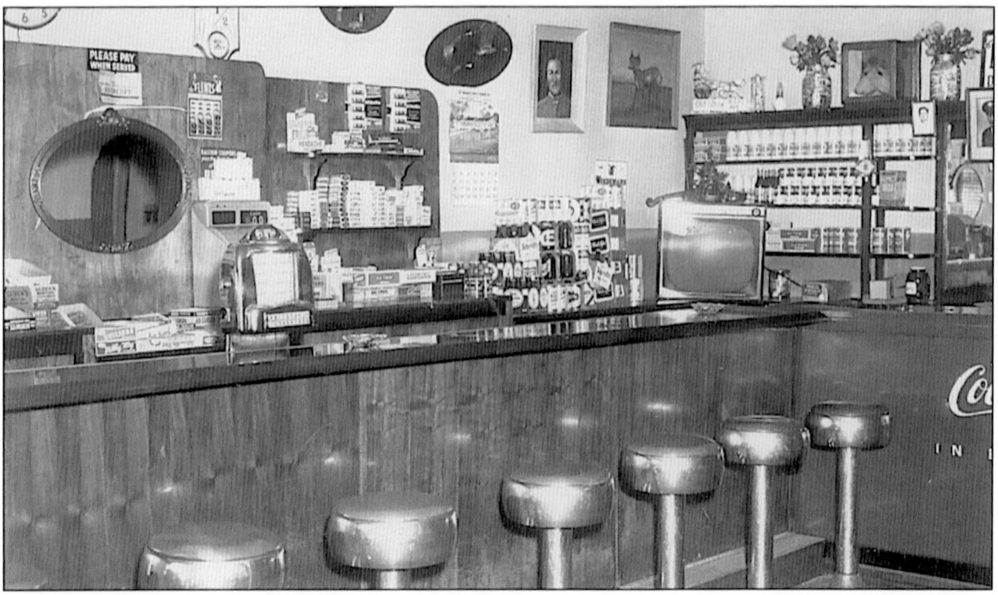

CONEY ISLAND RESTAURANT. This Grafton business was located along Latrobe Street and was noted for its hotdog sauce. Some say the restaurant had the best hotdog chili in the world. Opened and operated by a Greek immigrant, Angelo Soterion, the business was later inherited by his daughter Katherine and operated by her husband, Art Stravakis. The Latrobe Street building that once housed the Coney Island Restaurant is now home to the Bread of Life Mission. Many of the adjacent old buildings were razed. (Photo courtesy of Peggy Robinson.)

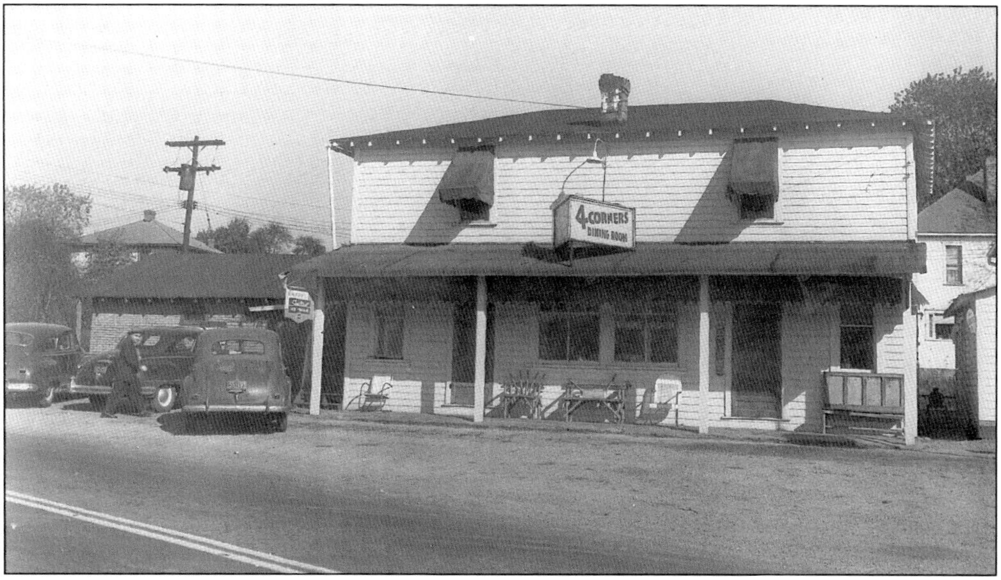

4-CORNERS RESTAURANT. The first 4-Corners Restaurant opened in 1938 in the above woodframe building, which burned in 1955. The present building was built in 1955. The original proprietors were the DeLanceys, followed by Allene Cutright, then the Joe Medricks, and next by Ray and Mabel Holbert. In 1965, A.R. "Dick" Leonard became manager until 1986, except for less than two years under Claudia Jennings. Since 1986, Paulette and Ellis Byers have owned and operated this Blueville intersection landmark. (Photo courtesy of Wayne McDevitt.)

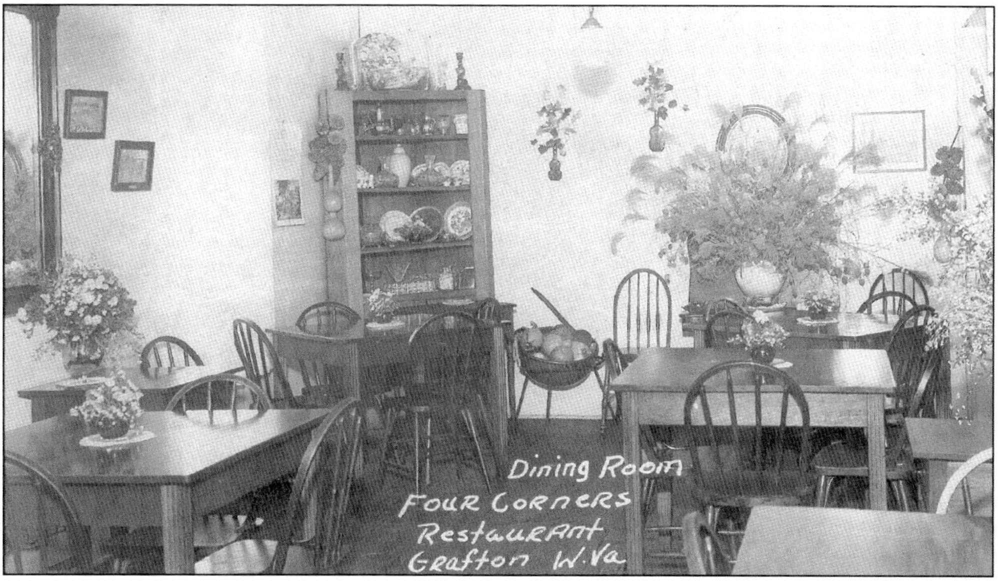

4-CORNERS RESTAURANT. This is an early interior view of the dining room of the 4-Corners Restaurant. The main dining room today features several scenic wall prints along the one side wall. It has an inverted interior sloping ceiling that comes down in the center and goes up toward the exterior walls. 4-Corners also has a second-level Mountaineer Room that is used for club meetings, receptions, and other group gatherings. The current owners recently added an exterior deck area for dining. (Photo courtesy of Wayne McDevitt.)

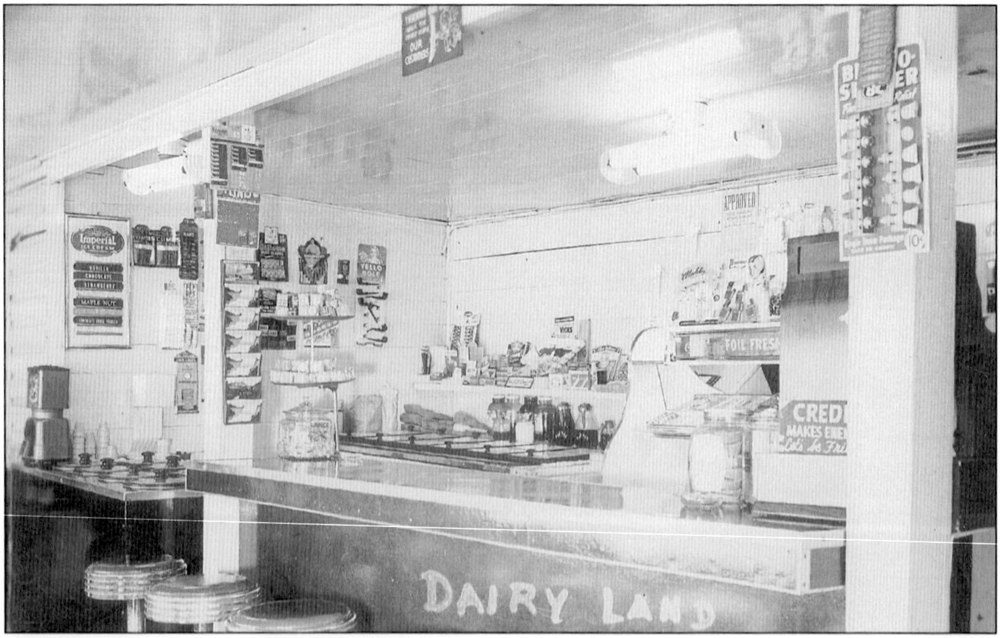

DAIRY LAND. In the early 1940s, Joe and Audra Mehlinger operated the service station at the intersection of Routes 50 and 119. Audra produced and sold homemade ice cream and this proved to be quite a popular entrepreneur business venture. In 1953, the business was transformed into Audra's Snack Bar and the couple operated it until they retired in 1967. Audra also is a member of the Harman family, which moved to Grafton in 1942. (Photo courtesy of Wayne McDevitt.)

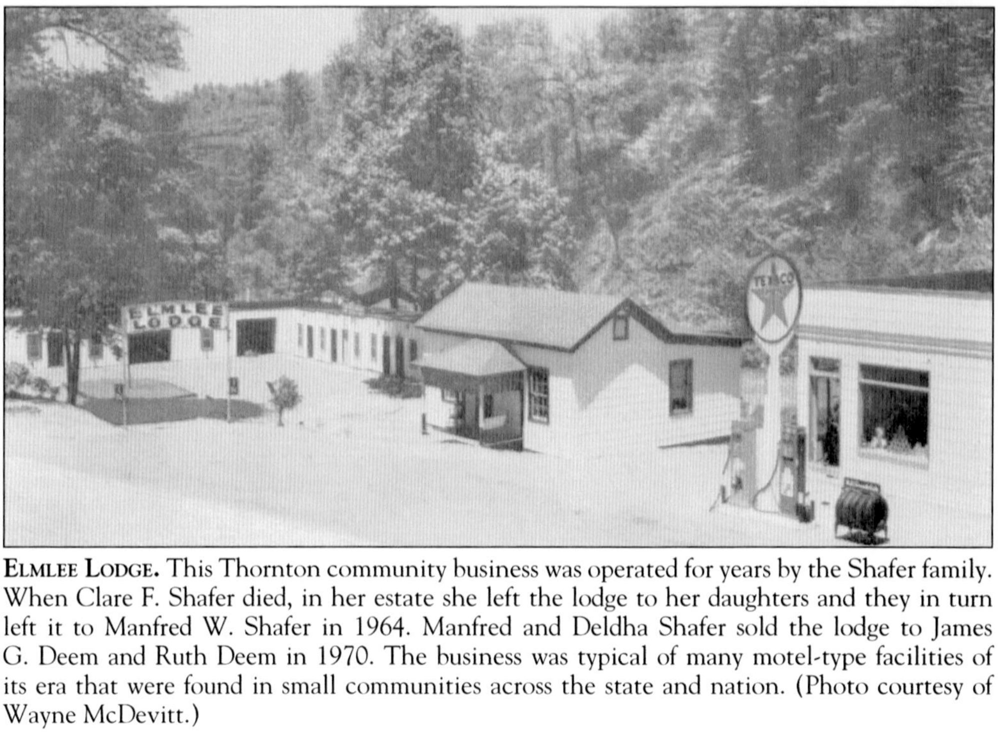

ELMLEE LODGE. This Thornton community business was operated for years by the Shafer family. When Clare F. Shafer died, in her estate she left the lodge to her daughters and they in turn left it to Manfred W. Shafer in 1964. Manfred and Deldha Shafer sold the lodge to James G. Deem and Ruth Deem in 1970. The business was typical of many motel-type facilities of its era that were found in small communities across the state and nation. (Photo courtesy of Wayne McDevitt.)

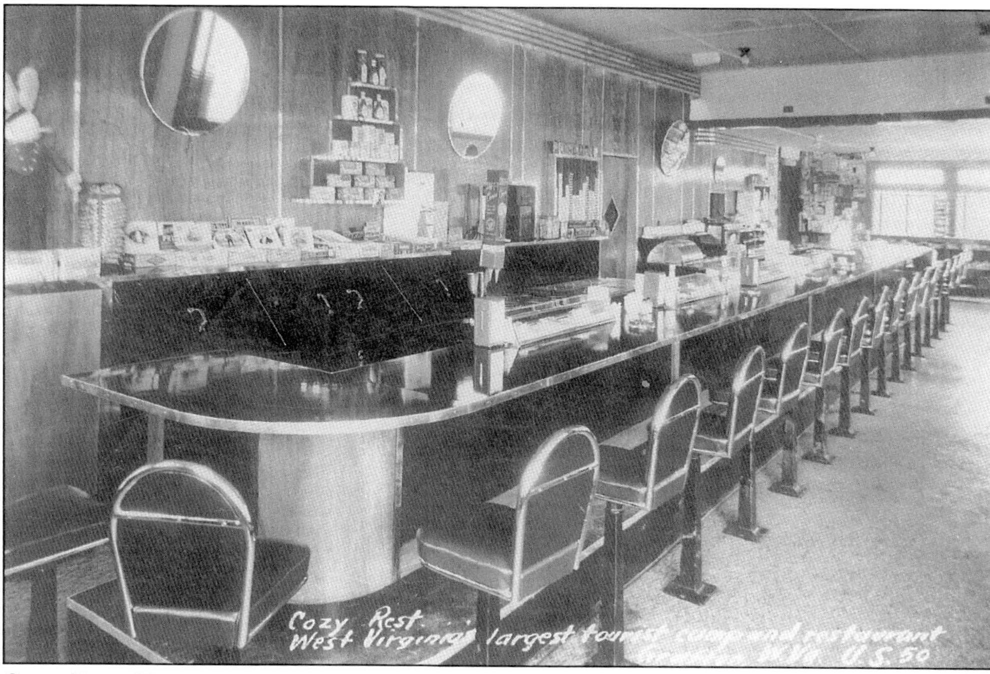

Cozy Rest Restaurant. In 1939, Debendarfer's Inc., was incorporated to provide eating establishments, lodging, and filling station services. This corporation owned and operated the Cozy Rest. The Route 50 business, just west of Pruntytown, was advertised as West Virginia's largest tourist camp. One of the business managers was D.W. Dudley. In 1961, the corporation's name was officially changed to Cozy Rest. On July 1, 1969, the restaurant was struck by lightning and the resulting fire destroyed the building. (Photo courtesy of Wayne McDevitt.)

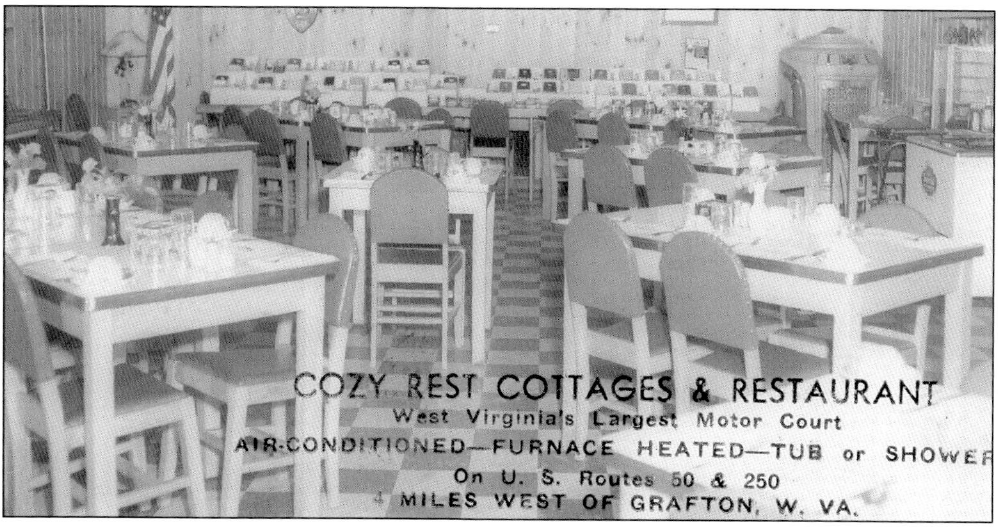

Cozy Rest Restaurant. This Taylor County business, which included a gasoline service station, restaurant, and cabins, was advertised for years as West Virginia's largest tourist camp. It was noted that the Cozy Rest cabins were modern cottages with baths. The buildings were air conditioned for the summer months and furnace heated for the fall and winter months. The restaurant served fine food for fine people. The owners/operators also offered restaurant space for private parties and banquets. (Photos courtesy of Wayne McDevitt.)

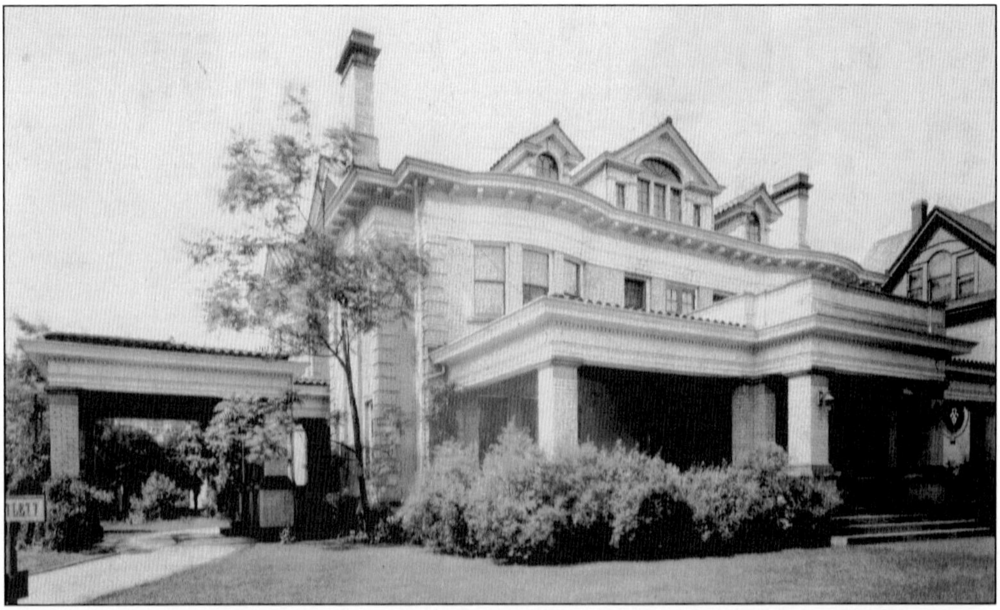

BARTLETT FUNERAL HOME. This mansion was built along McGraw Avenue in 1914 by sugar and wholesale grocery magnate Joseph Pugh. In 1928 it was purchased by G.T. Bartlett and he moved his funeral home into the mansion. Today, the historic home remains the Bartlett Funeral home, although it has had several owners. The business operated from 1908 to 1920 as the Perine and Bartlett Furniture and Undertaking Company. In 1920 the partnership dissolved and the furniture line was dropped. (Photo courtesy of G. Thomas Bartlett III.)

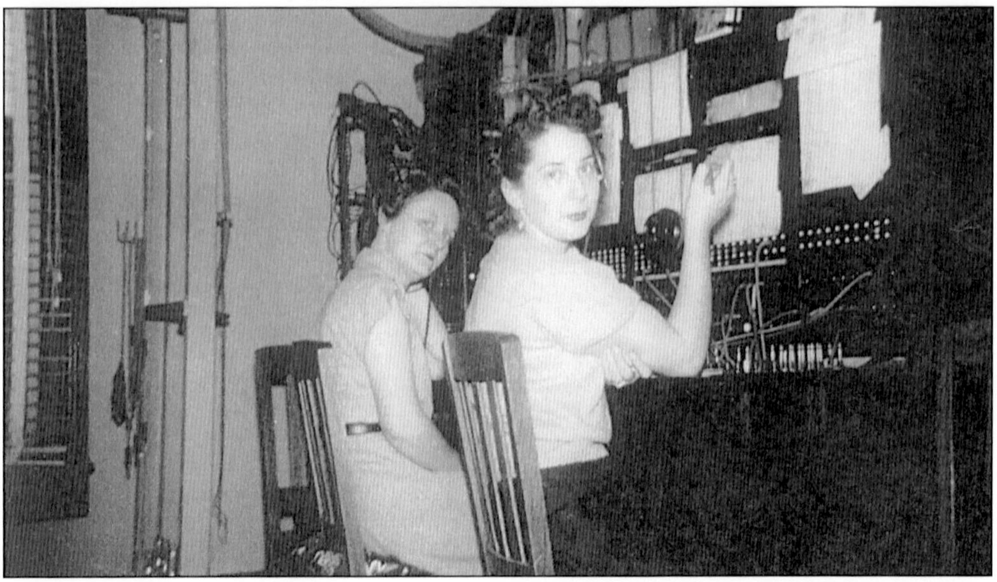

FLEMINGTON PHONE WORKERS. There was a time when every phone call included a chat with a friendly operator. Advances in technology now make it possible to call anywhere in the world simply by pushing the right numbers on your phone. While cell phones, various forms of wireless communication, home computers, and the Internet have increased our access to communication, many remain nostalgic for the good old days of this 1960 photo and the phone operators. (Photo courtesy of Geneva Phelps.)

Six

Government and Public Buildings

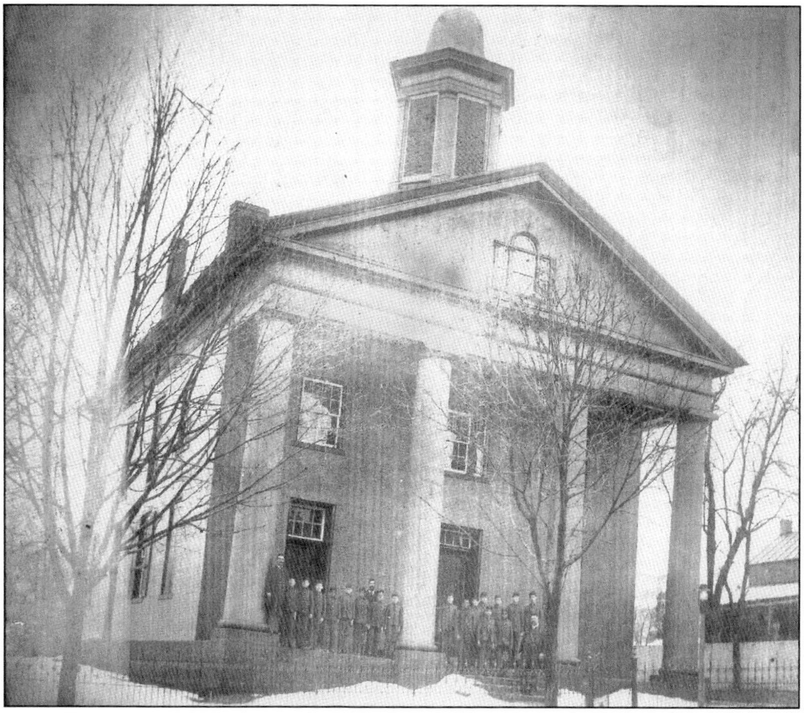

Pruntytown Courthouse. Pruntytown, the oldest community in what is now Taylor County, had its beginning in the late 1790s when it was known as Cross Roads. The village was issued papers of incorporation by the Virginia Legislature on January 8, 1801, and its name changed to Williamsport. On January 19, 1844, the Virginia General Assembly carved up Harrison, Barbour, and Marion Counties and created Taylor County. Williamsport was chosen as the county seat. A new courthouse was built and occupied by the county officials on March 22, 1849, having been under construction for three years. On Thursday, January 23, 1845, the name of the county seat was changed to Pruntytown. On October 8, 1878, a county vote was taken and the county seat was moved from Pruntytown to Grafton. After the move, an enlarged version of the old courthouse was used for years by the West Virginia Industrial School for Boys. In 1946 the structure was torn down and plans were made to develop the site as a park. (Photo courtesy of James Bolliger.)

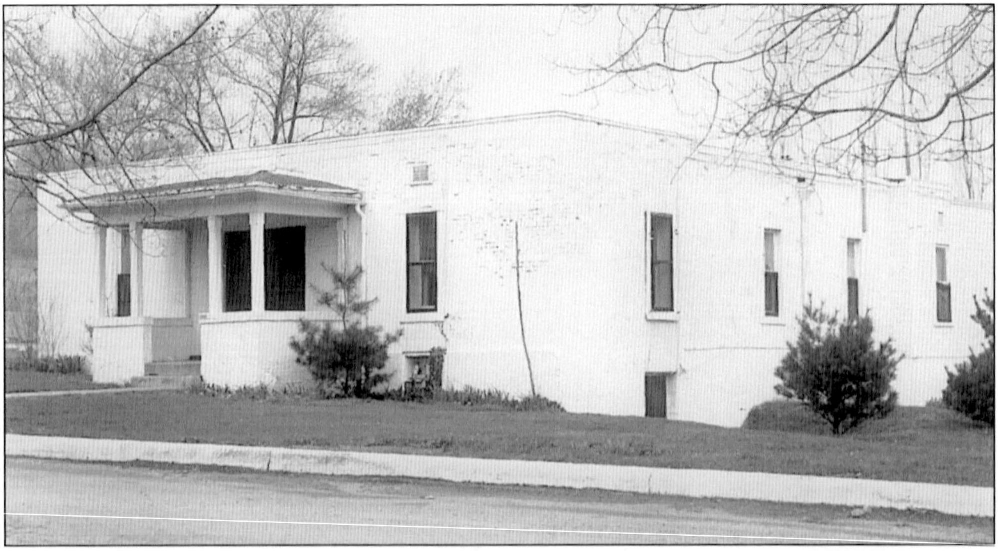

PRUNTYTOWN JAIL. Taylor County's first jail space was in a corner room of a Pruntytown home. It was leased by the court for a dollar a month. Zedekiah Kidwell received a contract for $1,984 to build public buildings, including a jail, and have them completed by November 1, 1845. As one of the conditions set for granting West Virginia statehood, the first slaves to be set free were released November 22, 1862, from the jail Kidwell built. That jail burned in 1864, and was replaced with the one shown above. (Photo courtesy of Peggy Robinson.)

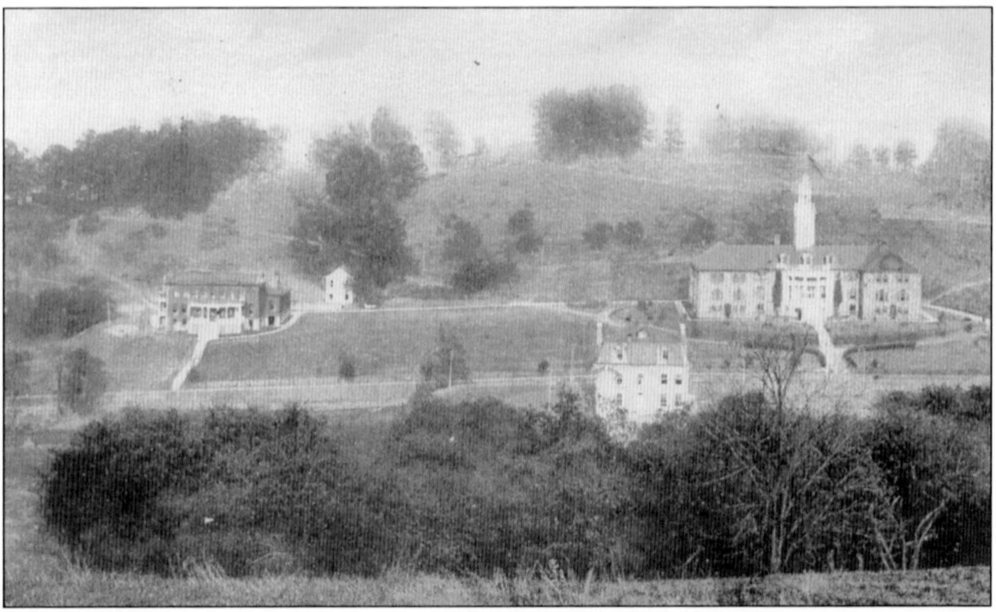

WEST VIRGINIA INDUSTRIAL SCHOOL FOR BOYS. This school was created in 1889 by the West Virginia Legislature as the West Virginia Reform School. The initial facilities were the old courthouse, jail, and sheriff's residence that had been abandoned in 1878 when the county seat was moved to Grafton. In May 1913 the name was changed to Industrial School for Boys. The facility continued to operate and expand its programs for many years. The last boys were moved to a Salem facility in December of 1982. (Photo courtesy of Wayne McDevitt.)

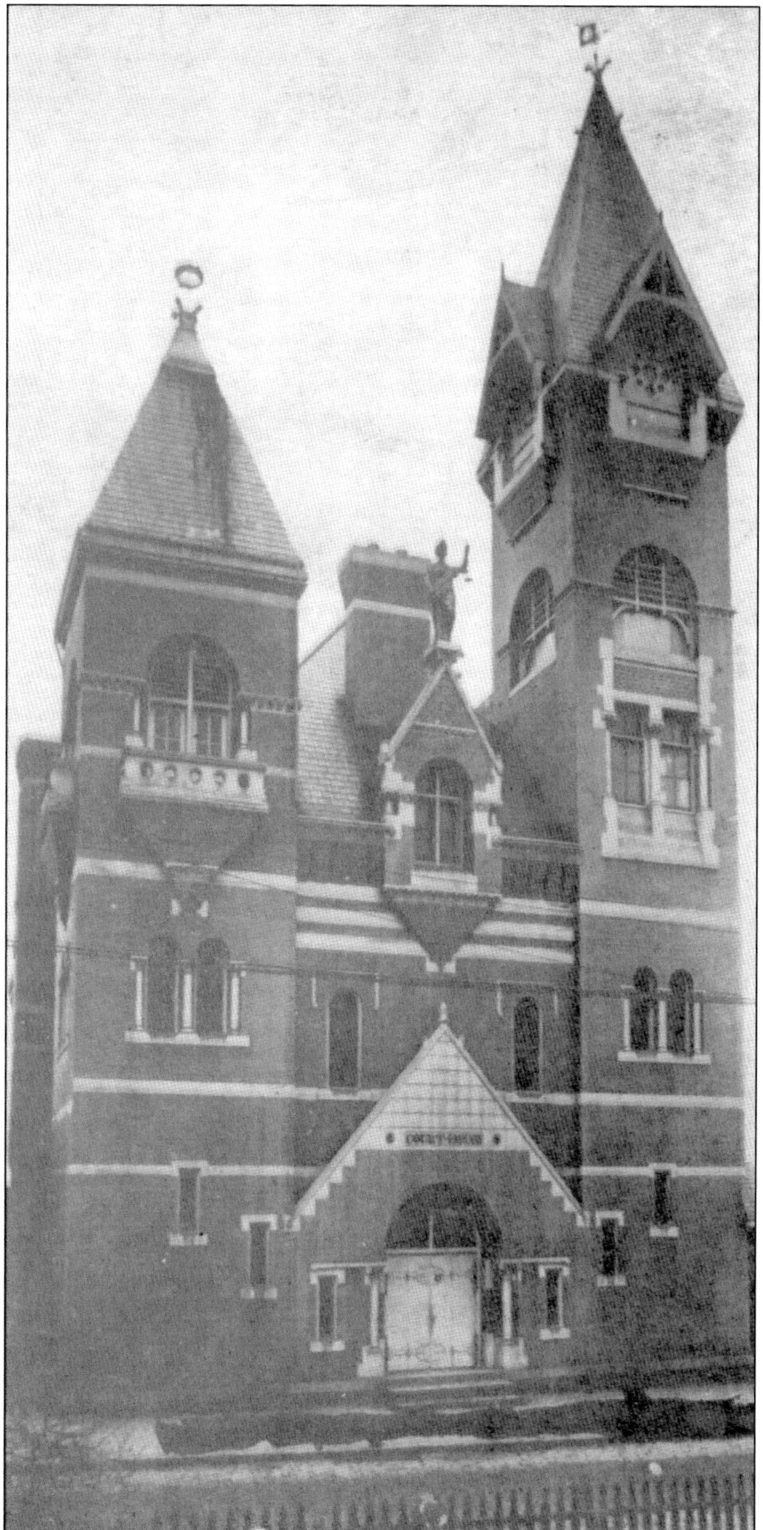

TAYLOR COUNTY COURTHOUSE. At a special election on Tuesday, October 8, 1878, the county seat of Taylor County was moved to Grafton. In November 1878, the first court session was held at Brinkman's Hall. The courthouse shown at right was completed in 1882. Adolphus Armstrong, clerk of the county and circuit courts, had been against moving the county seat and he refused to release or transfer the county records. But, the day after the election a team of men loaded the courthouse belongings on wagons and brought them to Grafton. At Grafton, the jail was in the courthouse basement until an adjacent jail and sheriff's residence were built in 1928. A courthouse annex was built. in 1976. (Photo courtesy of Wayne McDevitt.)

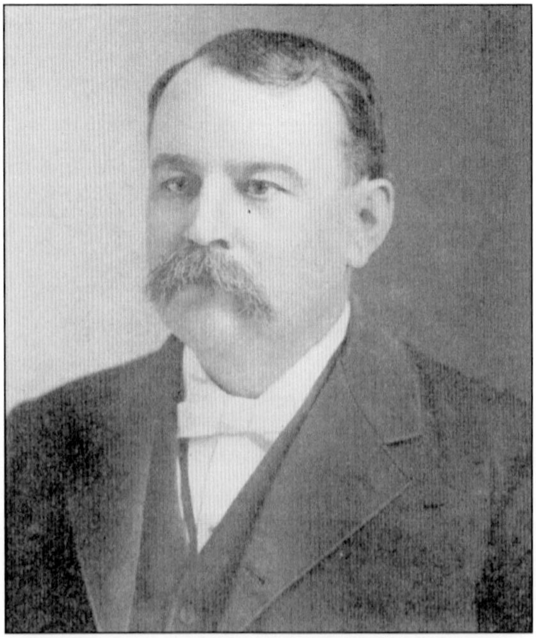

The Honorable Judge Marmaduke H. Dent (1849–1909)
(Reprinted from the 1890 publication of *Prominent Men of West Virginia* by George W. Atkinson, LL.D.)

Judge Marmaduke Dent (1849–1909). In 1870, Judge Marmaduke Dent became the first graduate of West Virginia University, and in 1873 he received the first Master's Degree from the University. He came to Taylor County to teach. He studied law books and was admitted in 1875 to the Taylor County Bar. During his career, Judge Dent held several legal positions, including deputy internal revenue collector under Col. John T. McGraw. This was prior to Judge Dent's election in 1892 to a 12-year term on the West Virginia Supreme Court of Appeals. John P. Reid, author of a book about Judge Dent's views, called him "the poet of American law." Judge Dent often quoted poetry in presenting legal arguments that were largely based on fundamental Biblical morality.

Judge John W. Mason (1842–1917). Mason came to Taylor County after the Civil War to practice law. By the mid-1870s, he was considered to be the most prominent attorney in Grafton. On July 4, 1876, at the Centennial Celebration, he presented what was most likely the first written history of Taylor County. Also in 1876, John T. McGraw entered Mason's law office, after his graduation from the Yale Law School. From 1889 to 1893, Mason served as commissioner of internal revenue with the administration of President Benjamin Harrison. After this, he moved to Fairmont and became a circuit court judge for 13 years. When Taylor County's Ira Robinson resigned from the West Virginia Supreme Court in 1915 to seek the governorship, Judge Mason was appointed to complete Robinson's term on the court.

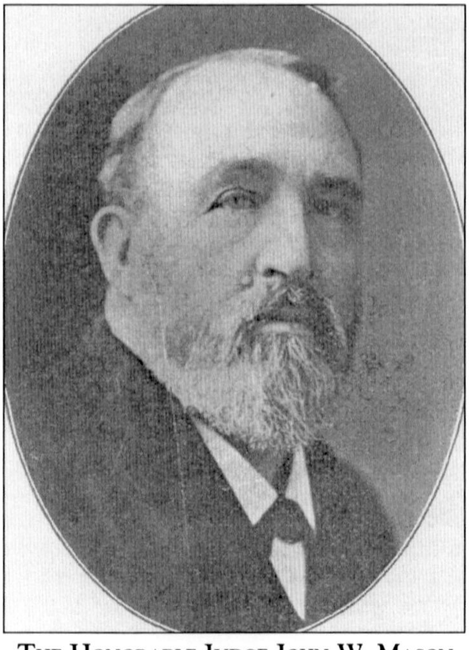

The Honorable Judge John W. Mason (1842–1917)
(Reprinted from a school reunion pamphlet.)

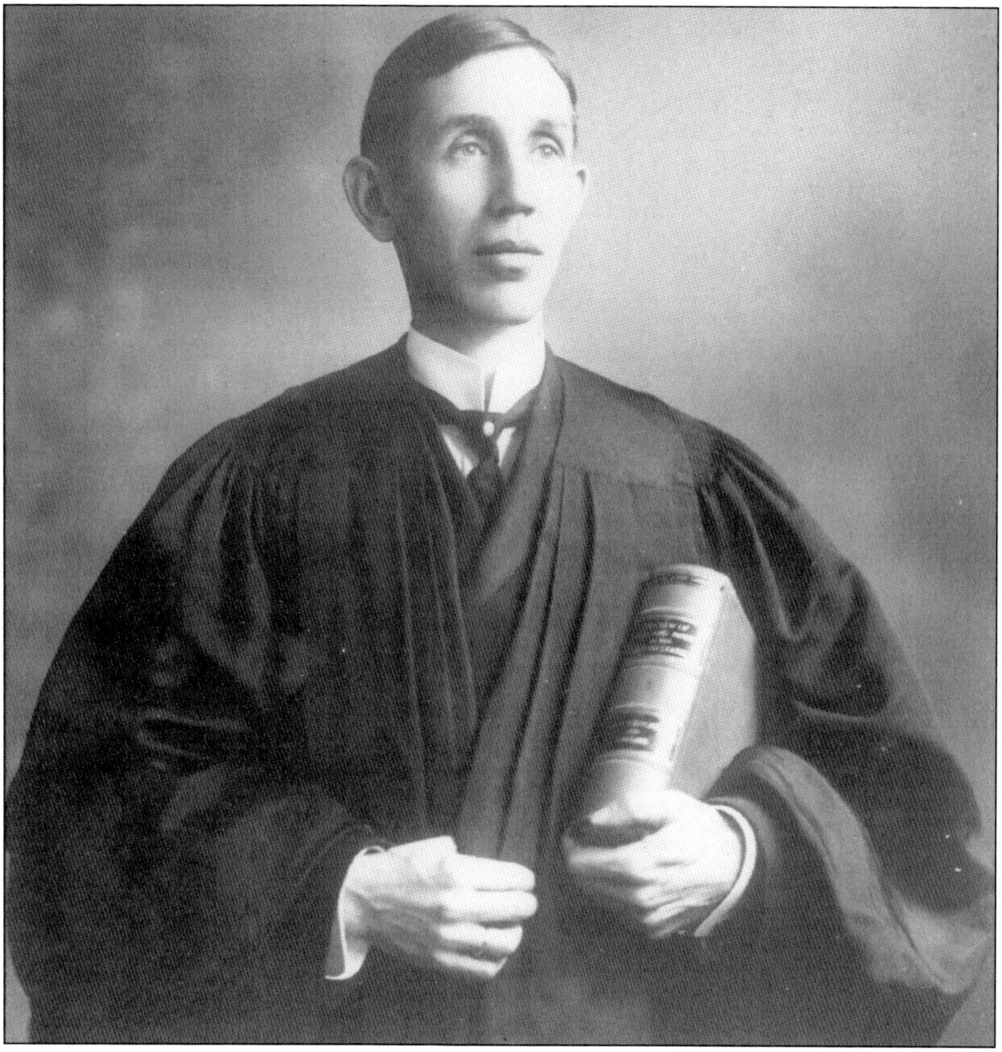

The Honorable Judge Ira Robinson (1869–1951). Judge Ira E. Robinson, a Taylor County native, was known for having a brilliant mind, high integrity, and for being an unselfish public servant. He was Taylor County prosecuting attorney from 1896 to 1900 and a West Virginia state senator from 1902 to 1907, when he was appointed to the West Virginia Supreme Court. Clyde B. Johnson inscribed in a gift copy of his 1914 book *Judge Ira E. Robinson—Statesman-Jurist-Orator-Poet.* He adhered to the Founding Father's view that the government should be run by the most capable, honest, unselfish people, rather than by short-sightedness populists. As a member of the West Virginia Supreme Court, he served as chief justice in 1910 and 1915. He resigned in 1915 to run as the Republican nominee for West Virginia governor. President Calvin Coolidge appointed Robinson as a special assistant to the attorney general and as a charter member of the Federal Radio (Communication) Commission. He was an associate editor on Barne's Federal Code in 1919, was a contributor to legal periodicals, wrote genealogical and historical articles, and spoke extensively on the decline of statesmanship in government. Anna Jarvis, founder of Mother's Day, found his help to be indispensable in her efforts to establish Mother's Day as a national holiday. The Adaland mansion in Barbour County, where Robinson lived from 1920 to the late 1940s, has been restored for public use. (Photo courtesy of Wayne McDevitt.)

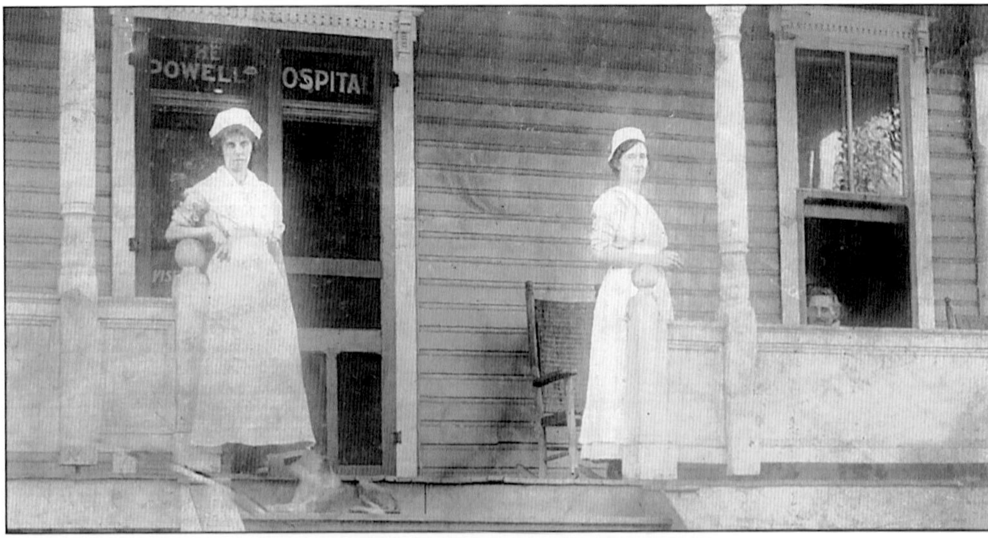

POWELL HOSPITAL. Dr. R.H. Powell purchased the old West Grafton Grade School in 1903. He used the wood frame structure as both a hospital and as his personal residence. The city of Grafton bought the facility in 1916. A new hospital was constructed at its present location along Route 50 at the intersection with Market Street. Over the years, Grafton City Hospital has been renovated and was expanded in the late 1960s. It now includes the Wallace B. Murphy wing, which is an extended care facility for the elderly.

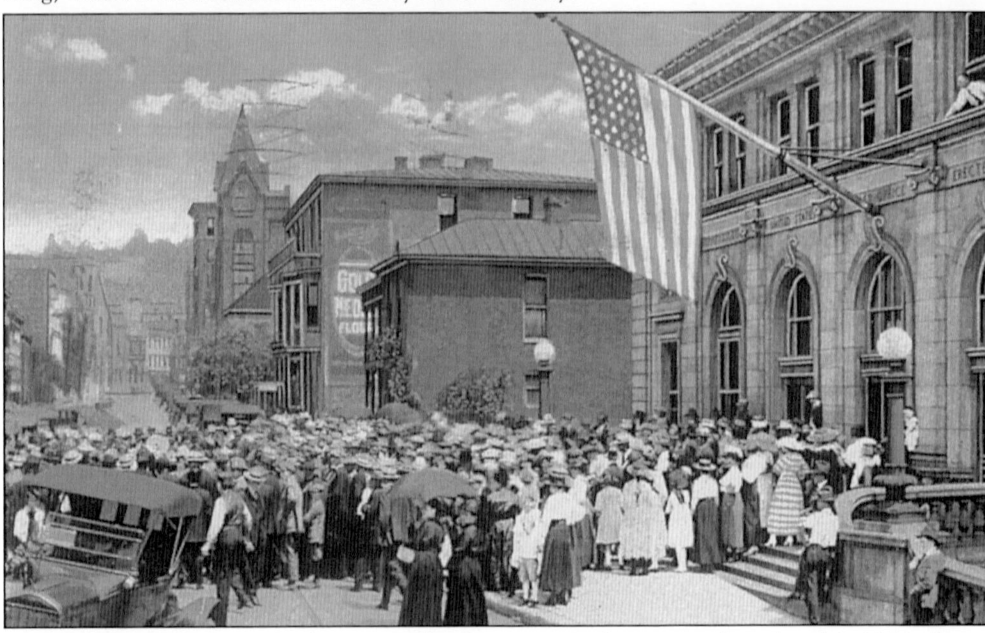

GRAFTON POST OFFICE. The first post office to serve Grafton opened on April 1, 1854, during the administration of President Franklin Pierce. At the time it served Grafton, VA. Shown above is the dedication and grand opening of the current post office, located at the west end of Main Street. The ground-breaking ceremony was June 1, 1913. The cornerstone laying was December 1, 1913, and the building was occupied on December 26, 1914. The contractor was the W.H. Fissell and Company of New York City. It remains in use today. (Photo courtesy of Peggy Robinson.)

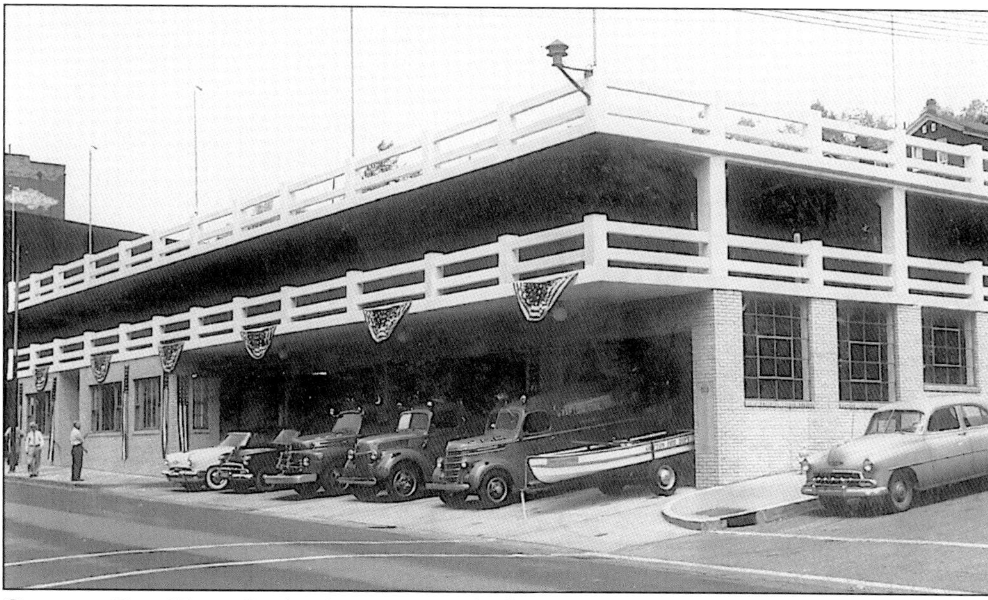

Grafton City Hall. Grafton's current city hall is located at Number One West Main Street, at the corner of St. John and Main Street. Built in 1953, the structure has Main Street level offices, along with housing the Grafton City Police and the Grafton Fire Department. The second and third levels of the structure are parking decks with an entrance off St. John Street to the middle level and off of Boyd Street to the top level. In 1953, A. Page Lockard was city manager and council members were Dorsey G. Bolyard, Lindsey T. Mahaffey, John W. Beall, Walter G. Robinson, and Homer A. Gatrell.

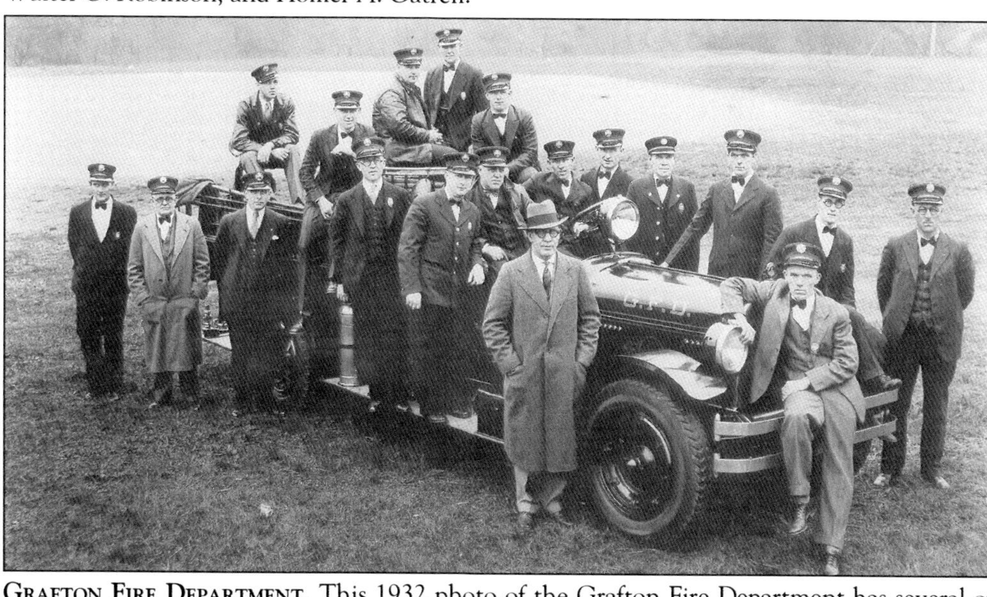

Grafton Fire Department. This 1932 photo of the Grafton Fire Department has several of the members identified by last name only. Included are M. Bailey, ? Bolton, ? Robinson, Chief Louis H. Greenwald, Smith, driver Harry Greenwald, R. Bennett, R. Paugh, Lawson DeLaney, driver R.G. Cole, R. Wittman, ? Jaco, driver R. Morrow, ? Clarke, ? Harrison, C. Burke, ? Hebb, and William R. Kraft. Also shown is Grafton mayor Charles O. King. Grafton has been served by firefighters almost from the time of its charter. (Photo courtesy of Wayne McDevitt.)

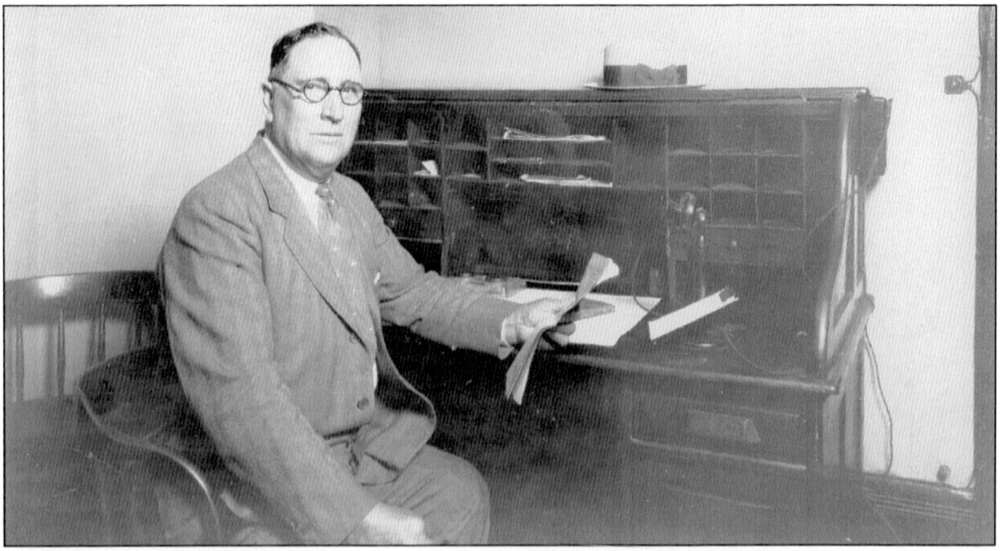

Taylor County Sheriff. William J. Mays is just one of the sheriffs to serve Taylor County over the years. When the courthouse was at Pruntytown, there was a sheriff's residence and jail. In those days, prisoners were segregated by race. After the courthouse moved to Grafton, the jail was initially housed in the courthouse basement. In 1928, the current jail was constructed. It has the sheriff's residence attached and faces Main Street. The residence has been converted into office space for the sheriff's department deputies. (Photo courtesy of Rick Reese.)

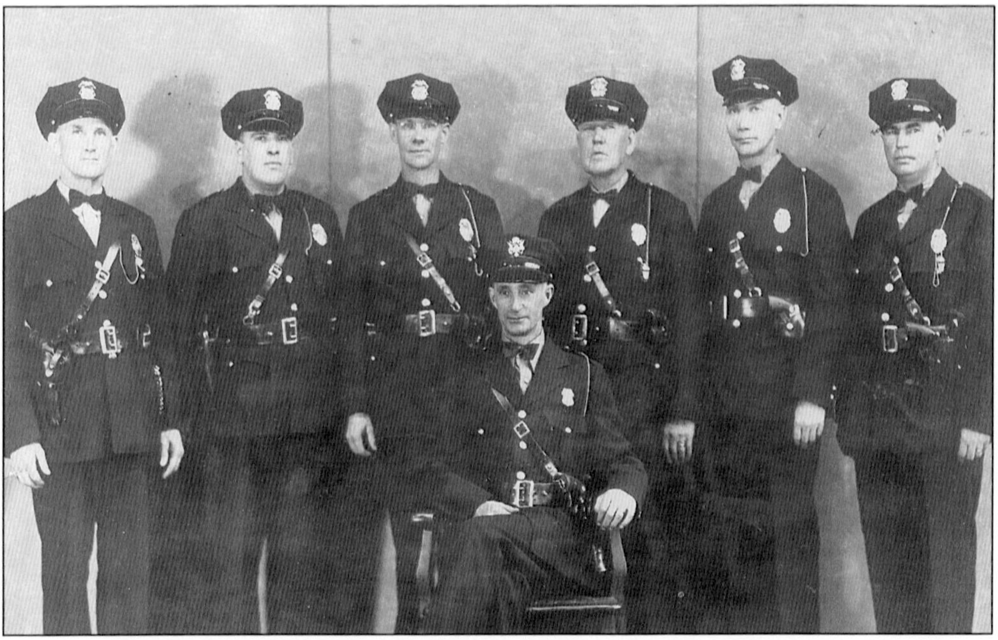

Grafton City Police. This photo is believed to be from the 1940s. The chief at the time was A.E. Charles Lockard. The other officers were Hugh Woodford, Norman Smith, Earl DeMoss, Clarence Silman, J.C. Helms, and Stafford Sturms. The city of Grafton has had a police force for many years. Taylor County is served by the Taylor County sheriff's department; it also has a detachment of the West Virginia State Police. All three law enforcement agencies are authorized to assist each other as needed. (Photo courtesy of Richard Utt.)

Seven

SCHOOLS AND EDUCATION

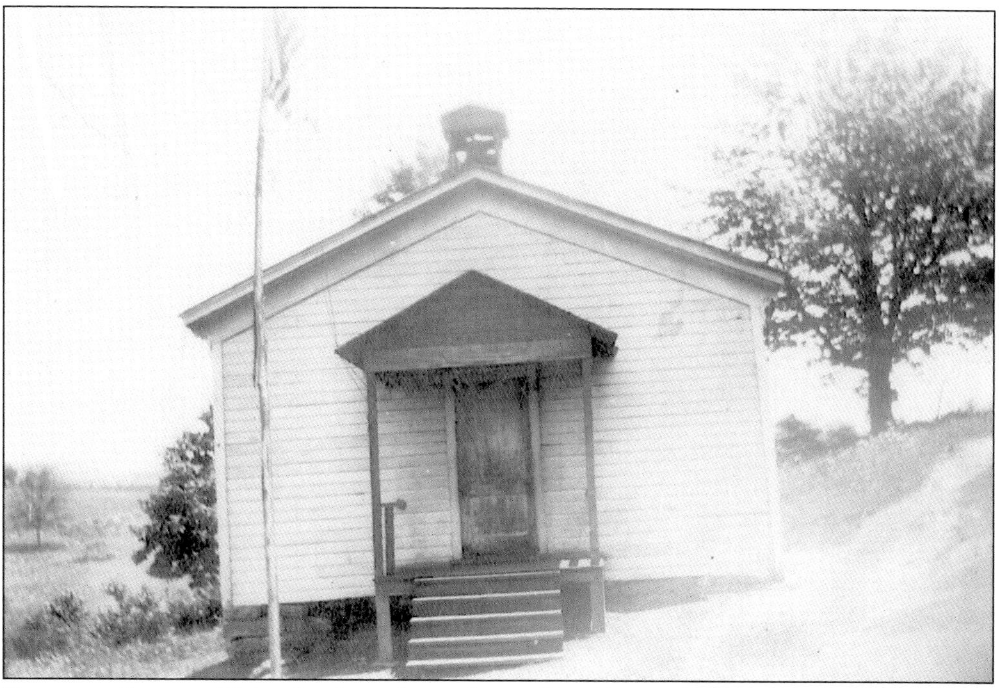

BARTLETT SCHOOL. This school was located near Doe Run and Pleasant Creek. It was torn down in 1936 because the land where it was located was going to be flooded by the construction of Tygart Dam. Students were transferred to the Pleasant Creek School. Ronald Knotts, John Poppalardo, Leo Moore, and Smith Lynch were some of the teachers who taught at the one-room Bartlett School. Enrollment was around 20 to 25 students. (Photo courtesy of James Kerns.)

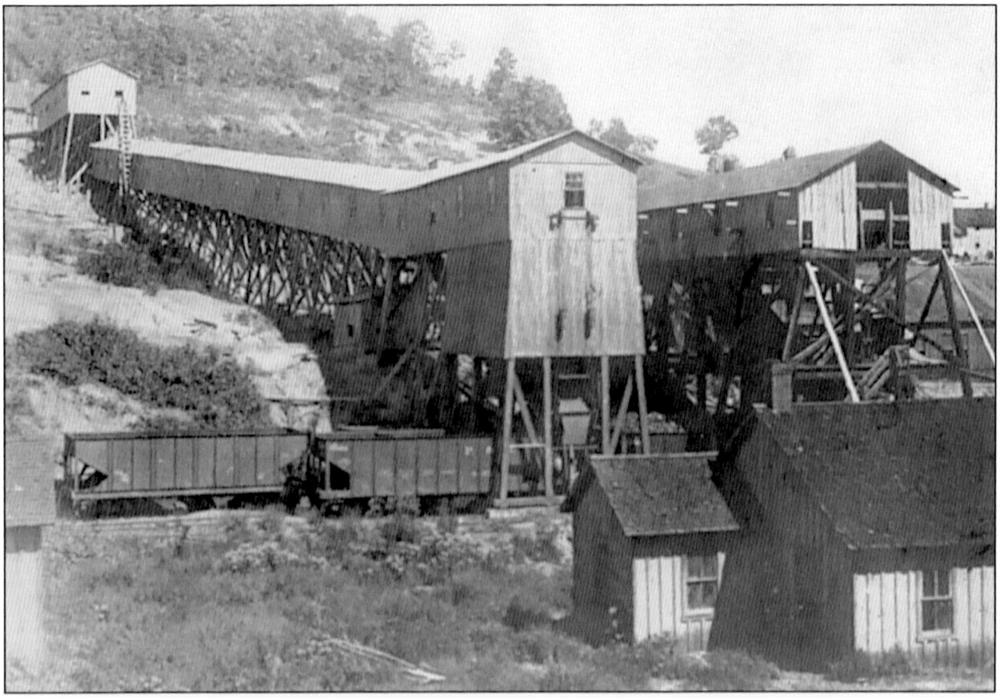

PITTSVEIN TIPPLE. The Pittsvein Coal Company, one of the larger mines in the Dogtown section of Flemington, was owned and operated by the Pittsvein Coal Company. In 1911, the general office for the company was at 15 Broad Street in New York City. The general manager was John Delaney, the mine superintendent was J.W. Davidson, and the mine foreman was George R.W. Johnson. Also in 1911, the company was recovering from a machine shop and powerhouse fire, but the buildings already had been rebuilt. (Photo courtesy of Geneva Phelps.)

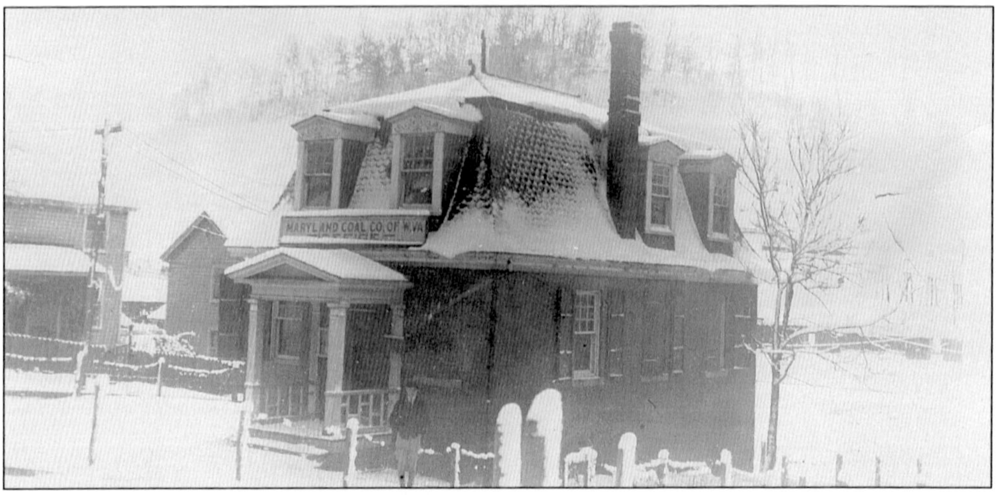

WENDEL COAL OFFICE. The Maryland Coal Company of West Virginia had its office at the community of Wendel in Taylor County. It was incorporated May 22, 1911, and Wendel is listed as its principal place of business. However, the five shareholders all gave New York City as their address. The company employed as many as 600 people at one time. It later became the Bailey Coal Co., after being sold in 1940. The office, which was located near the Yates Cemetery at Wendel, was demolished around 1990. (Photo courtesy of Wayne McDevitt.)

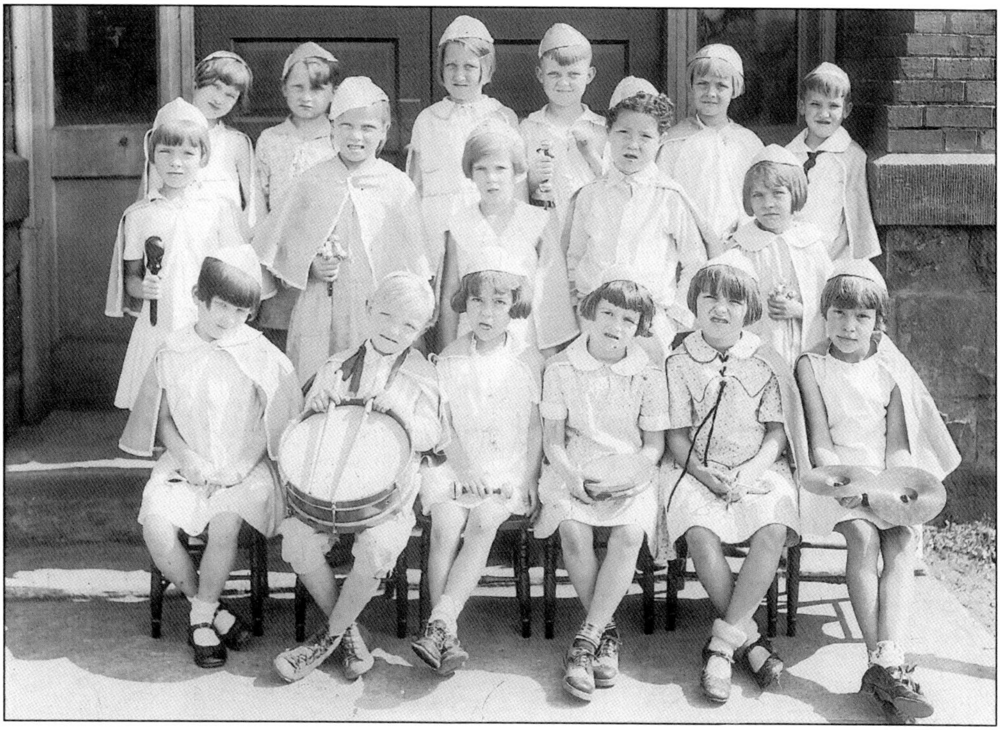

SOUTH GRAFTON SCHOOL. This school is one of the five ward schools listed by the 1910 Grafton Board of Trade. Addressing Grafton's educational facilities, the board of trade said, "Grafton offers splendid inducements along this line for capitalists who are looking for a place to locate industries, as the school advantages that can be had by the children of their workmen cannot be surpassed anywhere. The pride of Grafton is her schools and no one will make a mistake who comes here to educate his children."

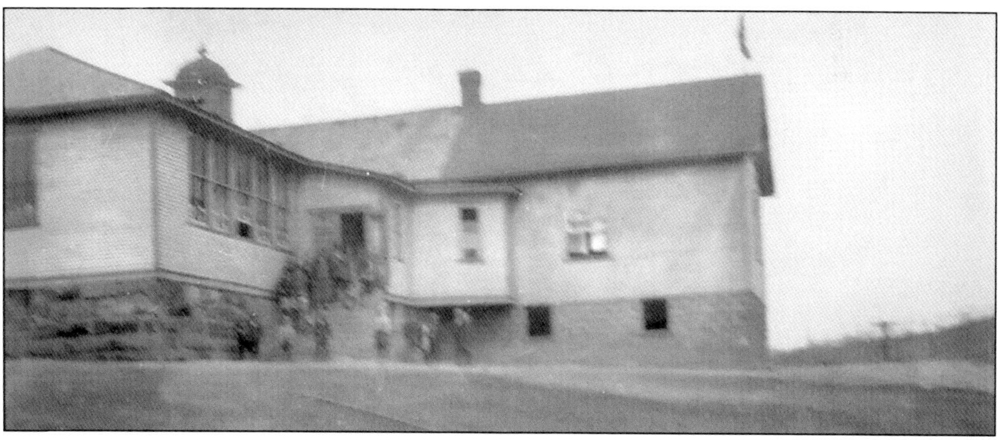

TYRCONNEL-ROSEMONT SCHOOL. This school served the area now known as Rosemont, beginning in 1909. Tyrconnell, a mining town, is gone. Its name was derived from a town in Scotland. When a new school building was built in 1912 to replace Tyrconnell, the schoolhouse name sign was taken down off of the old school, frame and all, and nailed to the gable end of the new school. By October 15, 1912, the name Rosemont School was used instead of Tyrconnell. On June 12, 1913, a bid of $115 was accepted from T.B. Haller to tear down the old school.

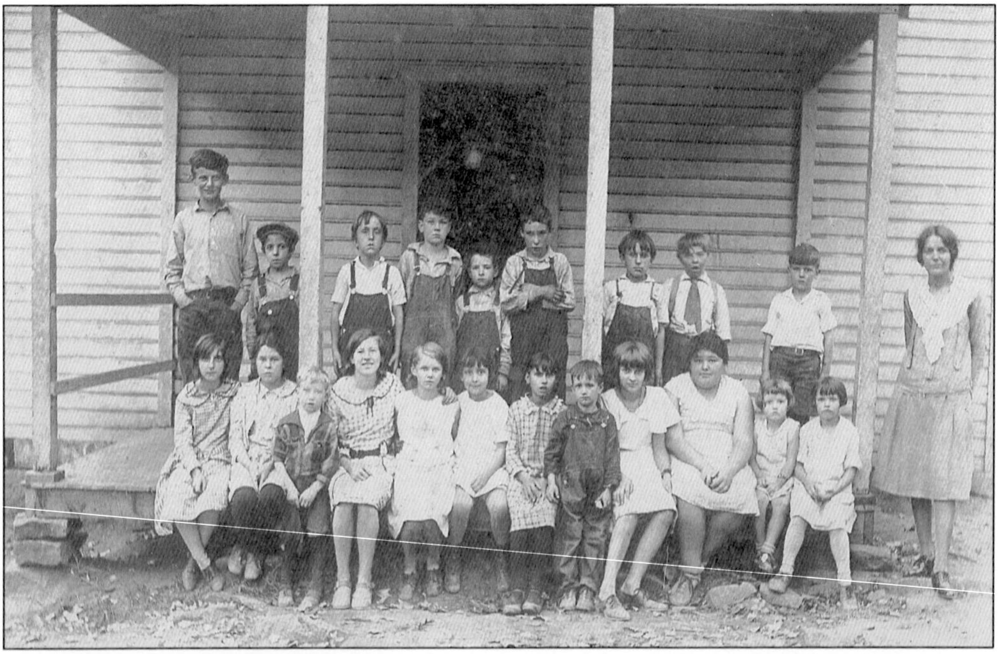

Westerman School. For the school year 1921–22, there were schools in each district of Taylor County. Westerman School was one of 17 schools in the Fetterman District. The other schools included Brown, Coffman, Haymond, Irontown, Keener, Laurel Run, Maple Run, Poe, Roderick, Westerman, White Day, Wilson, McConkey, Slab Camp, Blueville, Hardman, and Thornton. The teacher with this group of students is Florence Shaffer. The students remain unidentified. (Photo courtesy of Oleda Kite.)

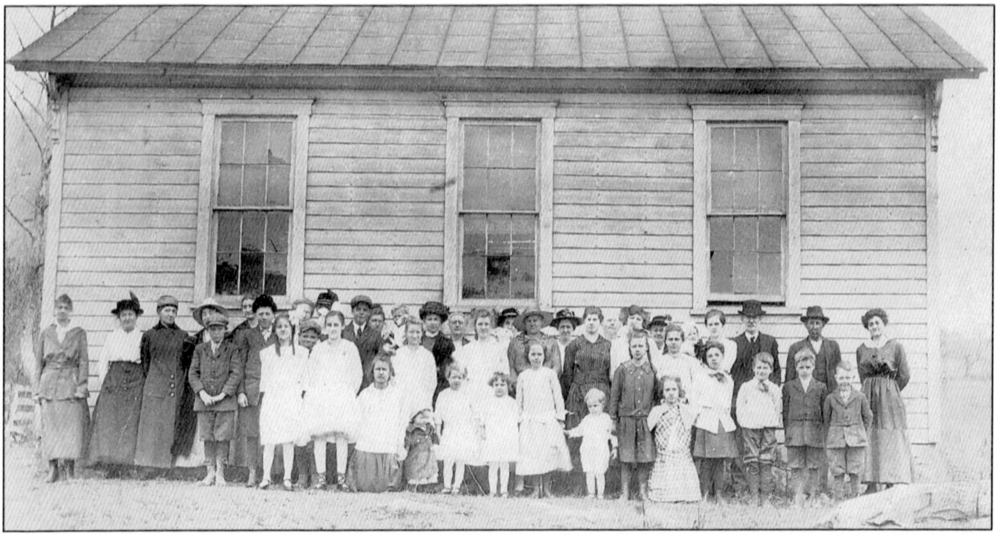

Yates School. Located in the Knottsville District, Yates was a stop on the rail line between Grafton and Philippi. Much of that area is now under water, covered when Tygart Lake was created by the construction of Tygart Dam. The school closed in 1923 and 36 students were transported to Park View by bus. In 1933, the county unit system was started. The district school boards were consolidated into a county board of education. During the first two years of consolidation, 15 one-room schools were consolidated with other schools.

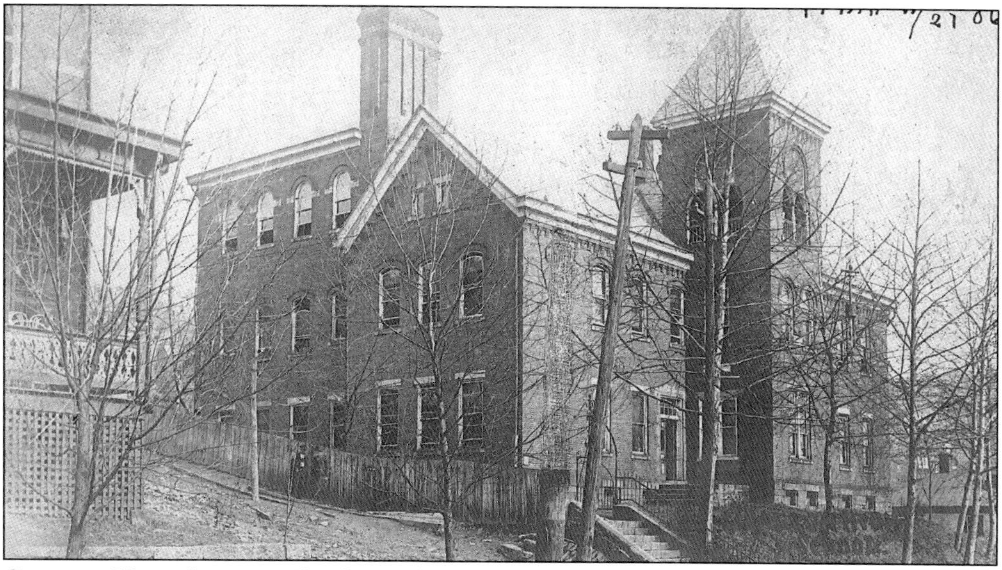

CENTRAL HIGH SCHOOL. The first public high school was a brick structure built in 1870, located along Wilford Street and known as the Central School. The structure contained four classrooms and served as a high school from 1884 to 1916. Two additional classrooms were constructed in the early 1890s. However, the building was overcrowded, and some classes were held in the West Side Elementary School building. Central lacked an auditorium and gymnasium and these activities were held at the Brinkman Opera House and the YMCA along Main Street.

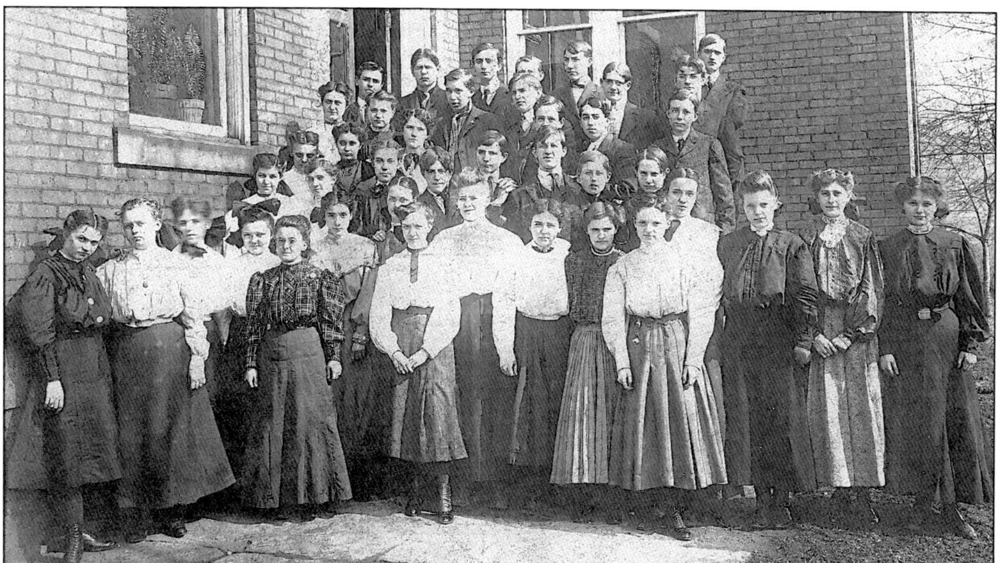

CENTRAL HIGH SCHOOL. The first class to graduate from Central High School was the Class of 1886, with four members. The first principal was U.S. Fleming, who served from 1884 to 1890. There were no graduates in 1893. The board of education realized that a new building to house the high school was a necessity. After failing on several occasions, the board persisted in its effort and on June 9, 1914, a bond election passed. Construction began in 1915 on a new high school building located along West Washington Street.

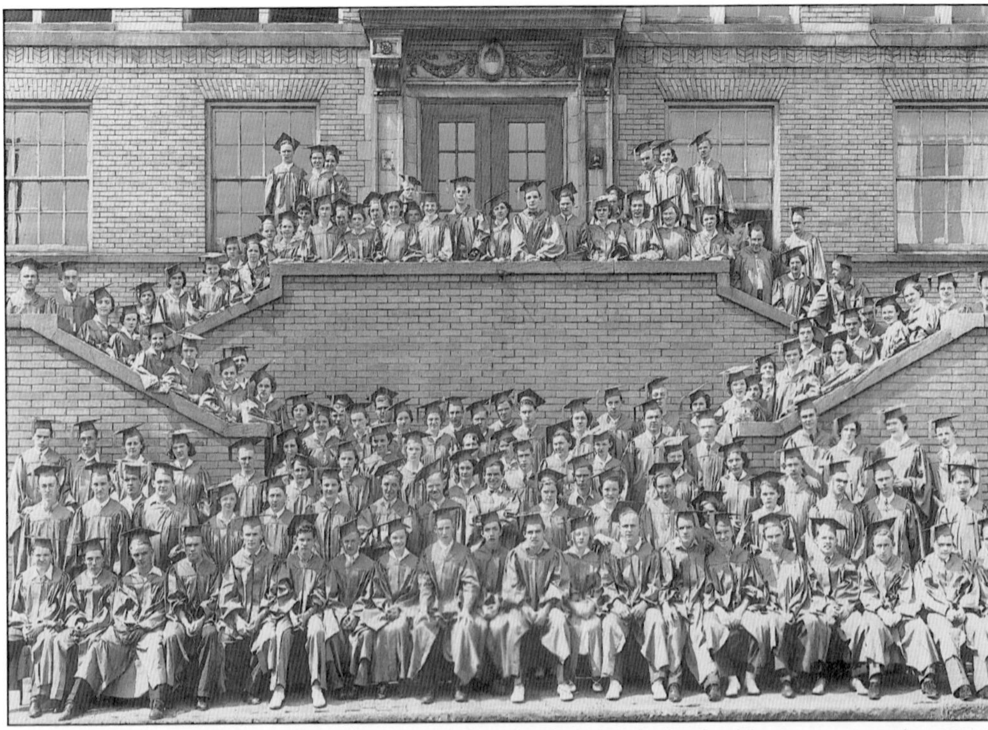

GRAFTON HIGH SCHOOL. Originally the Grafton High School, this building was started in 1915, and was completed and ready for occupancy in 1916 at a cost of $110,000. The new high school had 20 classrooms, an auditorium, gymnasium, and library. The school was built to house 400 students, but by the late 30s, enrollment reached the 800 mark. Once again the need for a new building was evident. After a new high school was built, the West Washington Street building became a junior high school and was later called Grafton Middle School.

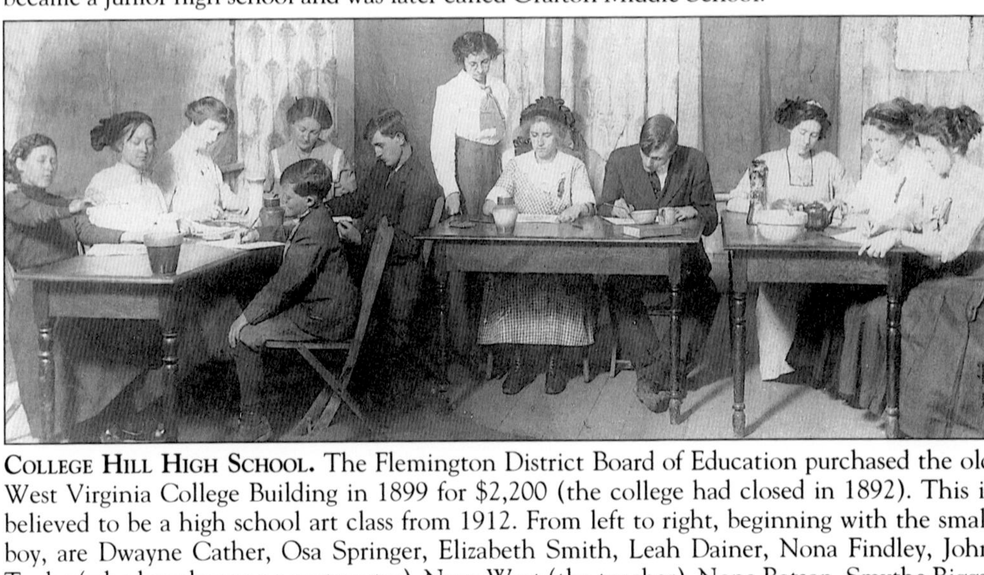

COLLEGE HILL HIGH SCHOOL. The Flemington District Board of Education purchased the old West Virginia College Building in 1899 for $2,200 (the college had closed in 1892). This is believed to be a high school art class from 1912. From left to right, beginning with the small boy, are Dwayne Cather, Osa Springer, Elizabeth Smith, Leah Dainer, Nona Findley, John Taxler (who later became a postmaster), Neva West (the teacher), Nona Batson, Smythe Biggs, Oma Springer, Hattie Smith, and Jessie Lawson. College High School was approved by the voters in 1902 and is believed to have been the first district high school in the state.

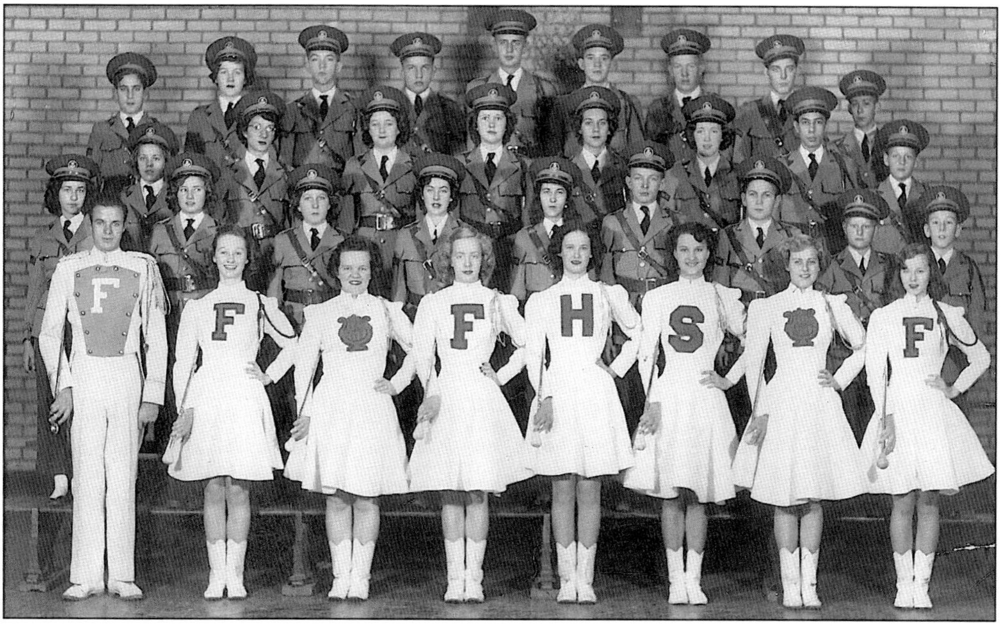

FLEMINGTON HIGH SCHOOL. FHS served the western part of Taylor County for many years before its 61st and final class graduated on June 3, 1990. The Taylor County Board of Education decided in late 1989 to close FHS on June 15, 1990. Economic and other factors were cited for the closing. A majority of the Flemington community, FHS teachers, and students opposed the closing and fought to keep the school open. It was a familiar scene across West Virginia as state board of education regulations by the 1990s favored consolidation.

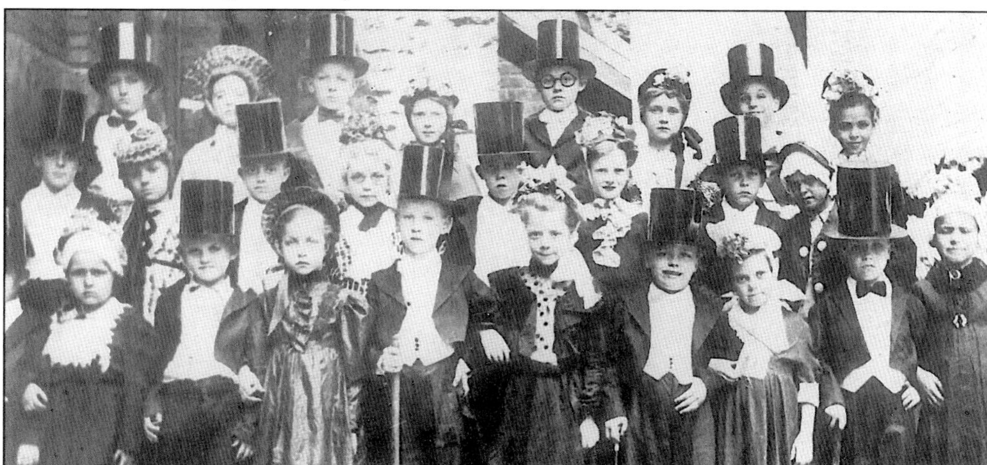

ST. AUGUSTINE SCHOOL. A Catholic school was established in Grafton in 1859. In 1966, grades 9-12 closed, but the elementary and junior high grades remained open until the end of the 1970 school year. In the above photo, students are dressed for a class play. From left to right are the following: (front row) Fred Ford, Bob Warder, Vera Litzinger, John L. Waters, Patty Ray Wrick, Charles Thayer, Jerry Dougherty, Mickey Tucker, and an unidentified student; (middle row) John Paul Grinnan, Anna M. Saccone, Charles B. Turner, Patty Smith, Bob Dougherty, Delores Pirone, George Haislip, and Louie Spino; (back row) Glenn Hussion, an unidentified student, Jim Ott, an unidentified student, Paul Robinson, Camilla Bradford, Jim Hyett, and MaryLou Kelly.

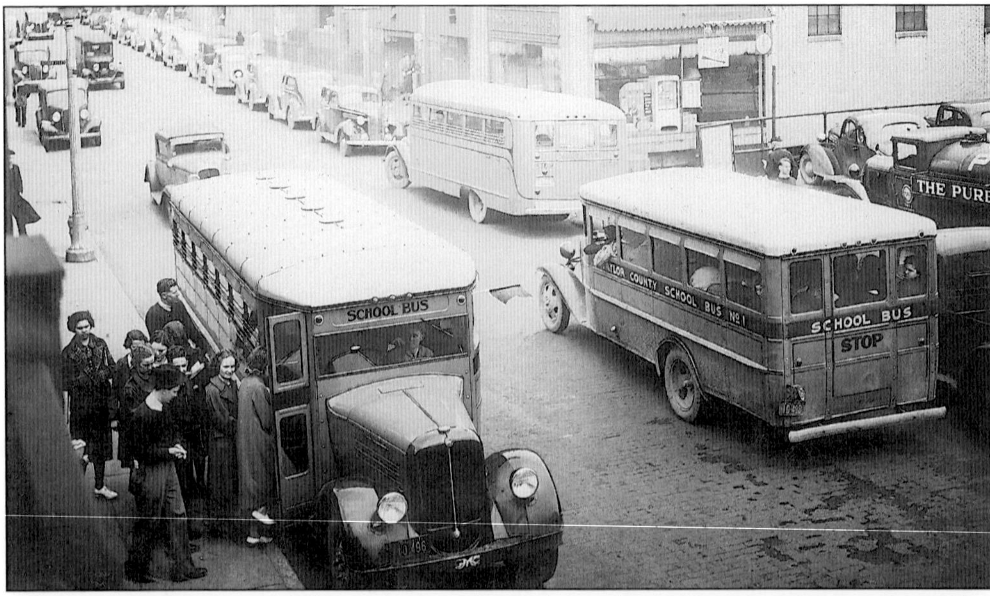

Main Street Buses. As early as the late 1800s, horse-drawn wagons started to be used to transport schoolchildren greater distances to school. With the arrival of the automobile, buses were soon manufactured and began service both as public transportation and for the transport of schoolchildren. In the late 1930s the need for school buses increased as small schools were closed and several new schools built, including Grafton High, Flemington, Haymond, Hepzibah, Knottsville, and Pruntytown elementary schools.

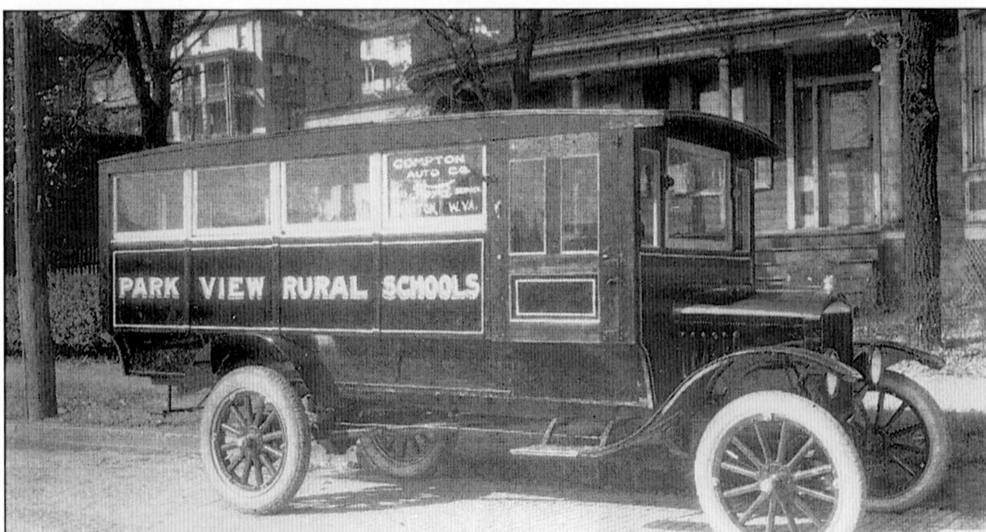

Parkview Buses. Shown above is a bus from the Park View School, which was part of the Knottsville District. In 1922, 80 pupils moved into a new four-room school. The principal was John Newcome. Teachers were Idella Rogers and Emma Leach. In 1923, the Yates School in the Knottsville District was closed and 36 students were transported to Park View by bus. The school term lasted eight months. In 1948, a hot lunch program was started. The school eventually closed and 54 pupils transferred to West Grafton School at the opening of the 1962 school term.

Eight

Churches, Homes, and Street Scenes

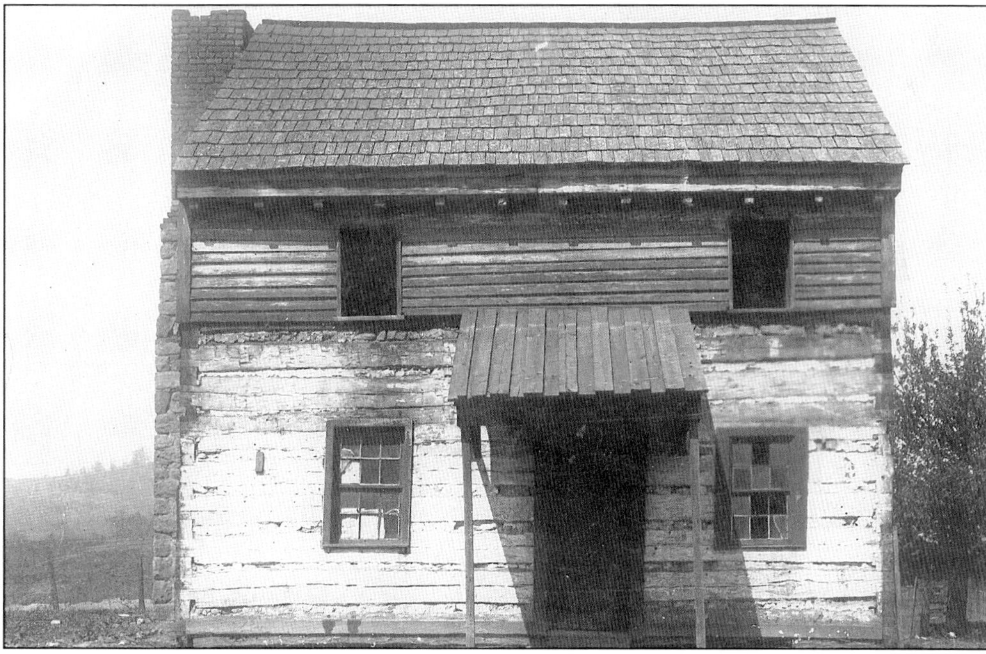

Early Log House. Land was procured in 1811 by Silas Stewart and his wife, Mary Anderson Stewart. They built a log home on the property, becoming the first permanent settlers of the later community of West Grafton. In 1835, the Stewarts sold the farm to the McKelvey family. They lived in the house for the next 11 years and then sold the farm to James Alexander Yates. He and his family lived in the log home until his death. His widow married William D. Mackin, who came to the area as a bridge contractor. He helped build the Wolman Truss Bridge, which crossed the Tygart River and Three Forks Creek, for the Northern West Virginia Railroad. In the 1870s the Mackins built a new home east of the National Cemetery and moved from the old log house. Over the next 20 years, various families resided in the log house. In the summer of 1898, a contract was given to raze the old Stewart cabin. The location is now the site of a service station at the west end of the St. Mary's Street Bridge. During demolition of the old log house, Charles A. Keener procured a piece of wood from one of the walls. He then had Charles Wells, an expert woodworker, turn the piece of wood into a gavel. The gavel was then presented to Judge W. Merle Watkins for use in Taylor County court. (Photo courtesy of James Bolliger.)

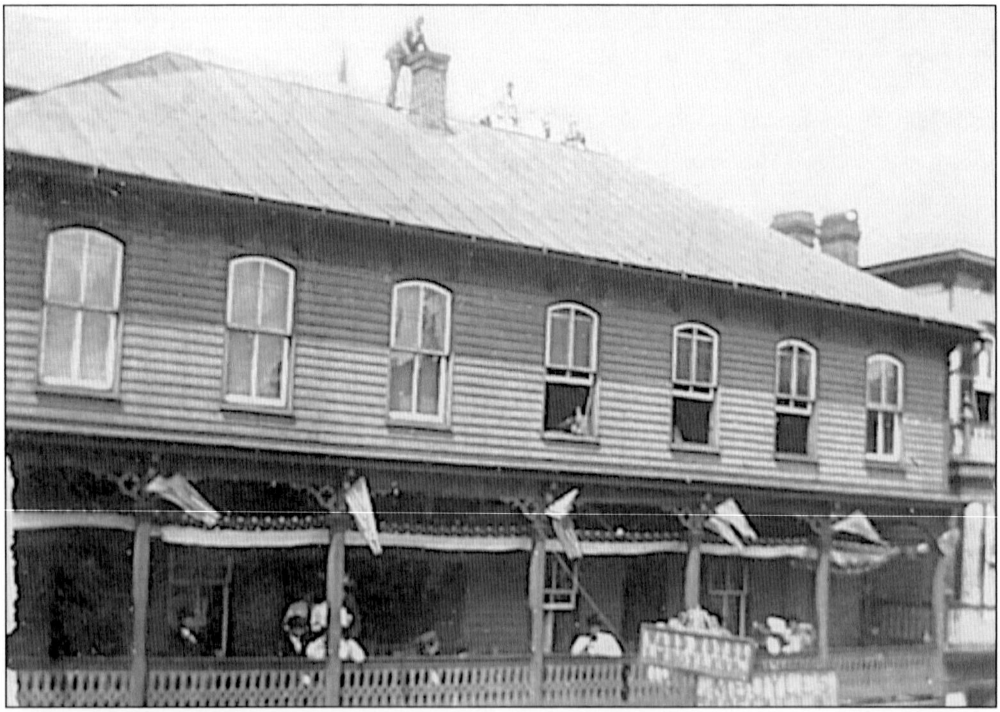

Ward Hotel. Charles Brinkman, Taylor County historian, says this building, with its antebellum architecture of the mid-South, was erected in 1854 by Capt. Thomas Perry, who operated it as the Perry House until his death. William I. Means operated the hotel during the Civil War until 1868. The hotel then passed to Thomas Mouse and his sister. They ran it until George W. Ward and son took it over. An L.M. Boyles, then his niece and many others, owned it before it was razed in 1954. (Photo courtesy of Peggy Robinson.)

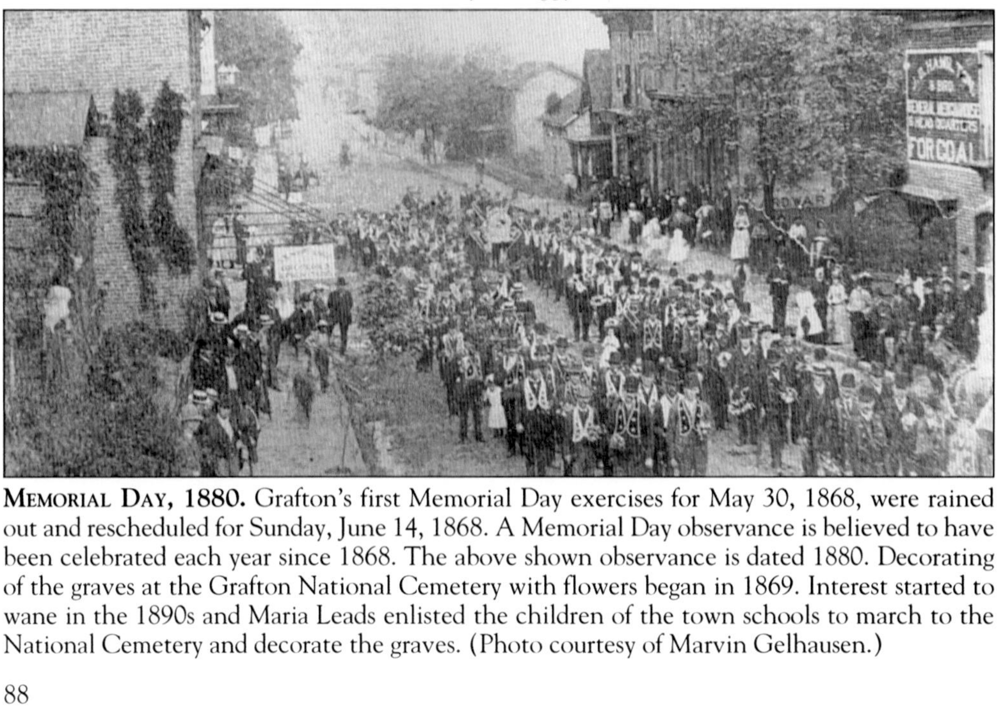

Memorial Day, 1880. Grafton's first Memorial Day exercises for May 30, 1868, were rained out and rescheduled for Sunday, June 14, 1868. A Memorial Day observance is believed to have been celebrated each year since 1868. The above shown observance is dated 1880. Decorating of the graves at the Grafton National Cemetery with flowers began in 1869. Interest started to wane in the 1890s and Maria Leads enlisted the children of the town schools to march to the National Cemetery and decorate the graves. (Photo courtesy of Marvin Gelhausen.)

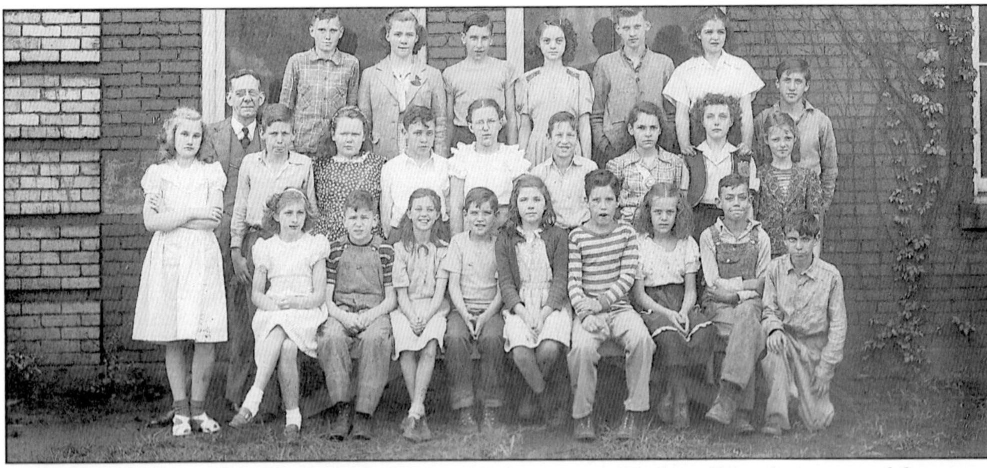

EAST END SCHOOL. East End School was also known as Grafton East. It is one of five ward school buildings listed in the 1910 Grafton Board of Trade book *Grafton, W.Va. Best Town, Best State.* Thos. H. Humphrey was superintendent of city schools at the time. He is quoted as saying, "The people of Grafton have always taken a great deal of pride in their public schools, and as a result, one of the best systems of public education in the state is found." One of the ward buildings was listed as being the finest ward building in the entire state. Pictured from left to right are the following: (first row) Charlotte Ann Williams, William "Bill" Clayton, Dakota Lanham, Glen Boyer, Shirley Martin, Robert "Bobby" Wolfe, Mary Shipp, Jimmy Tighe, and Stewart Keyser; (second row) Mary Alice Woodford, Eugene Stockett, Anna Kathryn Shelton, Charles "Buddy" Cox, Margaret Alberta Cox, Ronald "Ronnie" Poling, Rose Marie Lander, Barbara Louise Wagoner, and Anna Wilson; (third row) Principal Harry L. White, Don Williams, Willa Perone, William "Bill" Frey, Martha Poling, an unidentified student, Eilene Hawkins, and John Steadman.

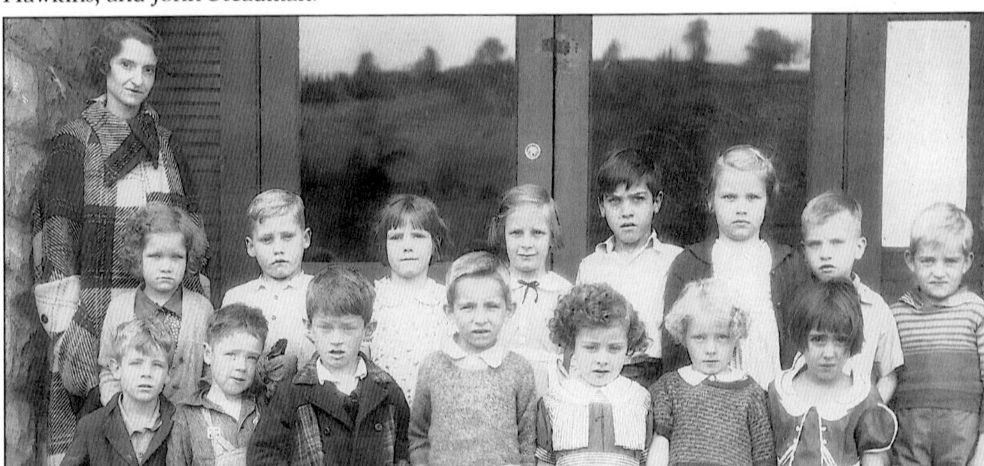

FIRST WARD SCHOOL. In 1856, Fetterman took the lead as the largest school in Taylor County. The Methodist Episcopal Church and the Masonic Temple were used as schoolhouses. The brick building above was built while N.F. Kendall was principal. S.H. Sommerville, Eugene Sommerville, and Mary S. Holden gave the ground for the building. When the school foundation was completed it was struck by lightning and half of it destroyed. When the building was almost complete, it was set on fire and burned. Albert R. Kelley was the contractor. The teacher shown is Helen Menear Smith. (Photo courtesy of Peggy Robinson.)

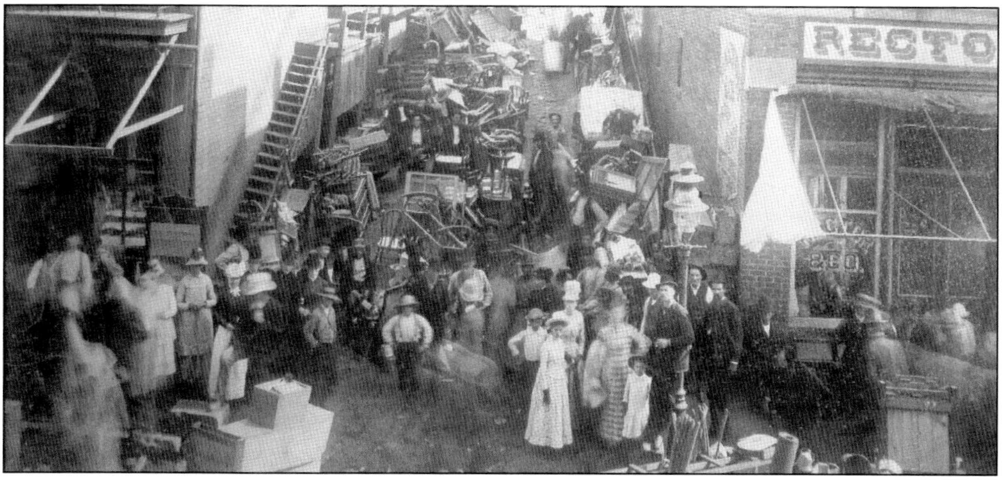

GREAT FIRE OF 1887. A disastrous fire occurred July 4-5, 1887. It broke out in the mid-afternoon on July 4 in a small ice cream parlor along Latrobe Street. After being put out, it started up again in the early morning hours and spread quickly, soon raging out of control, with up to 33 buildings on fire at one time. Appeals were sent across the state for help. B&O engine No. 73, with Patrick Flannery as engineer, left Parkersburg with fire fighting equipment and firefighters, reaching Grafton in record time. (Photo courtesy of Marvin Gelhausen.)

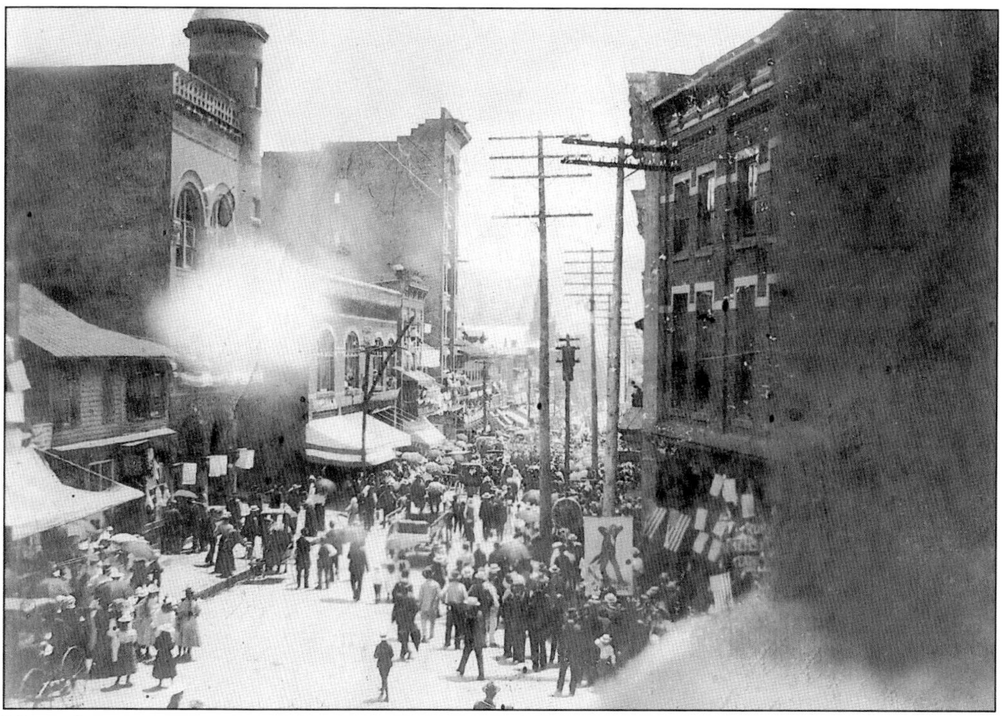

MAIN STREET IN 1895. In the 1890 census, Grafton had a population of 3,159, making it the sixth largest city in the state. In 1895, the date of the above photo, the B&O Railroad applied to Grafton City Council for the use of city water and agreed to pay $40 per month. On March 8, 1897, the town of West Grafton was annexed to Grafton. The town of Fetterman was annexed to Grafton on February 20, 1903. Grafton's population grew to 8,517 by the 1920 census, but its ranking among cities continued to fall. (Photo courtesy of Marvin Gelhausen.)

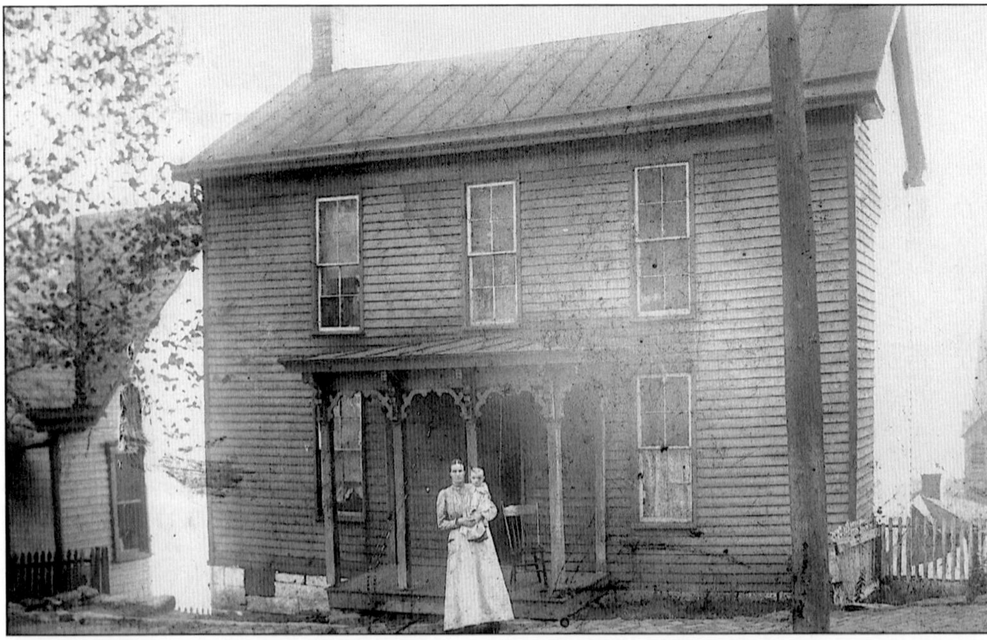

Wilford Street. An unidentified mother and child stand in front of a Wilford Street residence. This is a fitting portrait for the city where Mother's Day began. Notice the brick sidewalk and the cut stone foundation of the house. Also notice the church steeple in the lower right corner of the photo. This is believed to be the steeple of what is now the Church of the Covenant, along West Washington Street. That church is behind Andrews Methodist, which is now the International Mother's Day Shrine. (Photo courtesy of Ruth Mason.)

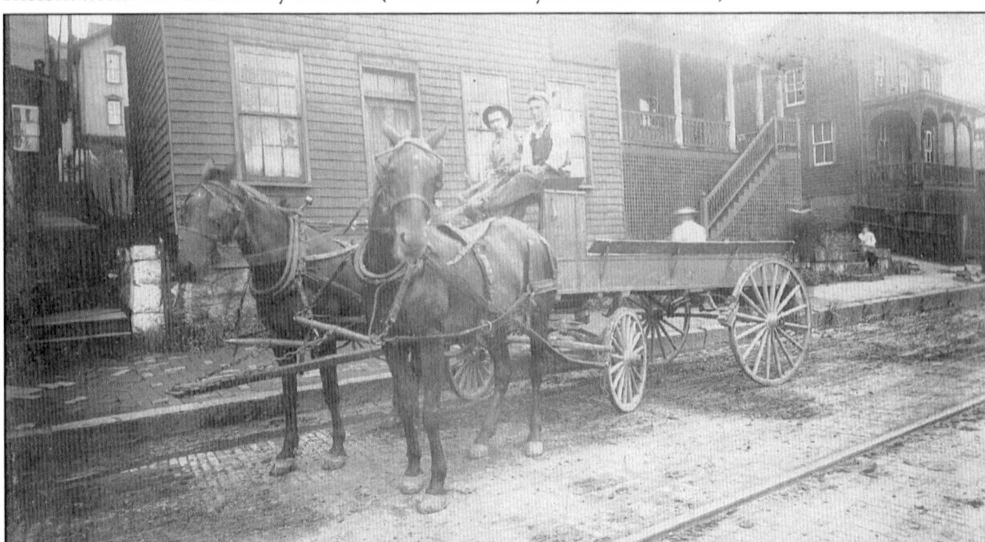

Horse and Wagon Days. Some of these structures along West Main Street, near the old Grafton Middle School steps, are still standing today and are unchanged enough to still be recognized from this photo. Notice the brick Main Street and one rail of the former street car line. Also notice the high cut stone curb from the roadway up to the brick sidewalk. Horse and wagon transportation also was used and provided most of the delivery services, getting goods to businesses and purchases to homes. (Photo courtesy of Norma Wyckoff.)

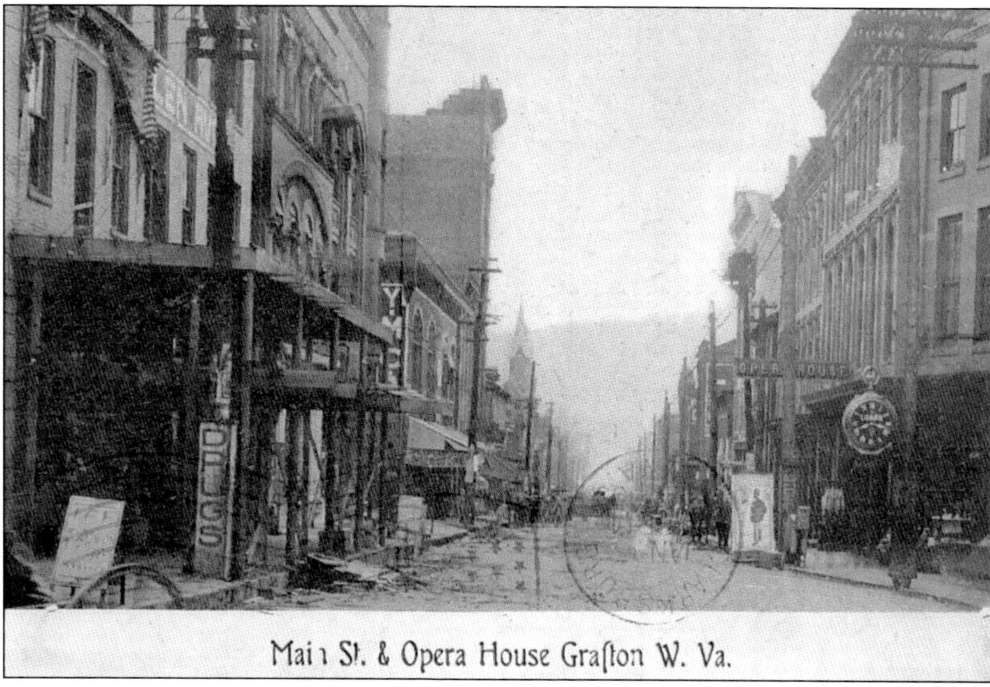

MAIN STREET LOOKING WEST. This postcard shows Main Street downtown including the former Blen Avon Hotel, the Joliffe building, the Merchants & Mechanics Savings Bank, the YMCA, the Loar Jewelry store, and the Brinkman Opera House. The opera house was destroyed by fire and rebuilt as apartments. The Blen Avon was renovated into apartments before being destroyed by fire, and the YMCA building was gutted by fire and its second story removed during the rebuilding. (Photo courtesy of Lois Heflin.)

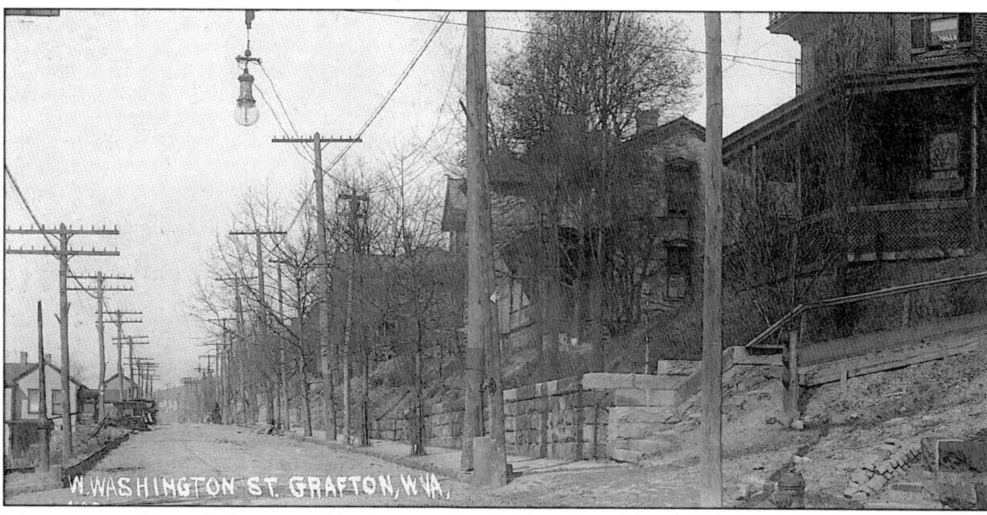

MARMADUKE DENT MANSION. The home of Judge Dent and his family along West Washington Street was a beautiful two-story brick structure. It was prominently featured in a 1898 sketch of the city by T.M. Fowler. The home was featured at the bottom center of the print. It was one of eight Grafton residences and four commercial buildings pulled out from the pictorial-type map. Fowler did similar prints of many cities. A biographical sketch of Dent is on p. 74. (Photo courtesy of Lois Heflin.)

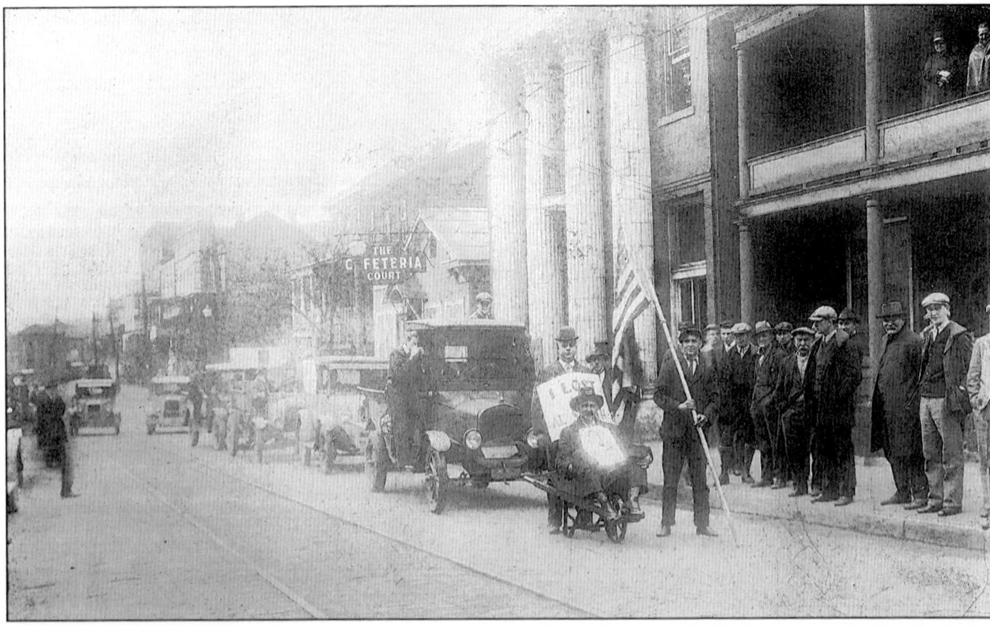

MAIN STREET LOOKING WEST. Carrying a sign believed to read, "I Lost to Al Smith," this unsuccessful candidate prepares to roll the winner down Main Street in a wheelbarrow. The scene is in front of the former Taylor County Bank building and the Cafeteria Court Restaurant that were located across from the Taylor County Courthouse. Notice the tracks for the street car line, the street lights, and the number of cars lined up. VFW Memorial City Post 3081 built on the site where the bank building stood. The building on the right was replaced by a filling station.

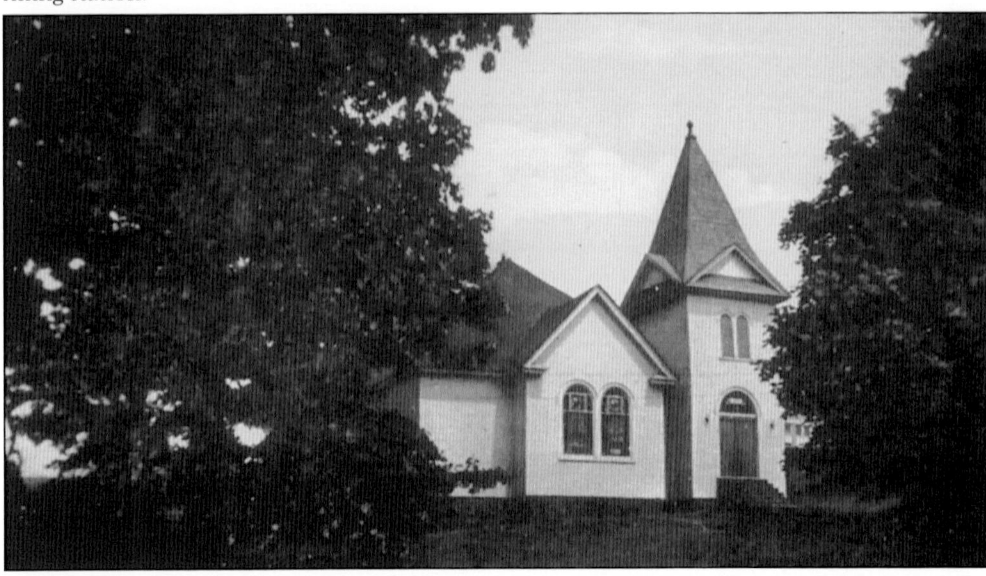

WARDER CHAPEL. After a merger in 1939 of the Methodist churches in Pruntytown, this structure became part of the holdings of the West Virginia Industrial School for Boys at Pruntytown. The WVISB used it for chapel services and other special events. However, the building was eventually razed. A cemetery behind the old church remains. (Photo courtesy of Wayne McDevitt.)

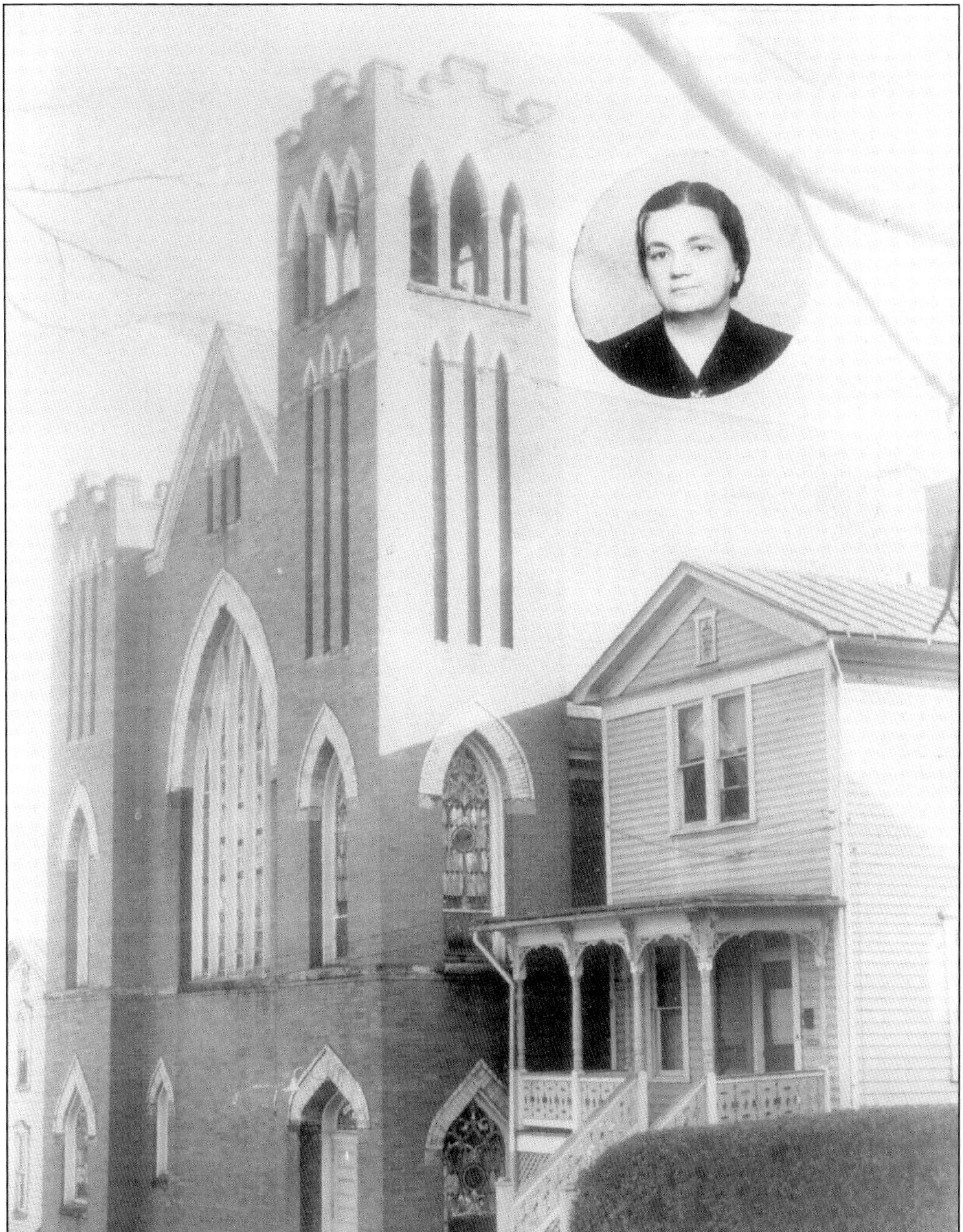

The United Brethren Church. In 1874, Lot No.78 in the Yates Plat of Grafton was purchased and in 1875, work was begun on the church building. The building was completed and dedicated by the Rev. Zebedee Warner in October. 1875. By 1905, the church had grown to the point where it was necessary to build a new and much larger building. The original building was moved to the back of the lot and became known as the back room. John C. Tibbets of Grafton was the architect and John E. Magill the contractor. It was dedicated by Bishop J.S. Mills, D.D., on May 26, 1907. Shown is Pastor Lois Luzader. (Photo courtesy of Marguerite Baugh.).

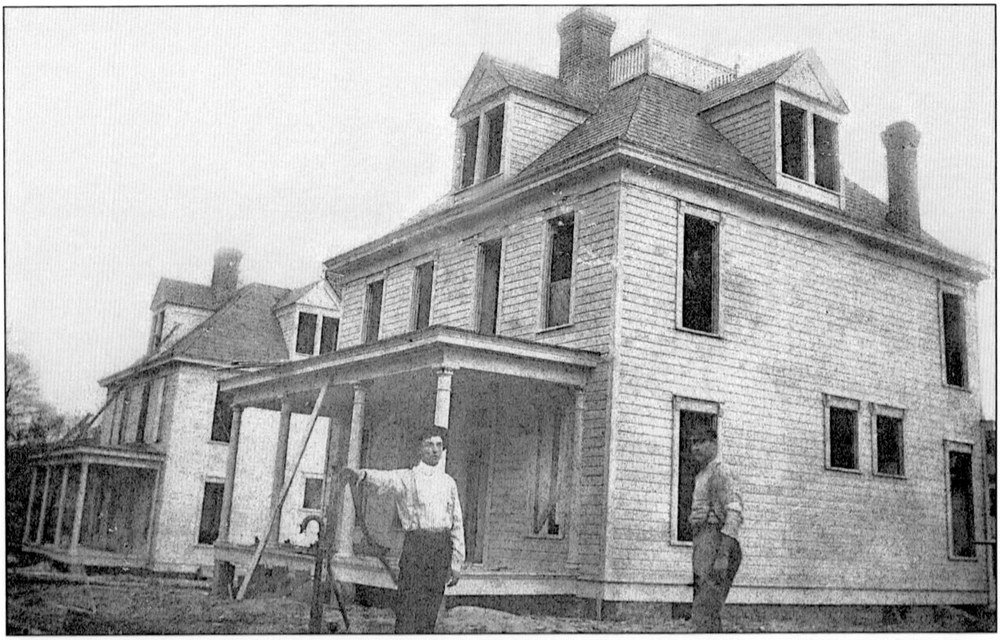

The Durbin Home. In a 1910 Grafton Board of Trade publication it was noted that Grafton real estate had steadily increased in value during the last 10 years, and many profitable investments have been made during that time. There was a larger percentage of home owners here than in any other city in the state, due largely to the liberal policy of the B&O Railroad Company in providing an easy-payment plan for the purchase of homes by their employees. Rents, taxes, and living expenses compared favorably with other cities of the state.

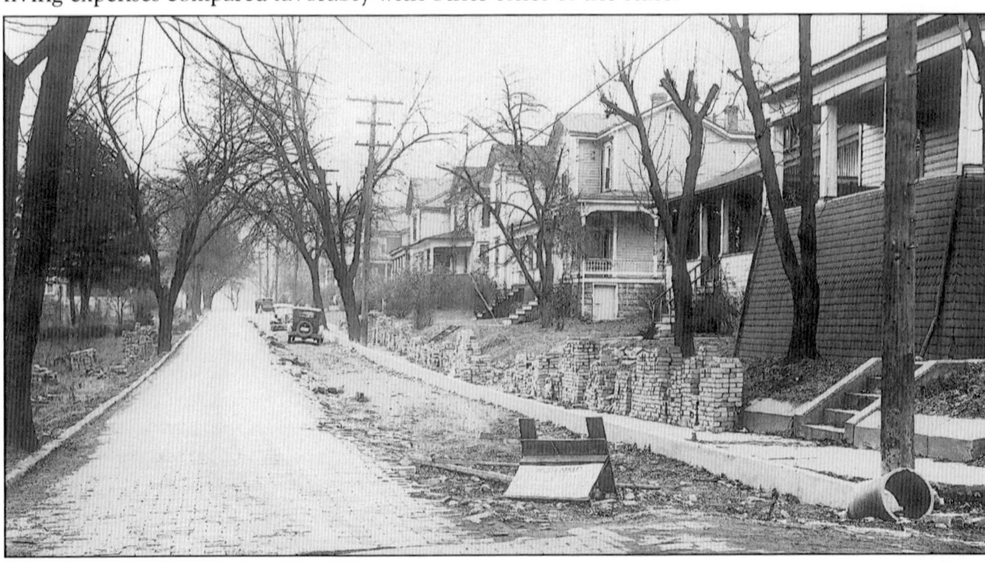

Brick Street Paving. The paving of streets with bricks became popular in the early 1900s. Shown above is a scene along one of the many streets in Grafton that was paved with bricks. Many of those streets were later covered with asphalt paving, but a few brick streets remain. One of particular interest is Mackin Alley behind the St. Augustine Social Center. This alley is being preserved because the brick paving was laid with certain bricks raised to provide horses a better foot hold while pulling heavy loads up the hill.

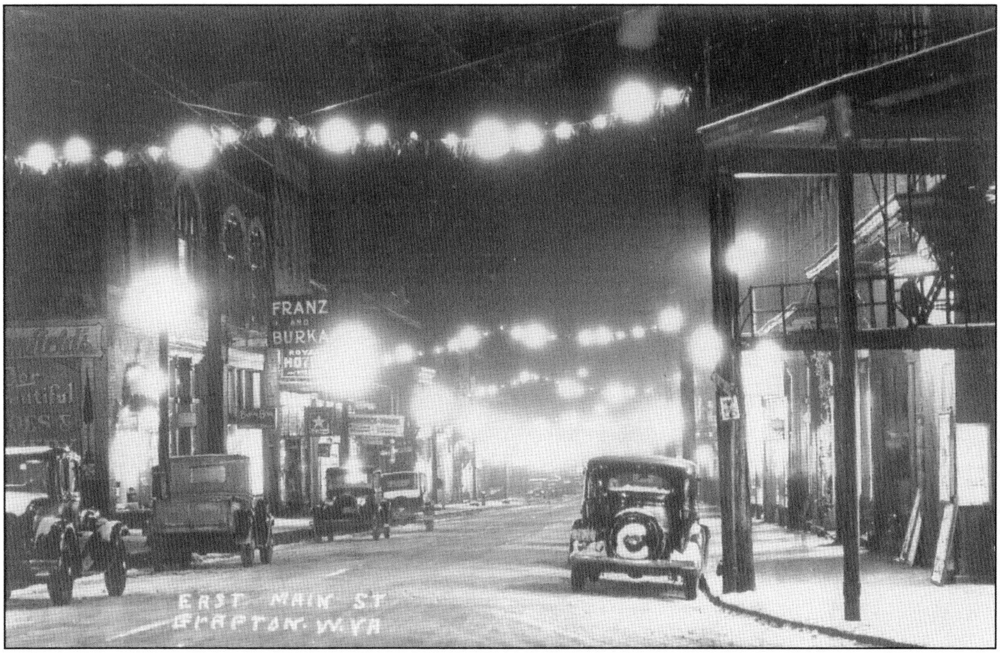

MAIN STREET IN THE 1930S. Shown is a scene looking west from the intersection of Main and Latrobe Streets. Like the rest of the country, the 1929 financial crash created hard times for the people of Grafton. The city's second largest industry, Hazel-Atlas glass, was shut down for most of the Depression. Railroad business was generally down. Only the First National Bank survived the banking crisis. The financially troubled streetcar system ended on March 31, 1934, and was replaced with bus services. (Photo courtesy of Wayne McDevitt.)

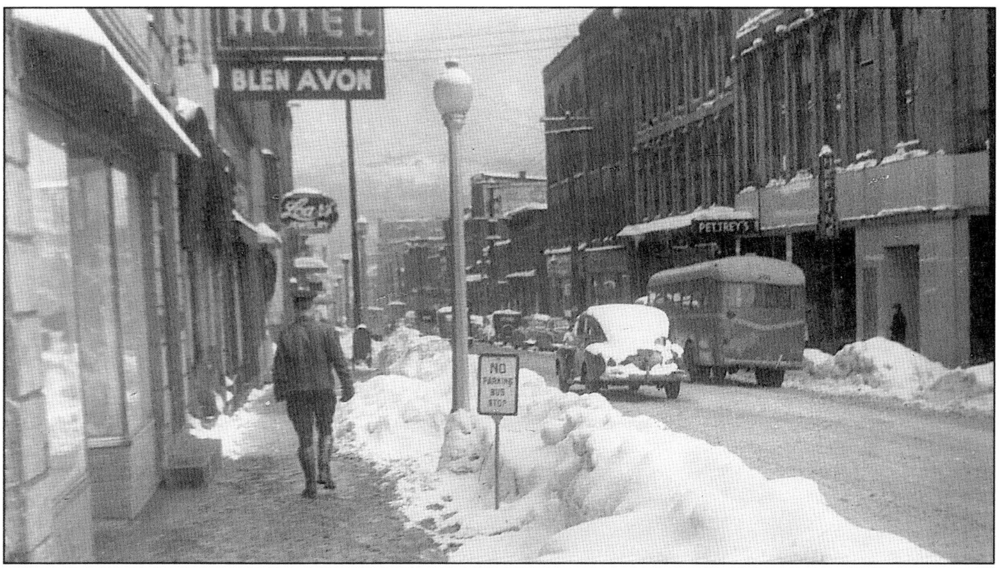

ONE BIG WINTER SNOW. It is not known when this snowstorm occurred, but the worst snow on record to hit Grafton and Taylor County arrived the day after Thanksgiving, November 26, 1950, with areas receiving up to 30 inches of snow. The extreme cold that followed hampered efforts to dig out and return to normal operation. The climate in Grafton and Taylor County is generally considered mild, not too hot in the summer, nor too cold in the winter.

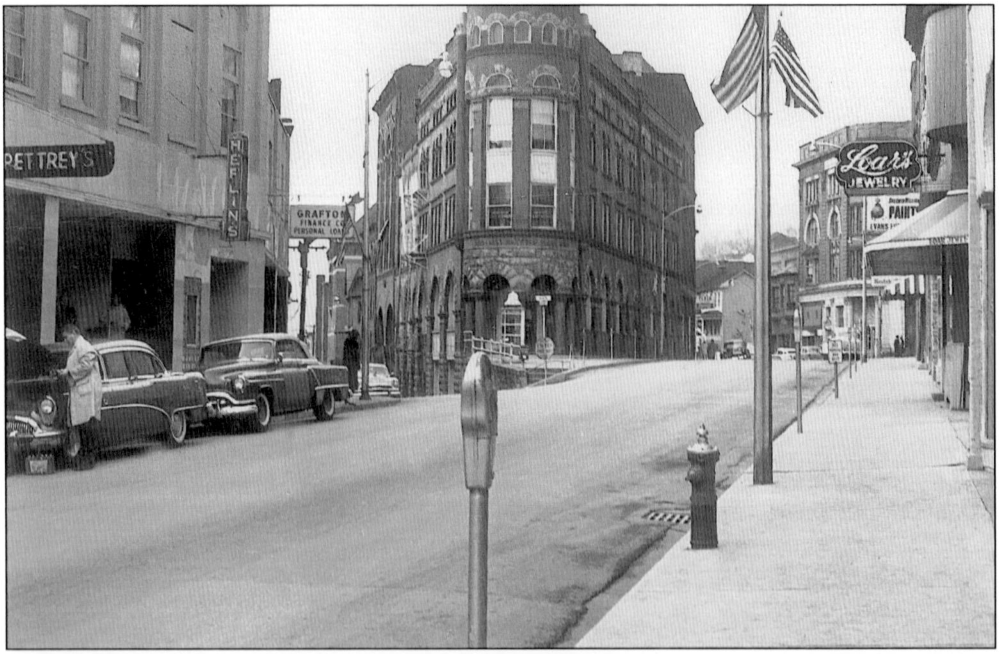

MAIN STREET. Grafton became a stopping over place for the unemployed who illegally rode the railroad boxcars during the 1930s. The mid-1930s decision to build Tygart Dam gave a boost to the local economy. Grafton, located in a steep valley with little air movement, was known for the amount of soot and cinders emmited by trains in the area. This problem eased as diesel engines were introduced, but fewer rail workers were needed as a result. (Photo courtesy of Marvin Gelhausen.)

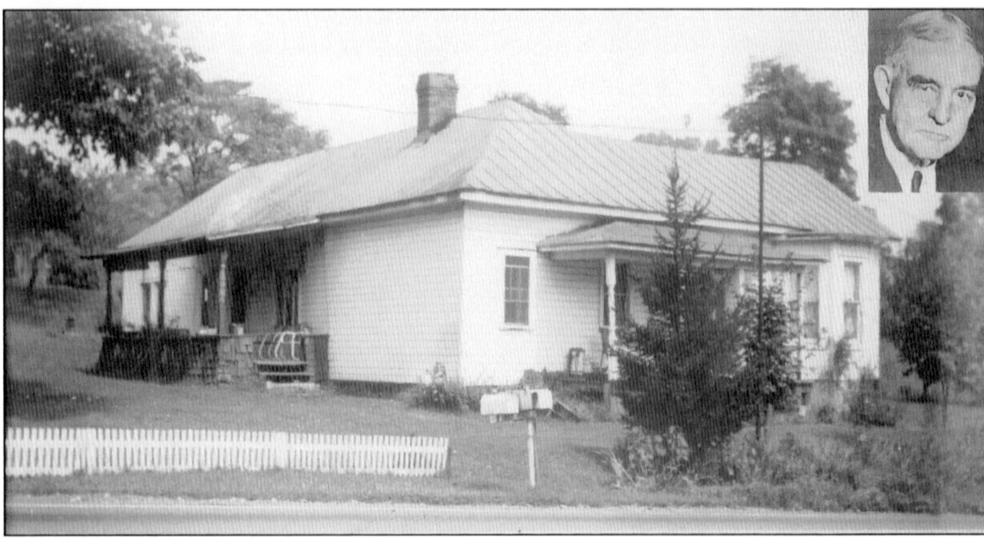

JOHN BARTON PAYNE. Considered to be the most outstanding citizen of Pruntytown from a national standpoint, Payne was born on January 26, 1855, to Dr. Amos Payne and Elizabeth Smith Payne. The family's two-room log house was part of the above residence in Pruntytown, but it has since been torn down. Payne served as secretary of the interior in the cabinet of President Woodrow Wilson, and from 1921 until his death in 1935, he was chairman of the American Red Cross. (Photo courtesy of Peggy Robinson.)

Nine

ENTERTAINMENT, PARADES, RECREATION, AND SPORTS

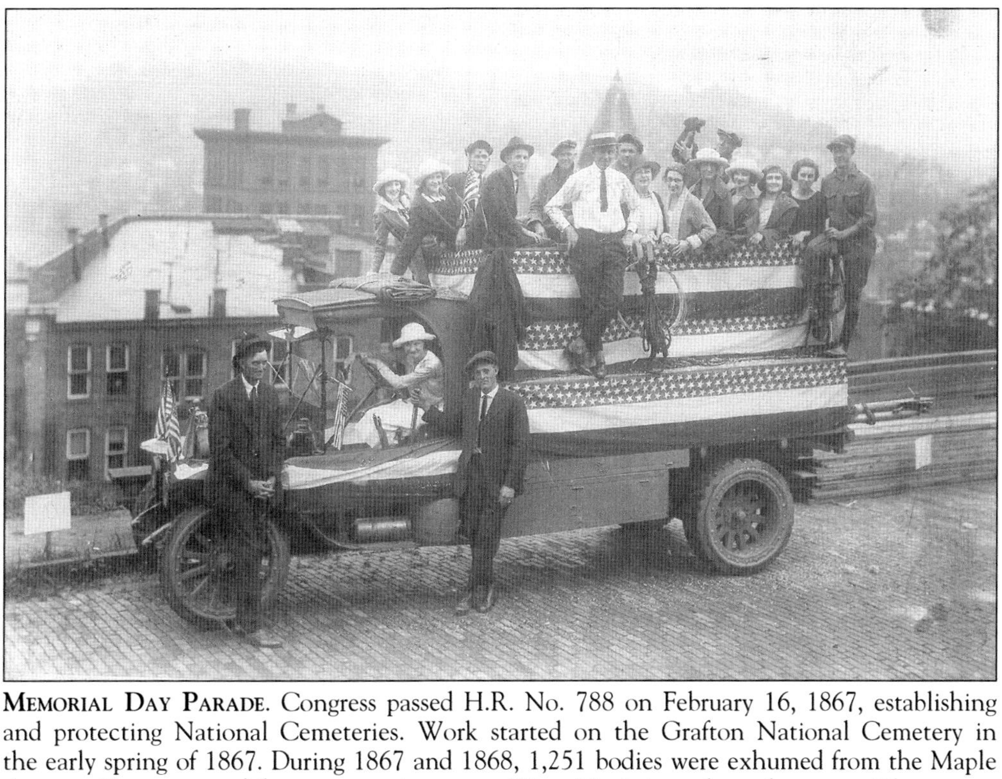

MEMORIAL DAY PARADE. Congress passed H.R. No. 788 on February 16, 1867, establishing and protecting National Cemeteries. Work started on the Grafton National Cemetery in the early spring of 1867. During 1867 and 1868, 1,251 bodies were exhumed from the Maple Avenue Cemetery and from cemeteries across West Virginia and nearby states. These were reburied at the new Grafton National Cemetery. The first Memorial Day parade was in 1868. It is not known whether or not the scene above is from an early Memorial Day parade. Grafton apparently has always been a city ready to have a parade as parades have been recorded over the years for various events and holidays. However, the Memorial Day parade is believed to be the city's oldest parade and it is still observed annually. (Photo courtesy of Wayne McDevitt.)

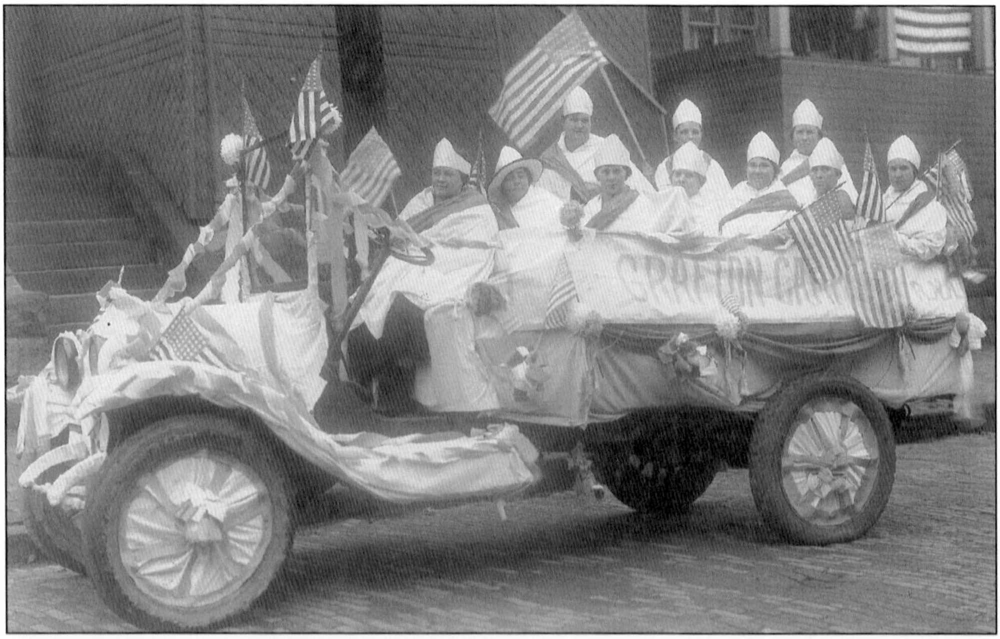

GRAFTON CAMP OF THE RNA. This photo of a parade entry is most likely from an early 1900 Memorial Day observance. Capt. Daniel Wilson, Maj. Jacob B. Brister, and Capt. Samuel Todd arranged for the first Memorial Day exercise at the new Grafton National Cemetery on May 30, 1868. However, days of rain resulted in the event being postponed until June 14. The first observance included a company of West Virginia veterans in military formation, lead by a martial band. (Photo courtesy of Wayne McDevitt.)

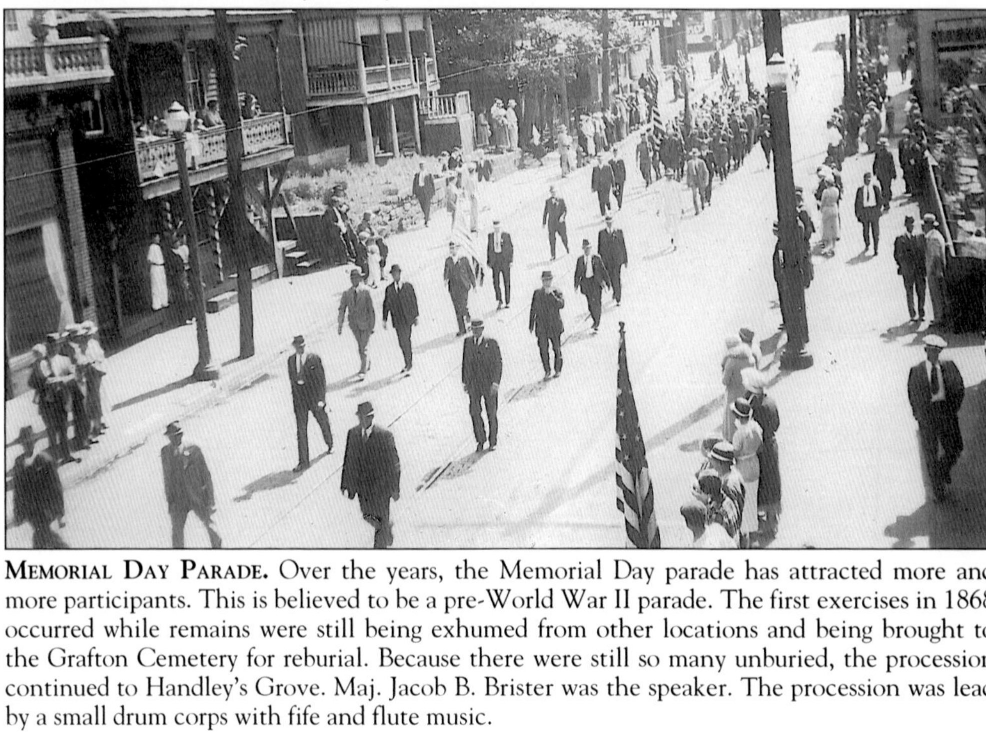

MEMORIAL DAY PARADE. Over the years, the Memorial Day parade has attracted more and more participants. This is believed to be a pre-World War II parade. The first exercises in 1868 occurred while remains were still being exhumed from other locations and being brought to the Grafton Cemetery for reburial. Because there were still so many unburied, the procession continued to Handley's Grove. Maj. Jacob B. Brister was the speaker. The procession was lead by a small drum corps with fife and flute music.

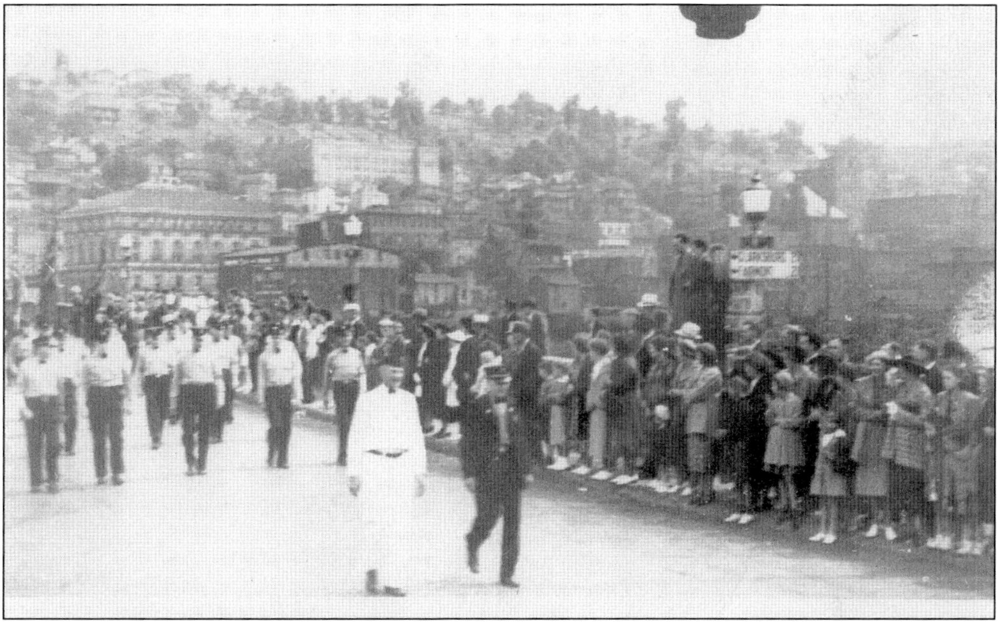

MEMORIAL DAY PARADE. This is a Memorial Day parade from the 1900s. The parade used the railroad bridge until a new public bridge was built across the Tygart Valley River in 1889 or 1890. After this, the parade did not have to travel down Latrobe Street. Arriving on the West Side, the parade route also stopped going out Pearl Street to the front of the cemetery and instead continued to Walnut Street and entered from the back of the cemetery. (Photo courtesy of Norma Wyckoff.).

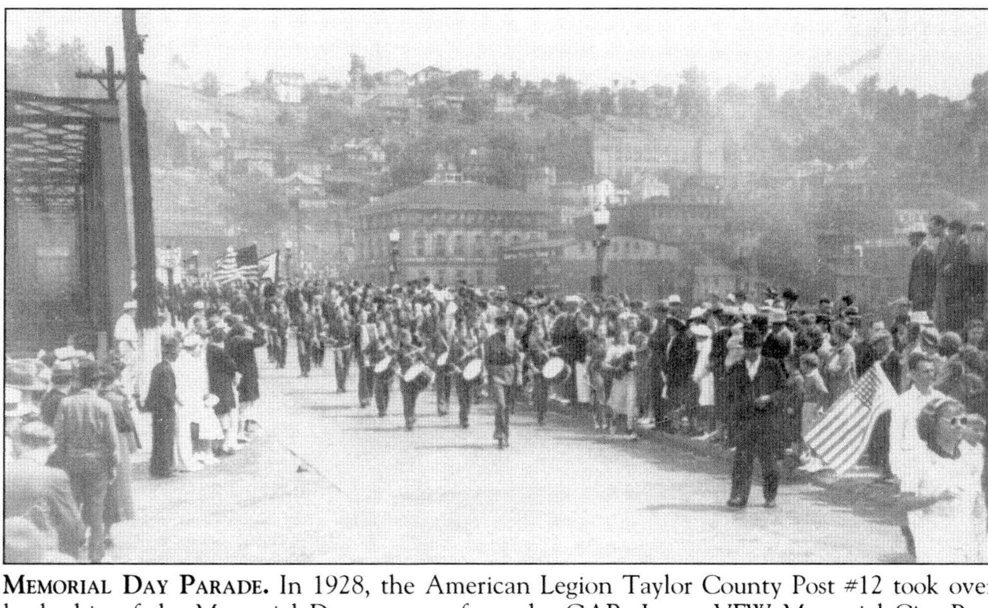

MEMORIAL DAY PARADE. In 1928, the American Legion Taylor County Post #12 took over leadership of the Memorial Day program from the GAR. Later, VFW Memorial City Post 3081 became more involved with the event. The 1893 speakers stand at the Grafton National Cemetery was removed in 1948. The superintendent's residence was built in 1876–1877 and was razed prior to 1959. An adjacent tool shed, built in 1893, was later used as the cemetery office. (Photo courtesy of Norma Wyckoff.).

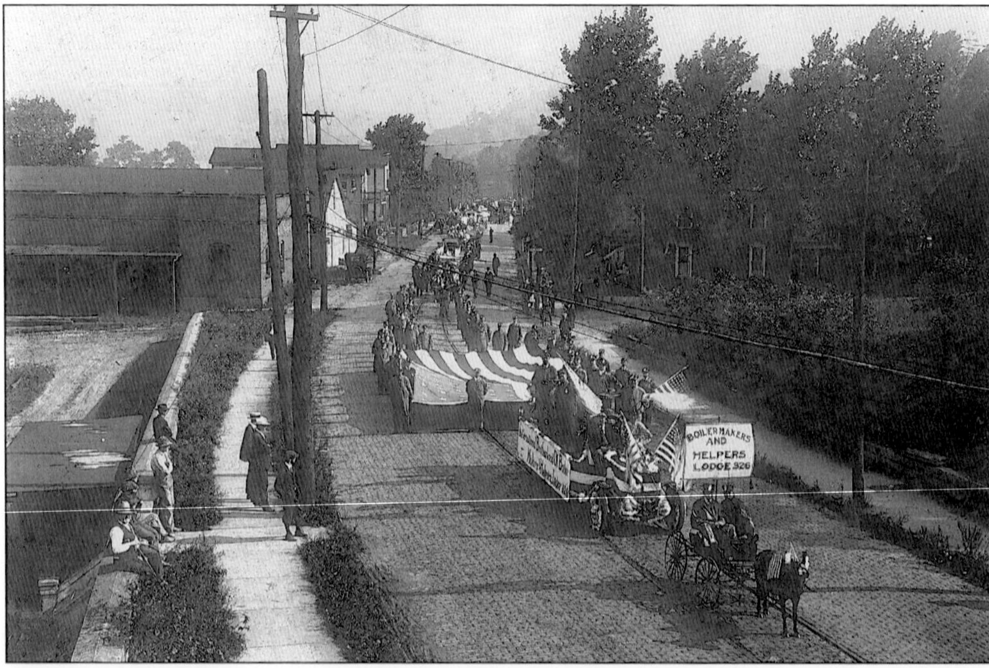

Memorial Day Parade. This is believed to be a Memorial Day parade scene, but the lineup is in the Fetterman area along West Main Street. Today, line up begins at the intersection of East Main and Bridge Streets and uses side streets in the area. Schoolchildren from pre-school and kindergarten through graduating seniors march and ride floats in the parade. In 1912, Grafton held its first homecoming week in conjunction with Memorial Day. The weekend remains a popular homecoming time for former residents.

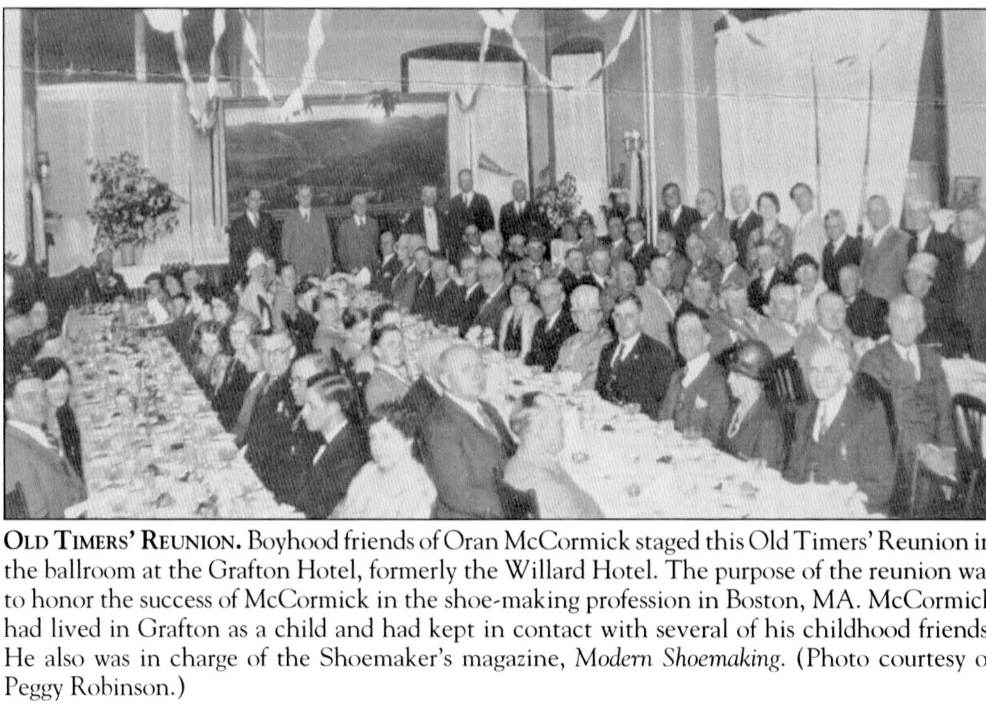

Old Timers' Reunion. Boyhood friends of Oran McCormick staged this Old Timers' Reunion in the ballroom at the Grafton Hotel, formerly the Willard Hotel. The purpose of the reunion was to honor the success of McCormick in the shoe-making profession in Boston, MA. McCormick had lived in Grafton as a child and had kept in contact with several of his childhood friends. He also was in charge of the Shoemaker's magazine, *Modern Shoemaking*. (Photo courtesy of Peggy Robinson.)

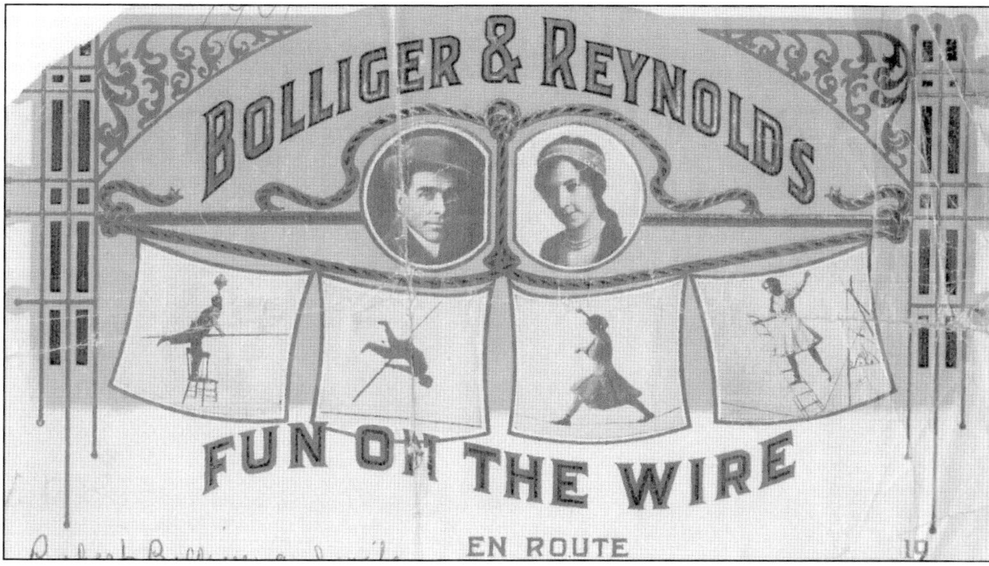

BOLLINGER & REYNOLDS. This photo is courtesy of James Bolliger, a contributor of several of the historical photos of Grafton and Taylor County that are published in this pictorial history. This high wire entertainment act was performed by Robert Bolliger and his wife. Robert Bolliger is the great-great-uncle of James Bolliger. The two wire artists were from Grafton. In addition to having had a number of entertainers with Grafton roots, the city for years attracted many popular entertainers to the Brinkman Opera House and other area entertainment outlets.

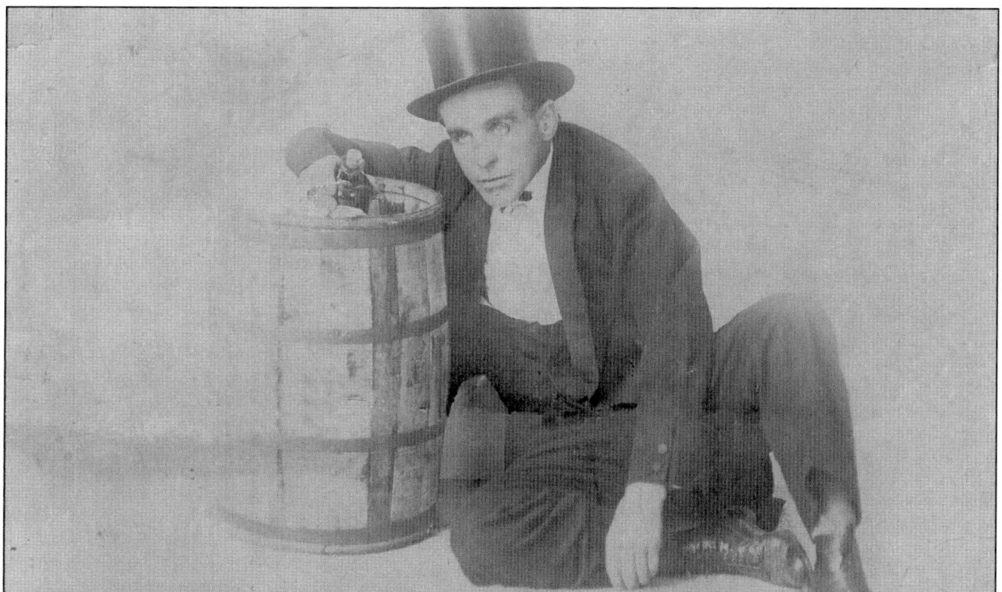

MR. BOLLIGER. On the back of the original of this photograph is written "Bolliger & Reynolds," but the man shown is not identified as Robert Bolliger, although it is believed that this is a photo of Robert Bolliger. Later, in the 1930s, William Doll, a native of Grafton, became a nationally known press agent. Doll had his own New York Press Agency and was best known for handling the press relations of the famous Ringling Brothers Circus. (Photo courtesy of Wayne McDevitt.).

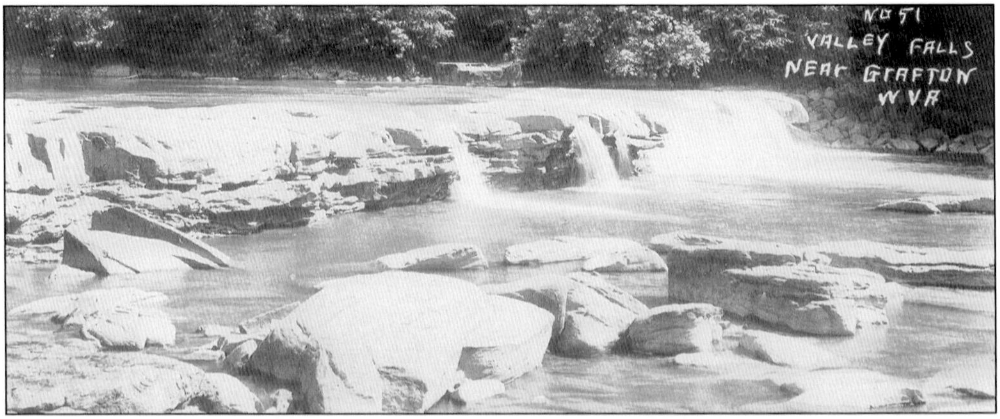

Valley Falls. In 1964, the Marion County side was established as a state park. The Taylor County side remains undeveloped. (Photo courtesy of Wayne McDevitt.)

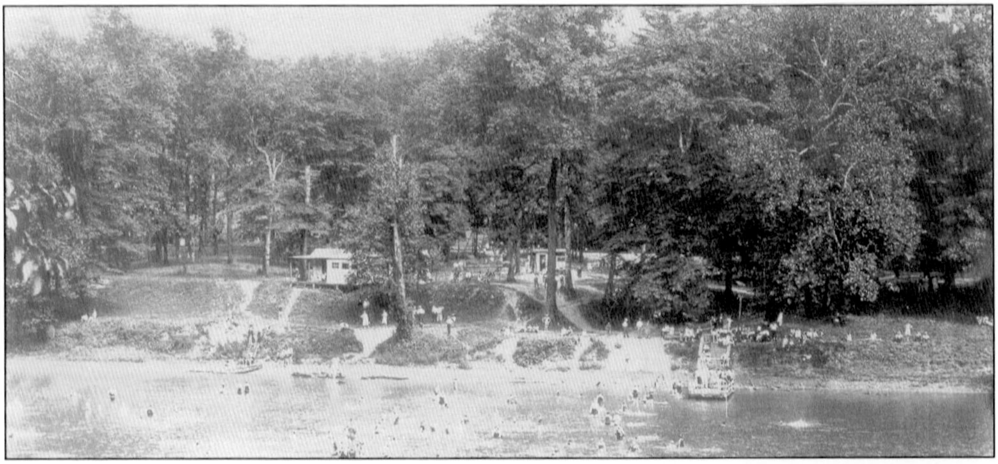

Grafton City Park. the park is now mainly a camping, fishing, and picnic area with two pavilions and a bathhouse. It was a popular recreation/swimming area prior to the Tygart Dam.

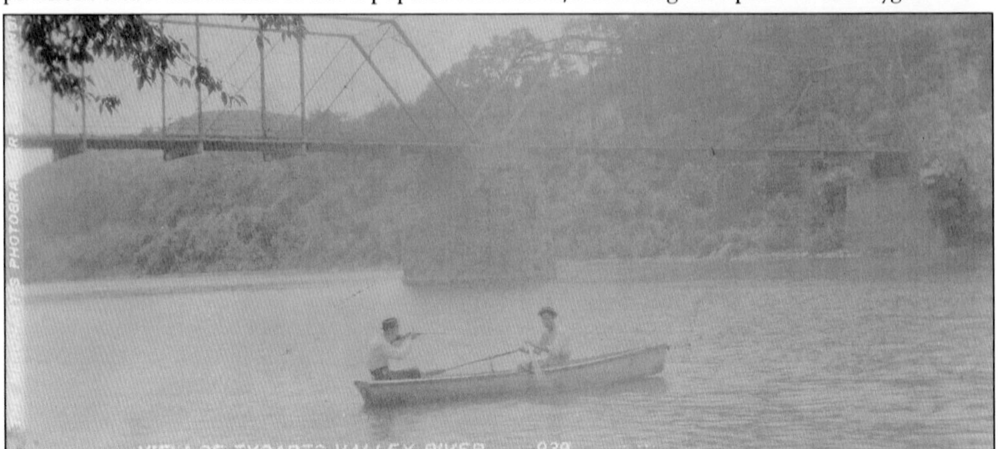

Fishing in the Tygart River. The bridge shown was built on the piers of the original covered bridge at Fetterman. (Photo courtesy of Wayne McDevitt.)

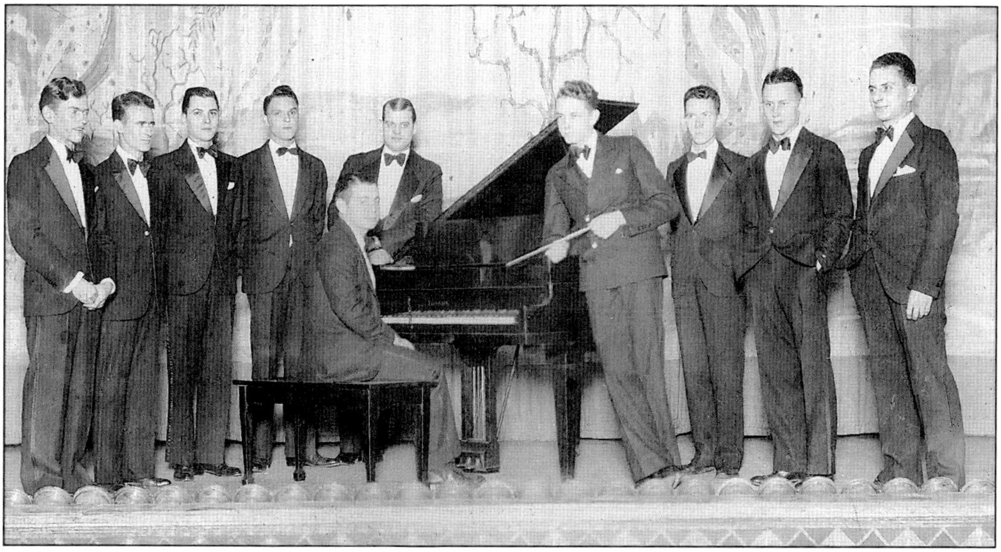

WELL-KNOWN ENTERTAINER. The Carson Howard's Collegian Orchestra is shown here *c.* 1929. From left to right are Davis Evans, Don Price, Julis Condus, J. Davison, Carson Howard, Bill Doll, Dick Monbody, and Phil Skoff. C. Samgth is sitting. William "Bill" Doll, a native of Grafton, was in this orchestra during his days at WVU. In the 1930s, Doll wrote a weekly syndicated newspaper column. Carried by *The Grafton News*, the column was titled "Manhattan Moments" and was about the activities of West Virginians in New York. (Photo courtesy of Marvin Gelhausen.)

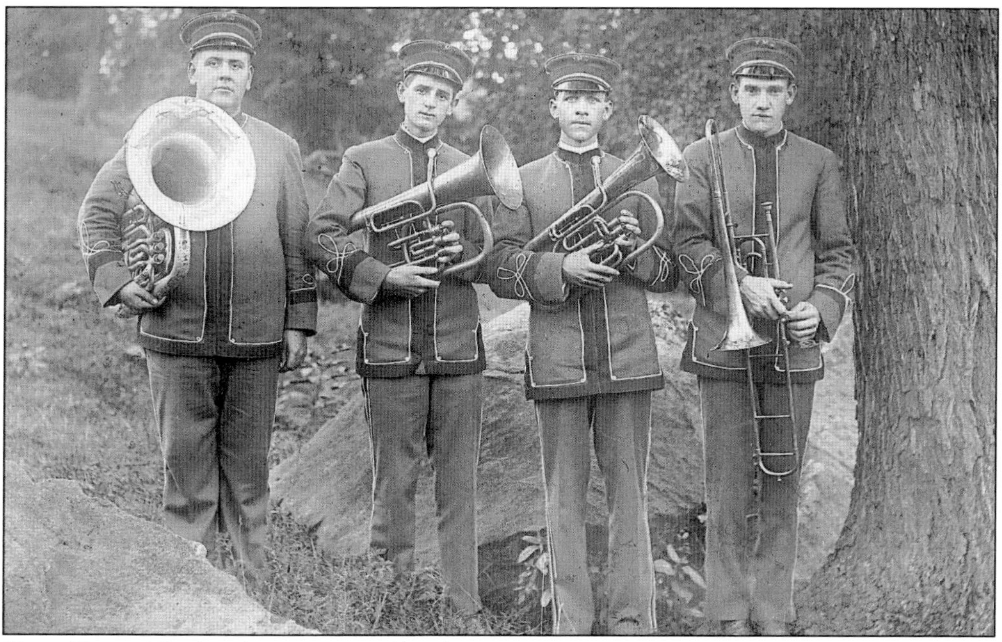

YATES BAND. The band was organized by the "Music Man," George M. Yates (1866–1940), who came to Flemington from Elkins in 1910. Yates is said to have touched almost every home in the area either through his teaching or his music. He composed music, especially marches, and frequently rearranged marches written by others. Several of his marches were accepted by the U.S. Navy. His arrangement of the "Star-Spangled Banner" was said to be a perfect success.

Official Program

for the

Centennial Banquet

HONORING THE GROWTH AND PROGRESS

OF THE

City of Grafton, West Virginia

March 15, 1856 --- March 15, 1956

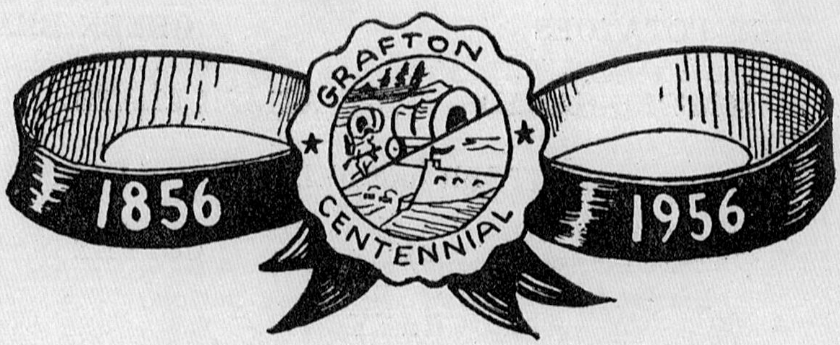

FIELD HOUSE, GRAFTON HIGH SCHOOL

Grafton, West Virginia

GRAFTON CENTENNIAL, 1956. From May 31 to June 6, 1956, Grafton celebrated its centennial under the chairmanship of George Shingleton. A community play, *Centurama*, that told the history of Grafton was presented as part of the celebration. Shown above is the cover of the official program for the Centennial Banquet that was held at the Grafton High School on March 15, 1956. Its purpose was to honor the growth and progress of the city of Grafton for the 100-year period of March 15, 1856, through March 15, 1956. (This program copy is courtesy of Darlene Ford.)

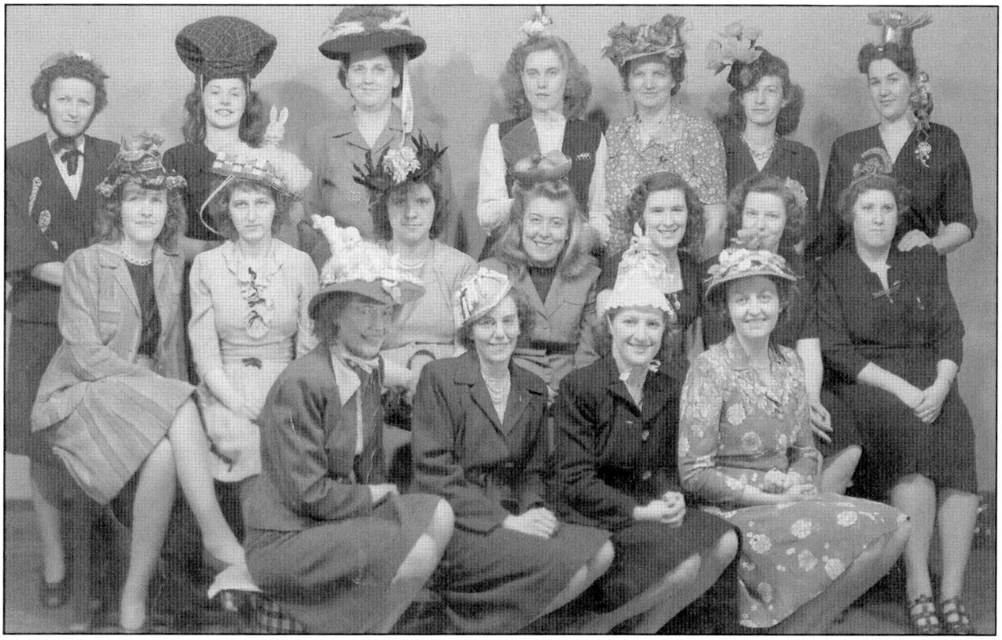

HAT LADIES. This was a mid-1940s hat party of the Delta Nu Chapter, Tau Phi Lambda, Supreme Forest Woodmen Circle. From left to right are the following: (front row) Beulah Belle Bailey, Marion Gough, Monford Cross Loar, and Louise Ringler Arble; (middle row) Grace Marie Bartlett, Clarabell Murphy Upton, Betty Keener Sinsel, Eleanor Green Weekly, Edith Jo Robinson Foley, Mildred Newcome Cole, and Miriam Isner Nestor; (back row) Pauline Sinsel Keener, Mary Poppalardo Jaco, Sarah Sayres, Evelyn Green Sinclair, Leona Zumbro, Flossie Johnson Goff, and Betty Hall Rinker.

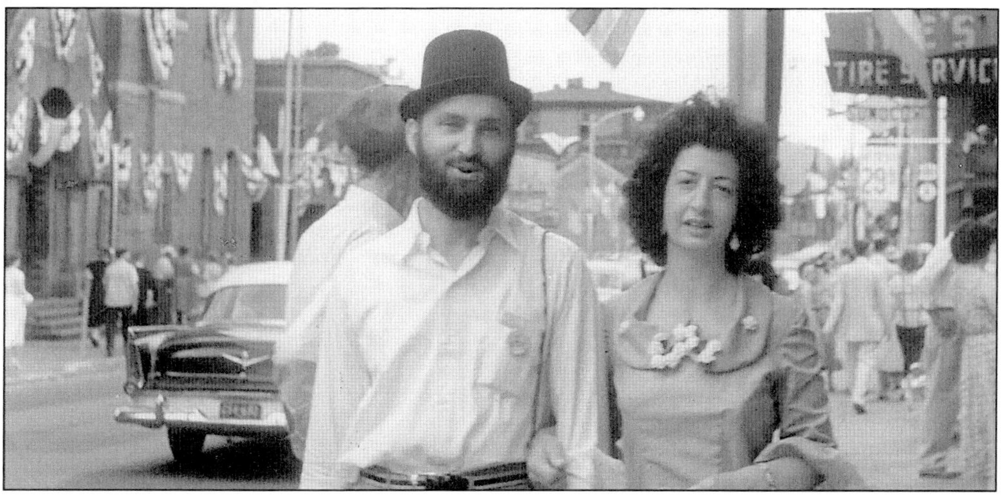

GRAFTON'S 1956 CENTENNIAL. Joe and Thelma Chis stroll along West Main Street across from the Taylor County Courthouse during the city's centennial celebration. The courthouse was decorated for Memorial Day as the celebration ran from May 31 to June 6, 1956. Behind the couple is Ike's Tire Service, a Main Street business that operated for many years until the death in January 2000 of owner Ike Rinker. The couple are in front of the Haislip building, which housed the offices of Dr. Charles Haislip, a Grafton physician. (Photo courtesy of Peggy Robinson.)

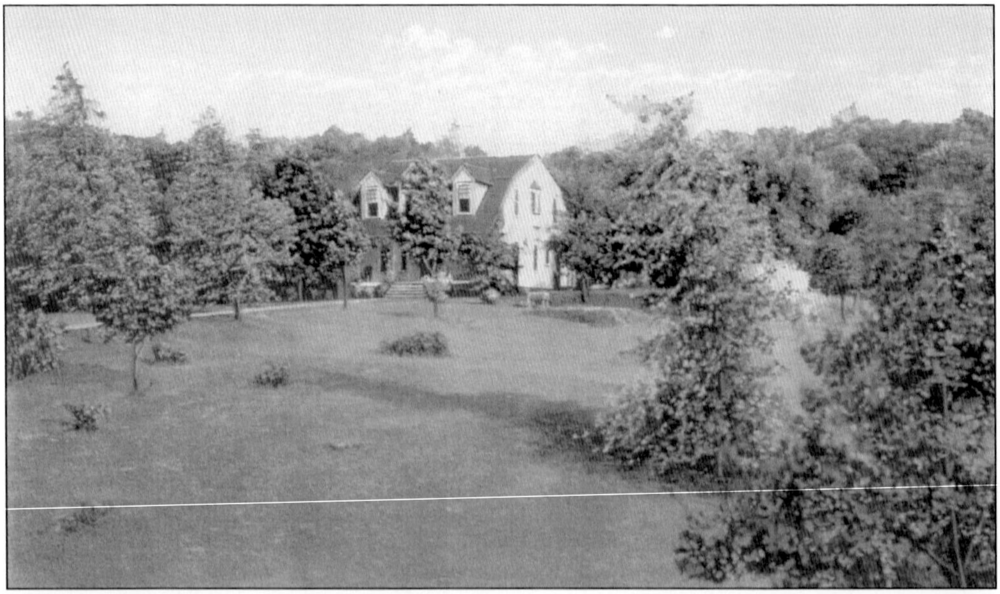

GRAFTON COUNTRY CLUB. This clubhouse that served the former Grafton Country Club is located along Route 310 that also is known as the Country Club Road. The golf course was not an 18-hole facility and was phased out when the Monongahela Power System had plans to build a power plant along the river at this site. Also, the course had competition from the Tygart Lake Country Club, which constructed an 18-hole golf course in 1967 and was open for the 1968 season. The proposed power plant was never built. (Photo courtesy of Wayne McDevitt.)

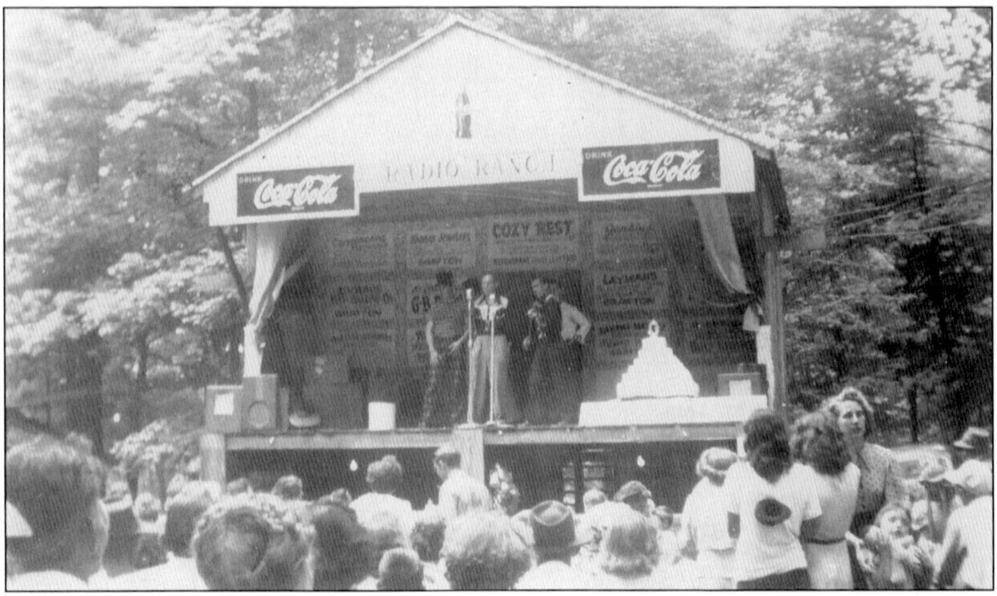

RADIO RANCH. This entertainment center was located along Wickwire Road, a short distance from its intersection with U.S. Route 119 North, near the new Grafton Wal-Mart. Many local and nationally known country musicians came to play and perform here at the Radio Ranch. This was during the heydays of Fairmont radio station WMMN and many of their performers played here. The above photo is believed to be from the 1940s. (Photo courtesy of Wayne McDevitt.)

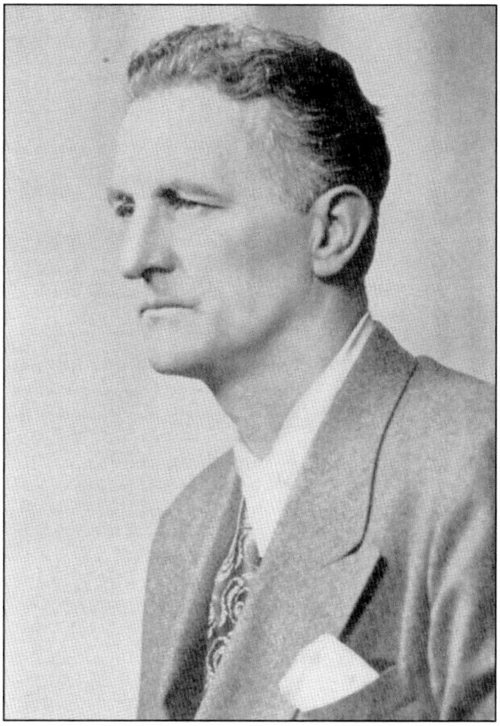

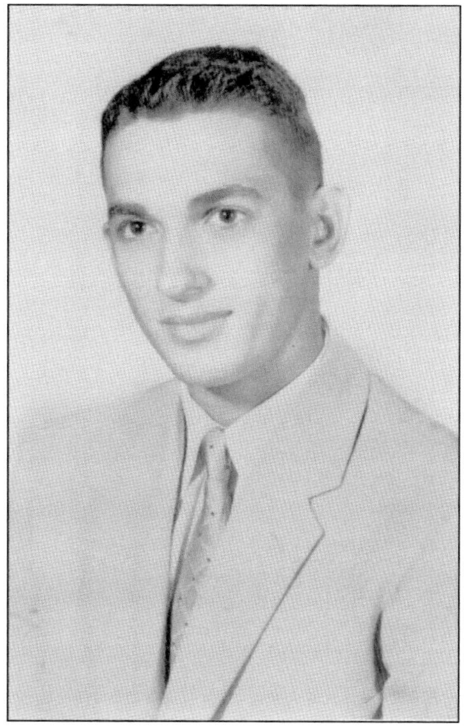

ABOVE LEFT: CLAIR BEE (1896–1983). Grafton raised, Bee was one of the most knowledgeable and successful basketball coaches ever. At Long Island University, he had a 81.9 winning percentage. Later, he became coach, general manager, and part-owner of the Baltimore Bullets. He was elected to the Basketball Hall of Fame. He was a sports writer.

ABOVE RIGHT: PAUL E. POPOVICH (1940–PRESENT). Flemington's Paul Popovich scored 2,660 points in four seasons, 1955–1959. He held the state record of all-time leading scorer in high school basketball until it was broken in 2000. He played 11 years in the Major Leagues for the Chicago Cub's, LA Dodgers, and Pittsburgh Pirates.

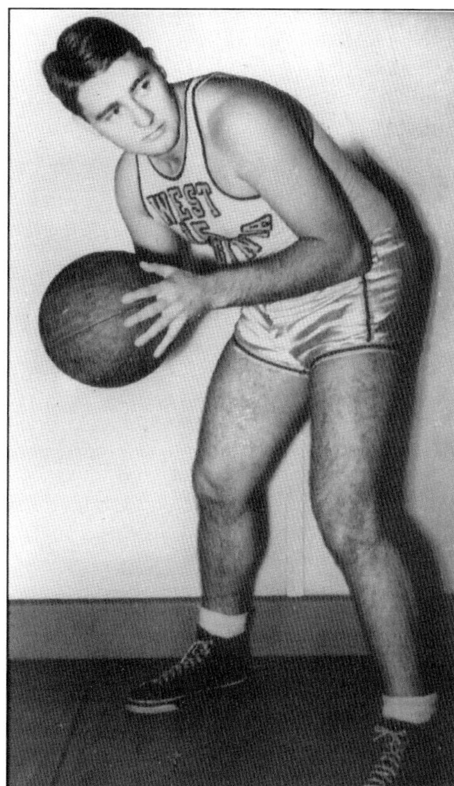

RIGHT: SCOTTY HAMILTON (1921–1976). Grafton's Scotty Hamilton, named an all-state basketball player in high school, went on to become WVU's first All-American basketball player. His 1942 team defeated Clair Bee's team to win the NIT Tournament Championship. Hamilton briefly played professional basketball and later coached. In 1966, he entered the West Virginia Sports Hall of Fame.

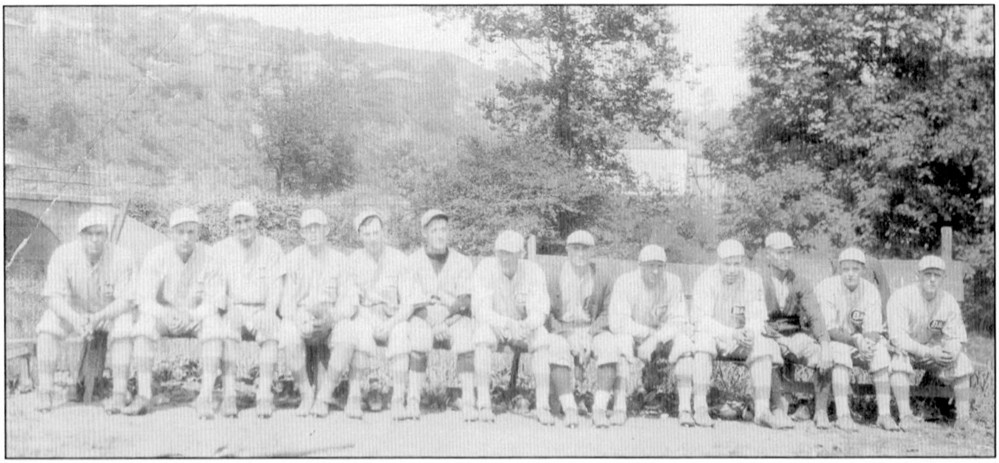

B&O Railroad Baseball. The names of individual team members are not available for this 1918 or 1919 photo, except for Clem Parr, team catcher, who is on the far left. The photo was taken from the sports grounds next to the baseball field at GHS. In August 1908, Col. John T. McGraw, George H. Hartley, and Charles Flanagan formed a stock company and bought the Scottsdale franchise of the Pennsylvania-West Virginia League for $10,000. The Fetterman Ball Park was the site of the first game, attended by 2,500 fans. (Photo courtesy of Wayne McDevitt.)

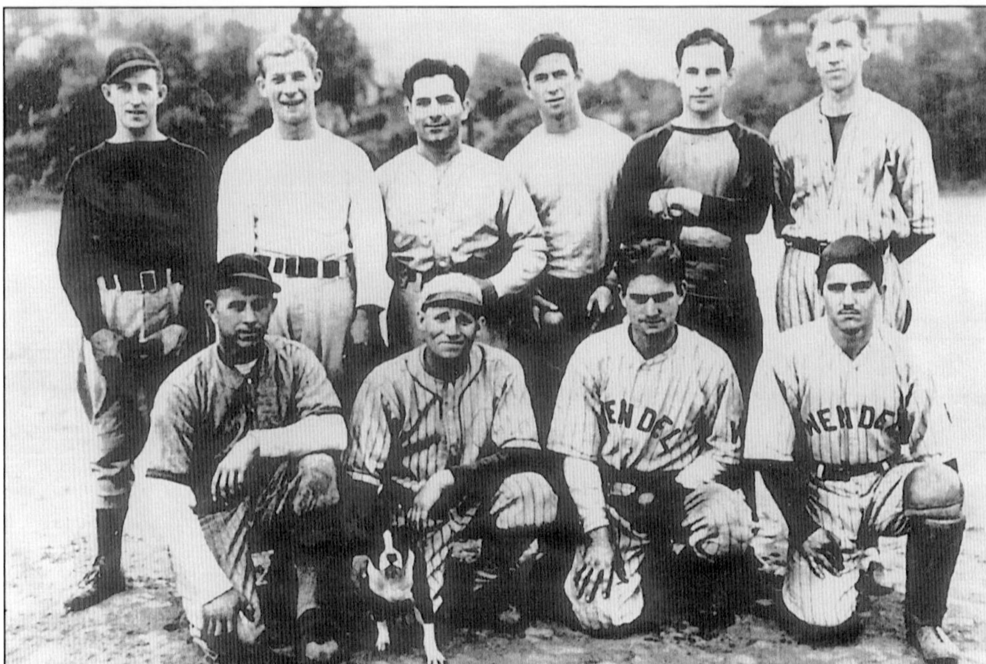

Wendel Baseball. The game of baseball in Taylor County has evoked the interest of players and spectators alike for well over 100 years. Perhaps the influx of men to build and man new industries resulted in a need for recreation. Whatever the reason, baseball was the "in" sport before the turn of the 20th century and remains popular today. The village of Wendel was settled around 1825 by the Yates family. The Maryland Coal Company bought land in 1903 and the community grew until the 1930s.

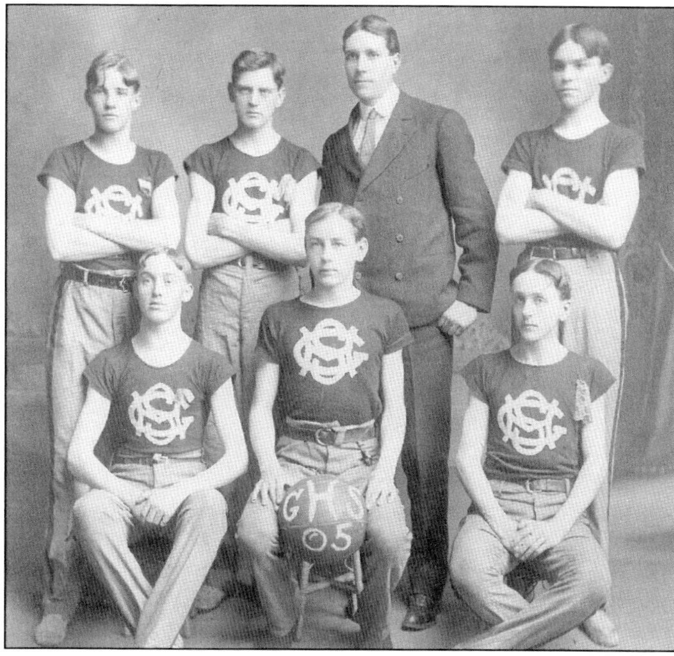

GHS 1905 BASKETBALL TEAM. From left to right are the following: (front row) Holmes Wyckoff, Edgar Doll, and Neil Heflin; (back row) Leslie Rogers, Clyde Richman, coach W. Merl Watkins, and Ward Lanham. This photo is from the time period that the high school was in the Central School Building along Wilford Street. That facility did not have a gymnasium and the Young Men's Christian Association (YMCA) building along Main Street was used, as were other structures around the city. (Photo courtesy of Larry M. Richman.)

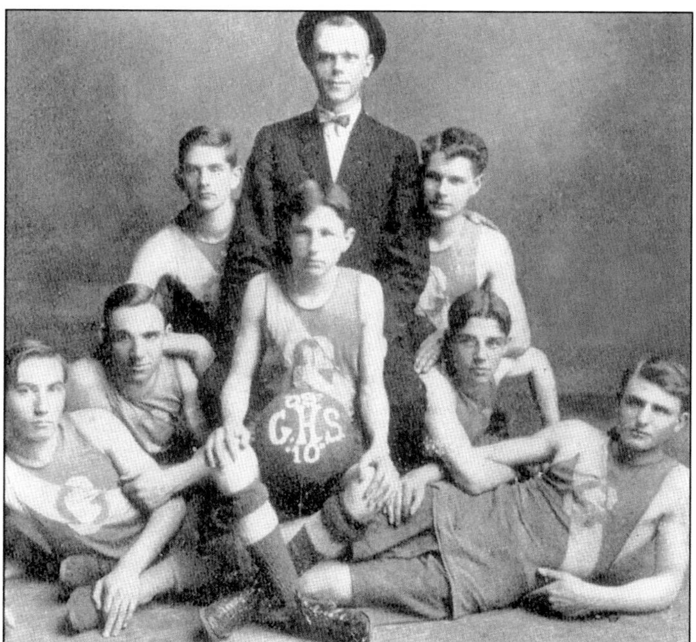

GHS 1910 BASKETBALL TEAM. This team had a 6-12 record. Squad members were center Fred Abbott, right guard Edwin Powell, left guard William Scull, right forward William Cassell, and left forward Charles Sinsel. The subs were Chauncey Helms, Harry Curry, Leslie Loar, and Herman Wilson. This was during the time period that the high school was in the Central School Building along Wilford Street. A new high school was built in 1914–16 along West Washington Street. (Photo courtesy of Rich Bord.)

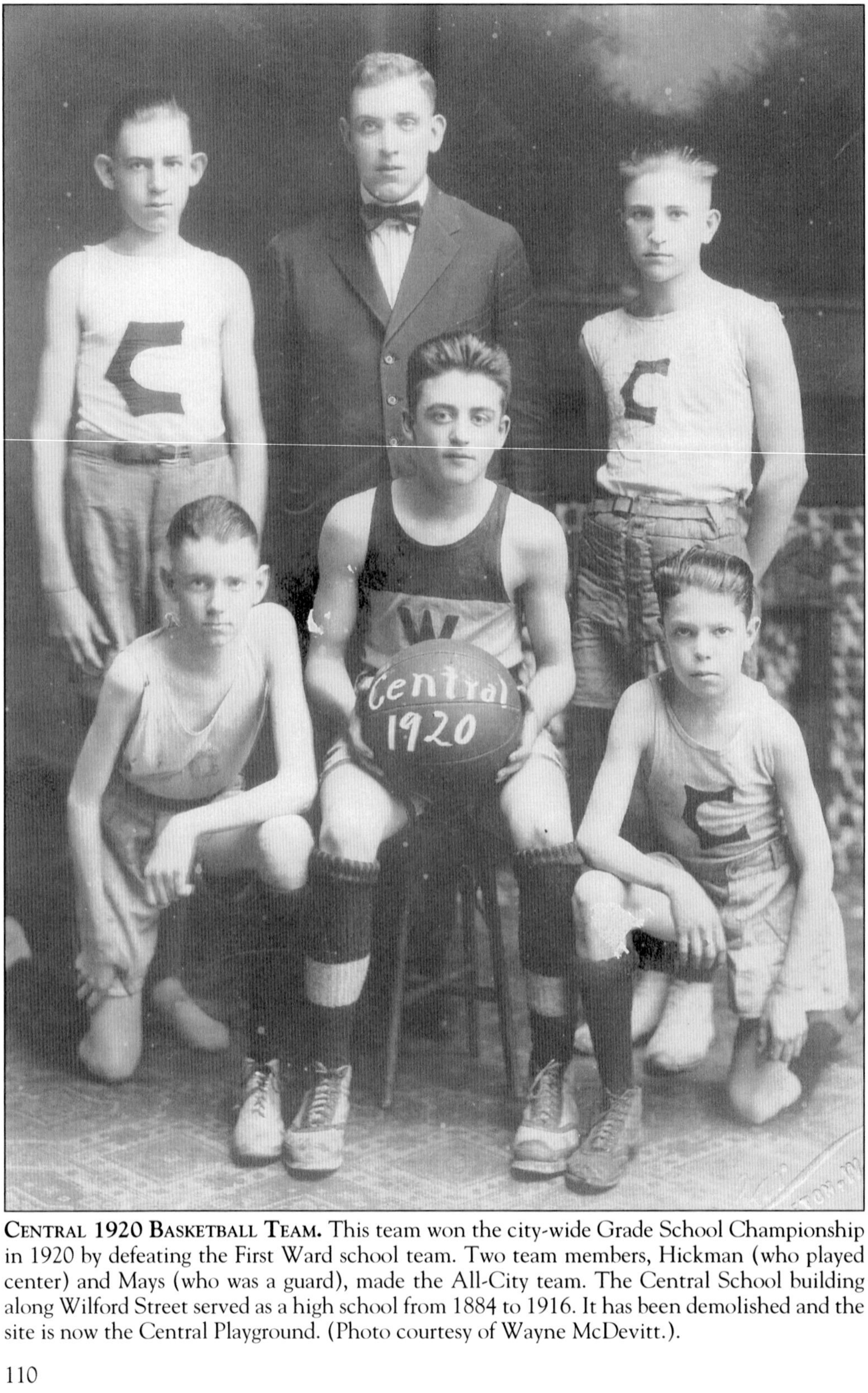

CENTRAL 1920 BASKETBALL TEAM. This team won the city-wide Grade School Championship in 1920 by defeating the First Ward school team. Two team members, Hickman (who played center) and Mays (who was a guard), made the All-City team. The Central School building along Wilford Street served as a high school from 1884 to 1916. It has been demolished and the site is now the Central Playground. (Photo courtesy of Wayne McDevitt.).

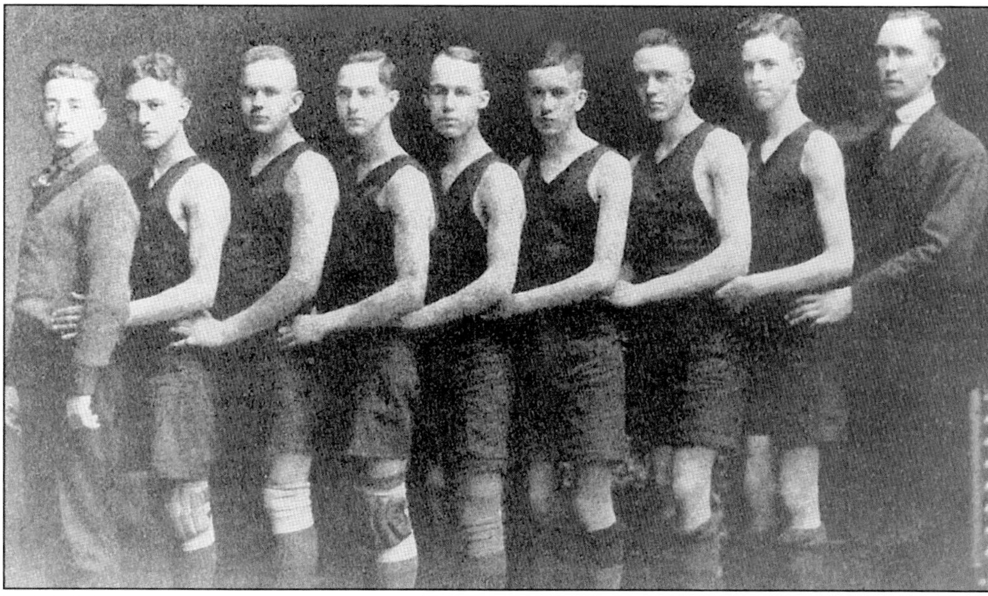

GHS 1920 BASKETBALL TEAM. Shown here are team manager William Copp, guard Clair Bee, forward Terring Heironimus, guard Henry Wehn, forward Richard Bartlett, forward Charles Kimmel, captain Ernest Clark, forward Robert VanHorn, and coach J.H. Colebank. This photo was taken when the high school was still located along West Washington Street. Built at a cost of $110,000, the Washington Street high school was ready for occupancy in 1916. It had its own gymnasium. (Photo courtesy of Rich Bord.)

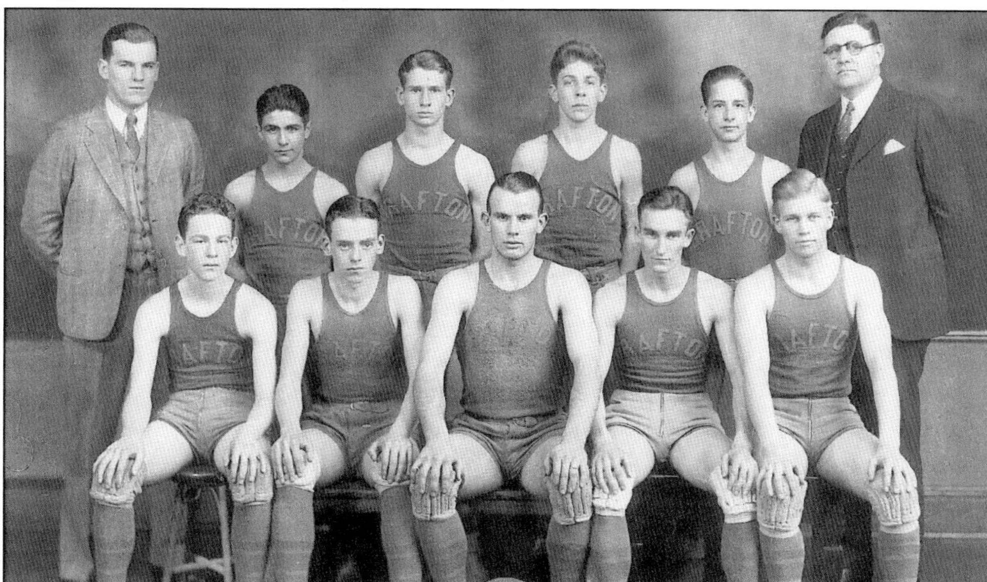

GHS 1931 BASKETBALL TEAM. Names of individual team members are not available, except for Richard McKinney, who scored over 250 points in 1931. Coach Randal H. McKinney (top left) had his hands full since he also coached the football and baseball teams. Lynn Faulkner coached the track squad. E.G. Kuhn, the principal, is shown in the upper right. The photo was taken when the high school was still located along West Washington Street. (Photo courtesy of Rich Bord.)

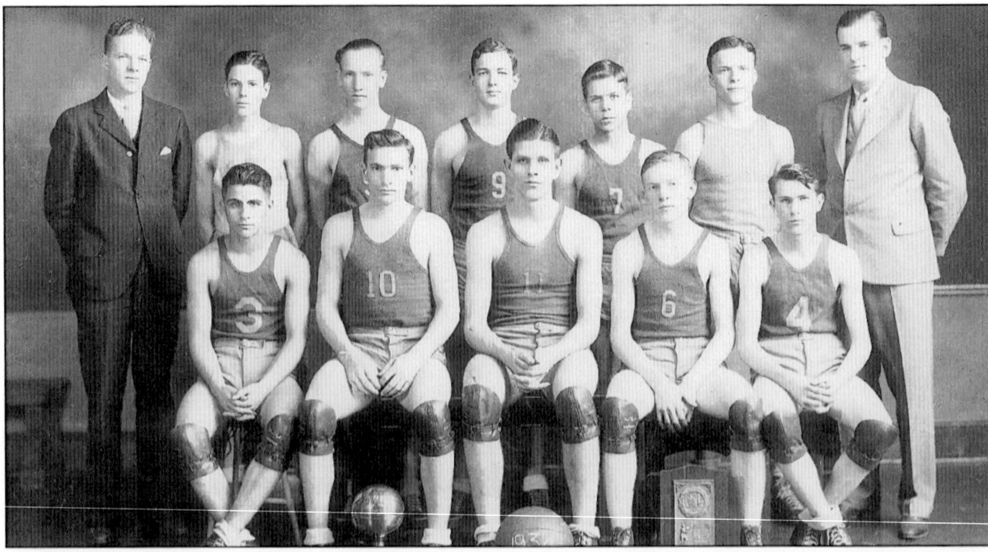

GHS 1934 Basketball Team. The varsity squad included forward Lobis, forward C. Peters, center Bolyard, guard Shahan, guard Stolzenfels, guard S. Peters, and guard Flanagan. In 1934 the high school was located along West Washington Street. The Grafton community was growing and the school was overcrowded. Industry started to pick up in the late 1930s. Carr China expanded its operations and the Hazel-Atlas glass plant returned to full production. The use of rail services also increased. (Photo courtesy of Rich Bord.)

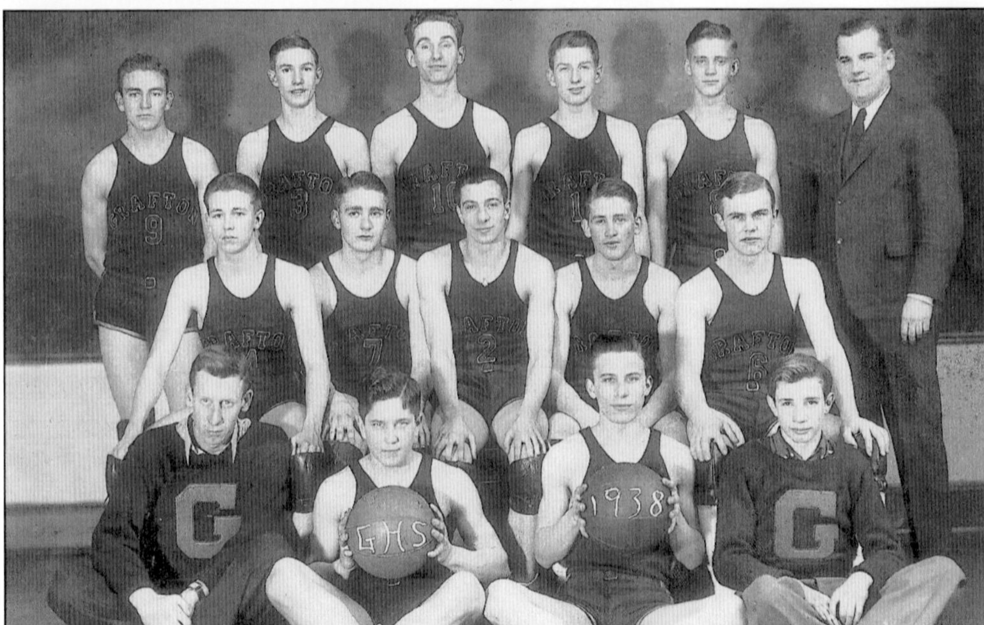

GHS 1938 Basketball Team. Floyd "Scotty" Hamilton led the 1938 Grafton High School basketball team to a runner-up finish in the state basketball tournament and he was named to that year's All-Tournament Team along with guard Denzie from Grafton. Earlier, in 1924, Grafton had a state runner-up team and that year a guard by the name of Heflin was named to the All-Tournament Team. In 1935, the present GHS fieldhouse was completed. It would later be named for Clair Bee. (Photo courtesy of Rich Bord.)

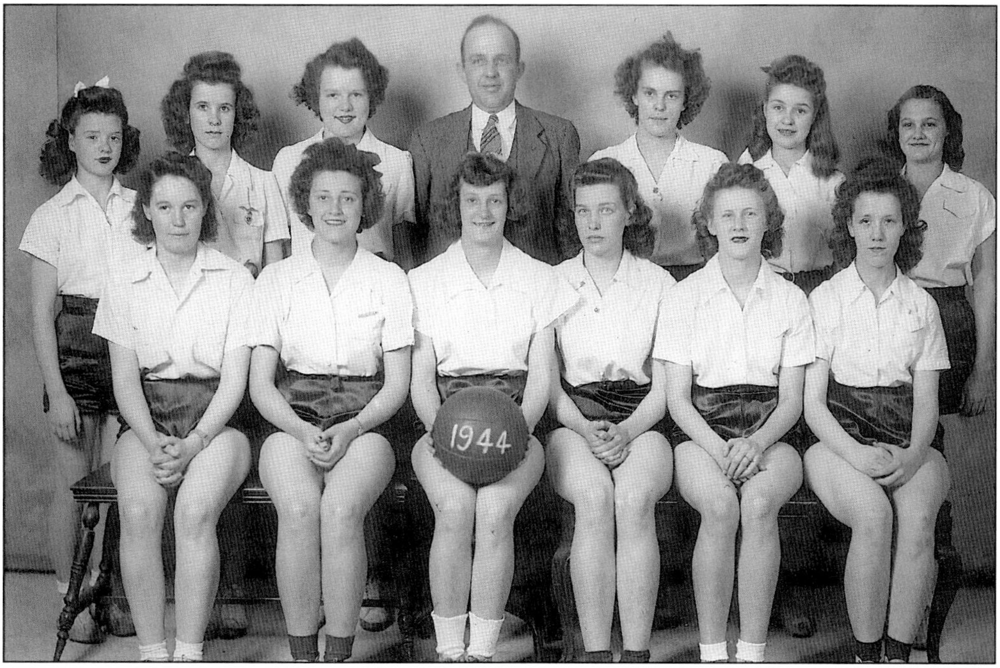

FLEMINGTON HIGH SCHOOL'S 1944 GIRL'S BASKETBALL TEAM. From left to right are the following: (front row) Helen Marteny, Ruth Mitch, Martha Ann Mitch, Marion Gaines, Helen Gozik, and Essie Longwell; (back row) Betty Jones, Betty Brown, Betty Dean Duval, Principal L.W. Talbott, Mary Etta Duval, Betty Christian, and Norma Glenn. The Class of 1929 was the last to graduate from the old college building at Flemington. In January 1930, students moved into the new Flemington High School. It closed in 1990. (Photo courtesy of Martha Ann Rus.)

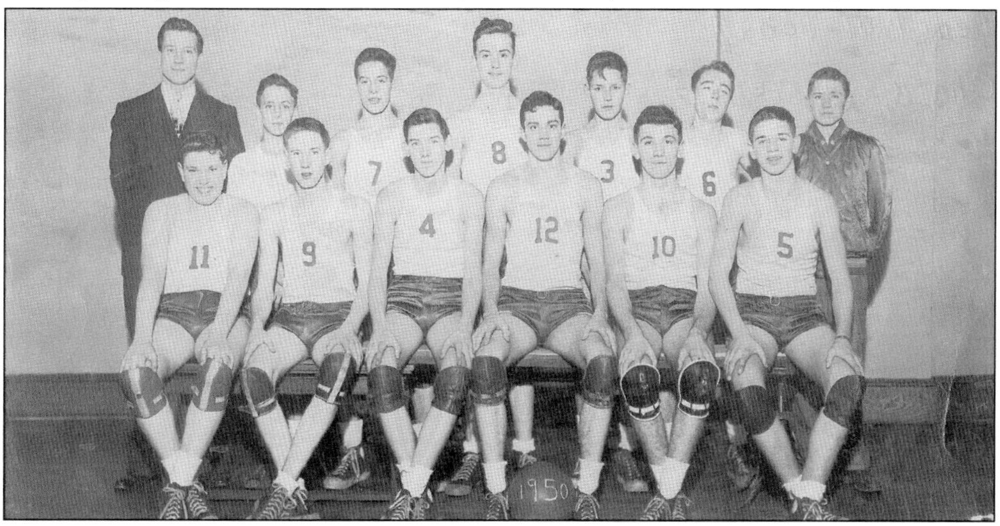

ST. AUGUSTINE BASKETBALL 1950. From left to right are the following: (front row) Frank Sandor, 11; John Waters, 9; Robert Dougherty, 4; Charles Turner, 12; Mick Turner, 10; and Gene Paul Behan, 5; (back row) coach Burner; Terry Tighe; Robert Colon, 7; Robert O'Conor, 8; Freddie Ford, 3; Charles Waters, 6; and manager Litzinger. The Catholic school was established in Grafton in 1859. In 1957, a gymnasium and auditorium building was dedicated. In 1966, grades 9-12 at St. Augustine School closed. (Photo courtesy of Darlene Ford.)

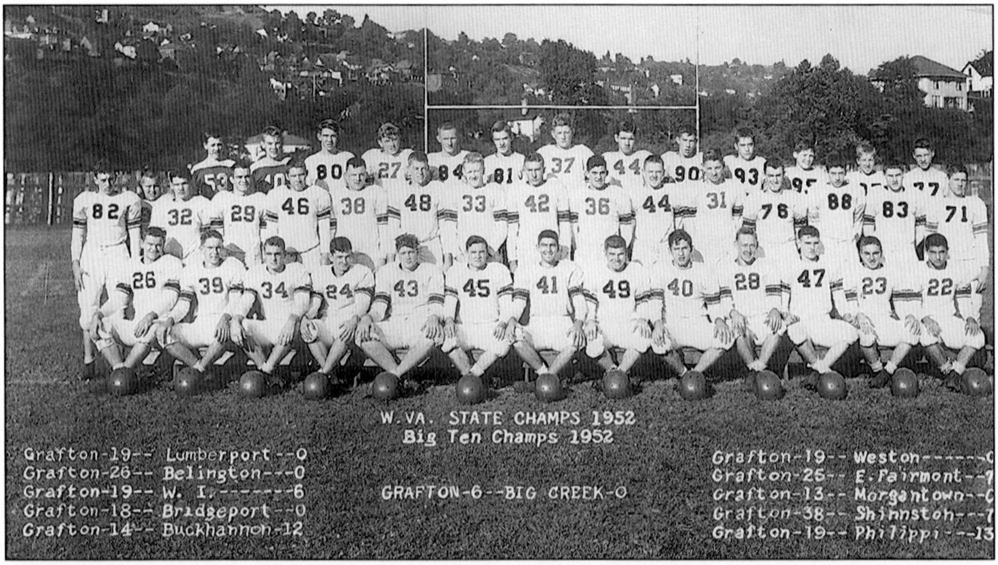

GHS 1952 FOOTBALL. This team was the West Virginia State Champs and Big Ten Champs. Only last names were available for most of the team members shown. They are, from left to right, as follows: (front row) Richmond, Mays, Tucker, Shafferman, M. Prunty, Lough, Dempsey, McCord, Knotts, Jennings, Williams, Bolliger, and Manno; (middle row) Stephenson, Nye, Maloney, Robinson, Wilson, Sandsbury, Hauser, Loar, Calfee, Luzadder, Mollohan, Shriver, Gooseman, Bennett, Heaton, and Jacobs; (back row) current managers Reed and Decker, Jenkins, Grey, C. Prunty, Steadman, Kent, B. Smith, Poling, H. Smith, and manager Morgan. (Photo courtesy of Rich Bord.)

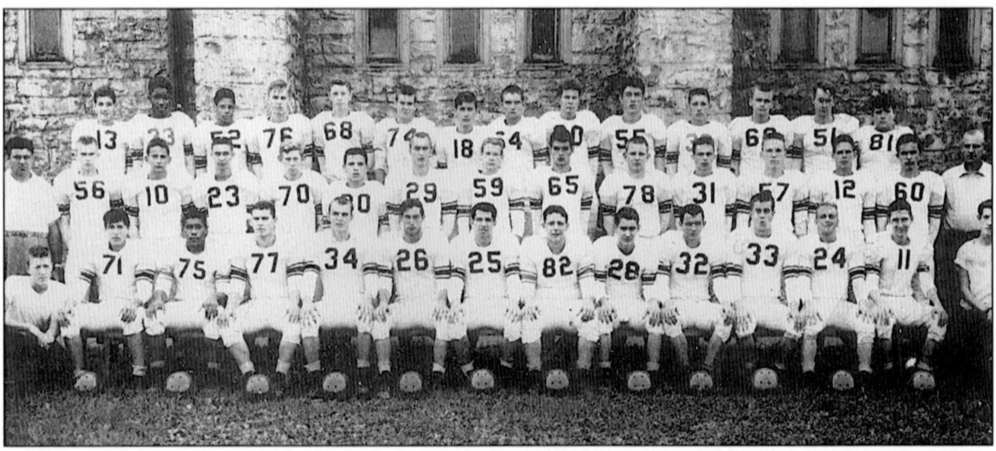

GHS 1956 FOOTBALL CHAMPS. The Grafton Bearcats were state champions and Big Ten crown winners for the second successive year. From left to right are the following: (front row) manager Russell Isner; 71 Garner; 75 B. Garrett; 77 Cuppett; 34 Michel; 26 Hershman; 25 Newhouse; 82 Dean; 28 Nicholson; 32 Posey; 33 Scragg; 24 Fred Knotts; 11 Walter; and manager Albert Wetzel; (middle row) assistant coach Lawrence Spadafore; 58 Lord; 10 Jaco; 23 Custer; 70 Colebank; 80 R. Robinson; 29 Jones; 59 Costolo; 56 Murphy; 78 Bush; 31 Ringler; 57 Lloyd Shriver; 12 Burdett; 60 Trouzcy; and coach Randall McKiney; (back row) 13 Millnovich; T. Garrett; 52 Jackson; 76 Danny Jacobs; 68 Bowman; 74 Jackson; 18 Cross; 64 Carl Knotts; 30 Haislip; 55 Rutherford; 39 Charles Morgan; 69 Marah; 51 Pratt; and 81 Martin. (Photo courtesy of Rich Bord.)

Ten

AN OVERVIEW OF TAYLOR COUNTY

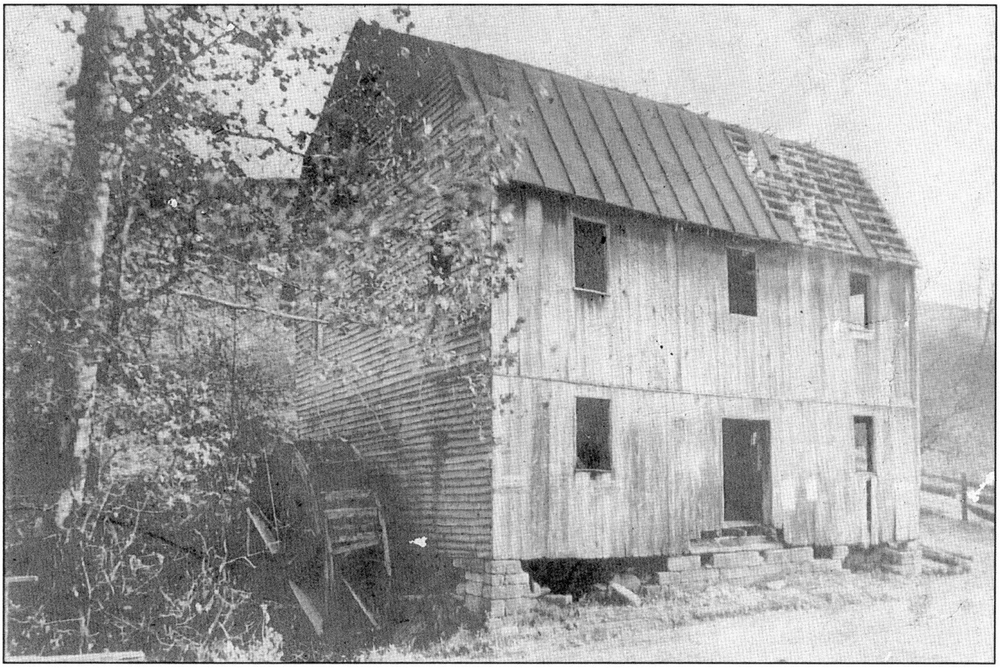

BOOTHSVILLE MILL. This mill, which has been gone for many years, was located on a small creek in the Taylor County section of Boothsville. Mills were popular in the late 1800s and early 1900s. Several mills were located in Taylor County. They primarily ground grain. The Fortney Mill on Three Fork Creek, Lyons District, Preston County, was built by Jonothan David Fortney. He owned and operated the mill until his death on July 4, 1885. It was then operated by John Wesley Fortney. Harold G. Fortney (b. 10/11/1902) of the Oak Grove community of Taylor County was the last member of his immediate family to be born at Fortney's Mill in neighboring Preston County. Fortney's Mill both ground grain and had an "up-and-down" saw that cut wood. In 2000, Fortney turned 98, having retired after working in coal mining, as a shop man for the B&O Railroad, and several years of employment with the West Virginia Industrial School for Boys at Pruntytown. In later years, Fortney's Mill became a popular swimming and recreation area and many from Taylor County enjoyed visiting the old mill area. (Photo courtesy of Wayne McDevitt.).

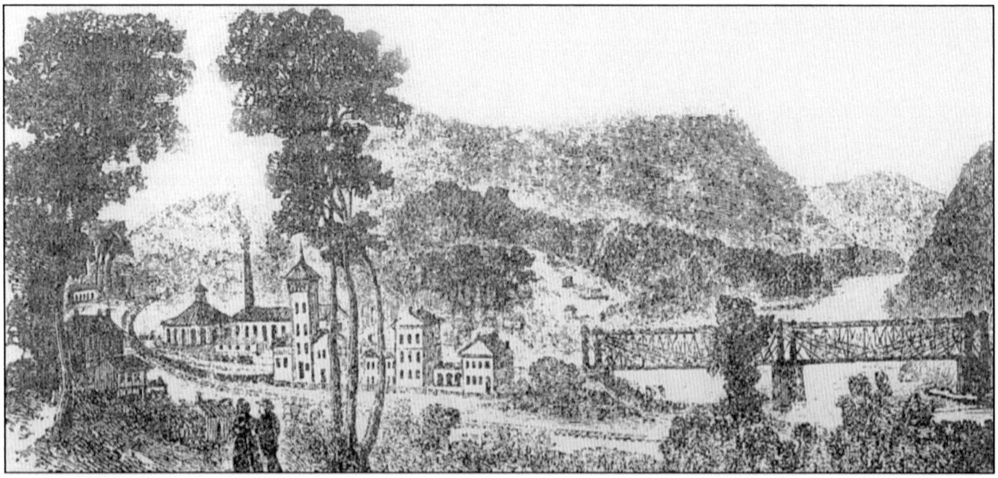

EARLY GRAFTON. In the above sketch, Grafton's ties with the railroad are noted as the city is listed as being at the junction of the Baltimore & Ohio Railroad with the Northwestern Virginia Railroad. In 1857, the B&O took control of the Northwestern Virginia Railroad. The Fetterman shops and roundhouse were razed by fire and moved to Grafton. A site between the rail lines was excavated and work started on a passenger terminal and hotel building. It is shown in the above sketch. (Photo courtesy of Peggy Robinson.)

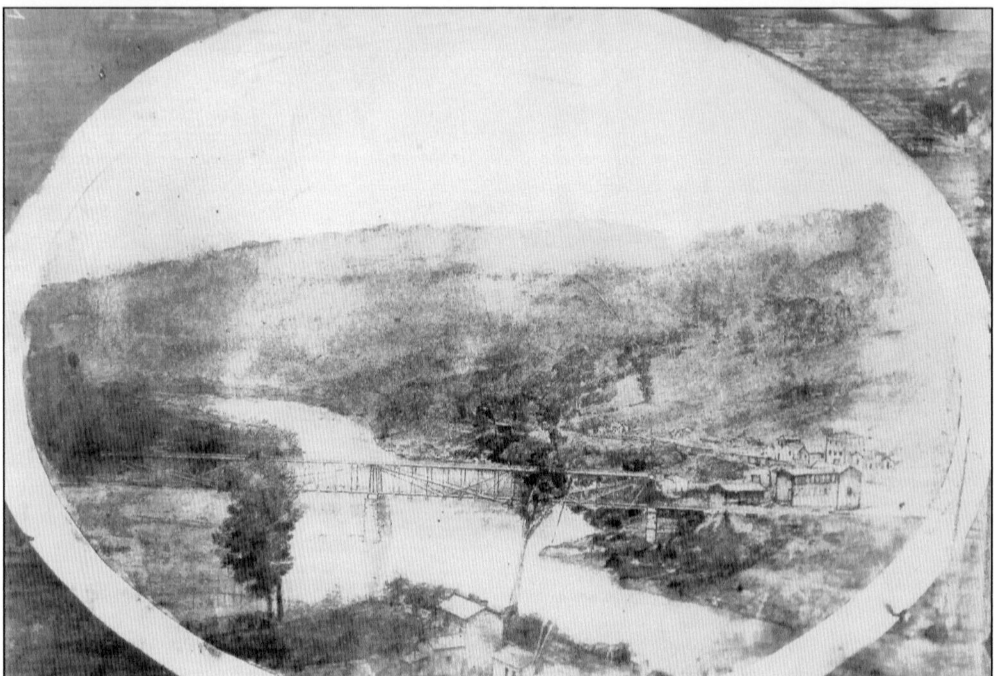

GRAFTON IN 1859. The influence of the B&O Railroad on Grafton is evident in this photo as the only bridge crossing the Tygart Valley River is one carrying rail traffic. In 1852, the land on which Grafton is built was surveyed and the town started. The principal street was Railroad Street and the first three houses were built along this street, fronting the railroad. The state of Virginia gave Grafton a charter on March 15, 1856. The "Junction" often added to Grafton was quickly dropped since the charter only used Grafton. (Photo courtesy of James Bolliger.)

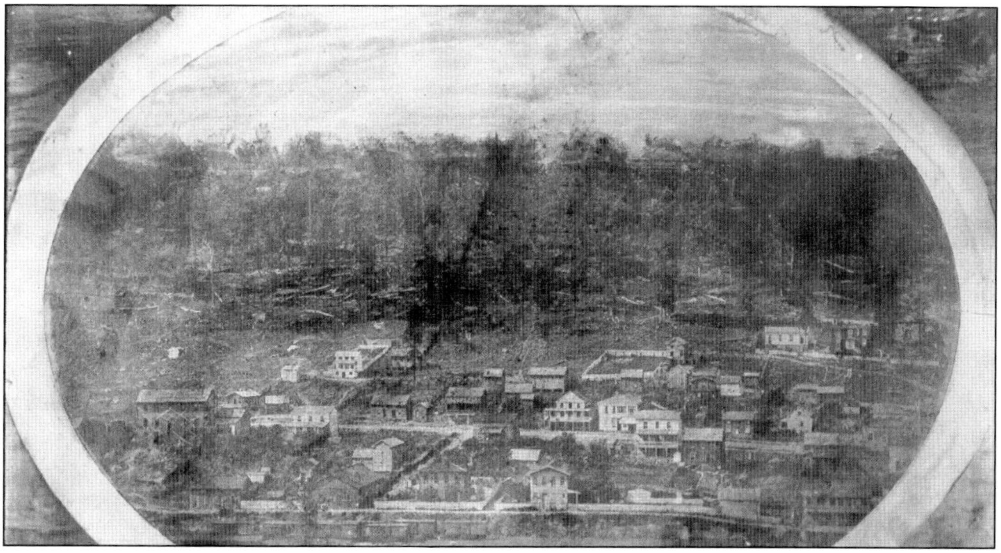

GRAFTON IN 1859. Simeon Siegfried started the first newspaper in Grafton in 1859, and later sold it to George R. Latham, who changed its name to *The Western Virginia(n)* from its former name, *Grafton Sentinel*. An 1847 Act of the Virginia Legislature stipulated that the road should reach or cross Tygart Valley River within 3 miles of Three Fork Creek. At the time this area was mostly uninhabited. The nearest settlement was at Valley Bridge (later Fetterman) on the Northwestern Turnpike, approximately 2 miles away. (Photo courtesy of James Bolliger.)

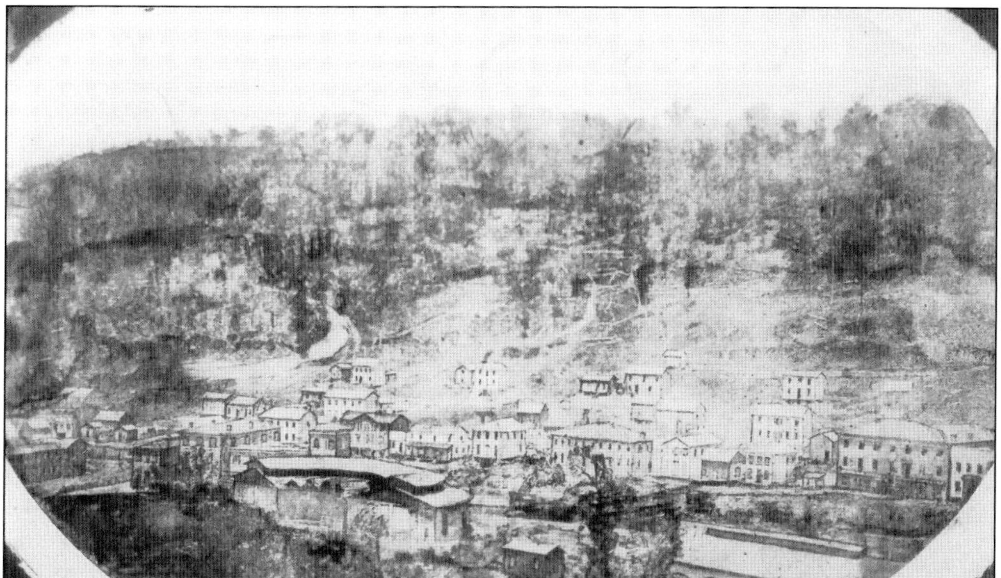

GRAFTON IN 1859. The Virginia Legislature granted a charter to the Northwestern Virginia Railroad Company, which was incorporated on February 14, 1851. Plans were to build a rail line from the main stem of the B&O to Parkersburg. Initial plans were to connect the line at Fetterman, which had been known as Valley Bridge. The B&O had shops at Fetterman and also there were stagecoach connections to the Northwestern Turnpike. However, the asking price for Fetterman land was too high and the connection was made at Grafton. (Photo courtesy of James Bolliger.)

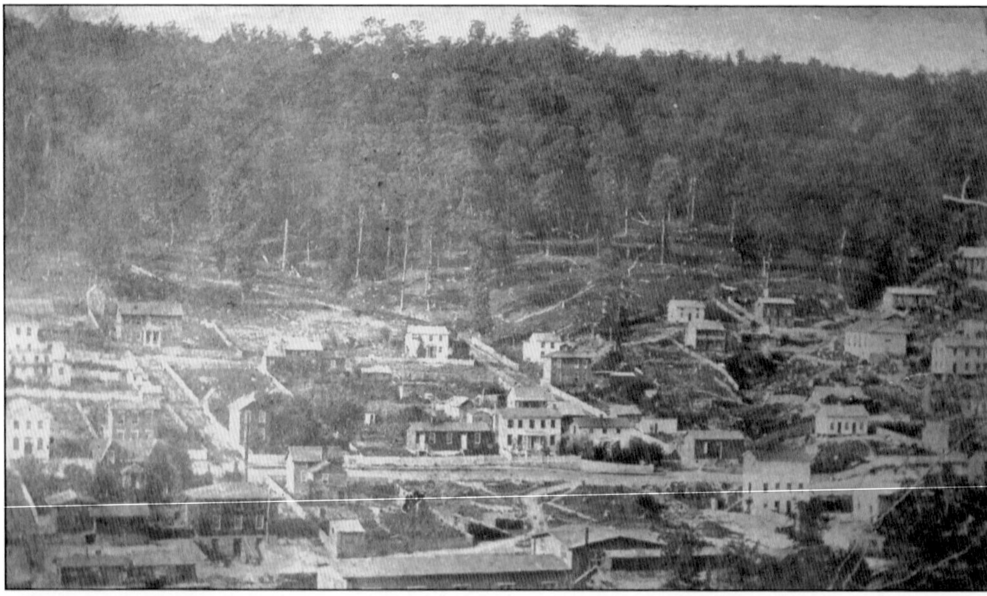

GRAFTON IN 1859. In its earliest days, supplies had to be hauled through the woods from Fetterman to Grafton. Thomas McGraw, one of Grafton's first settlers who came with the first construction train of the B&O, opened the first store on Railroad Street on May 1, 1852. In 1853, several houses and stores were built. George R. Latham opened the first school in Grafton the following year. On February 1, 1857, the B&O took over the liabilities and management of the Northwestern Virginia Railroad. The line opened in 1857. (Photo courtesy of James Bolliger.)

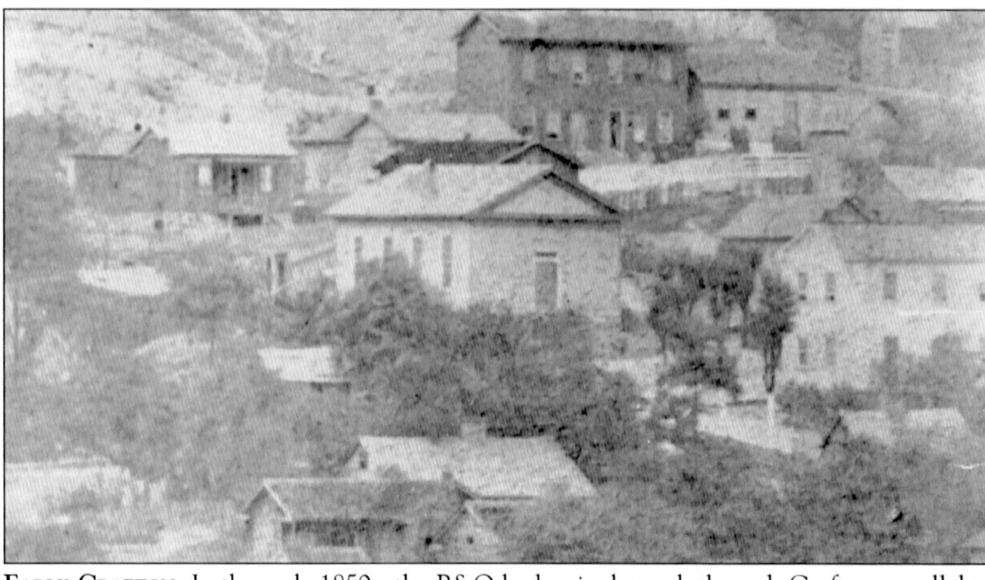

EARLY GRAFTON. In the early 1850s, the B&O had a single track through Grafton, parallel to Three Fork Creek, but the company's right-of-way extended to Elizabeth Street (later known as Main Street). This accounts for abandonment of the early sections of Railroad Street, which had been the first city street. In 1857, Methodists bought a lot at Washington Street and Indian Alley and built a small church building that was used by all of the Protestant denominations of the city. (Photo courtesy of James Bolliger.)

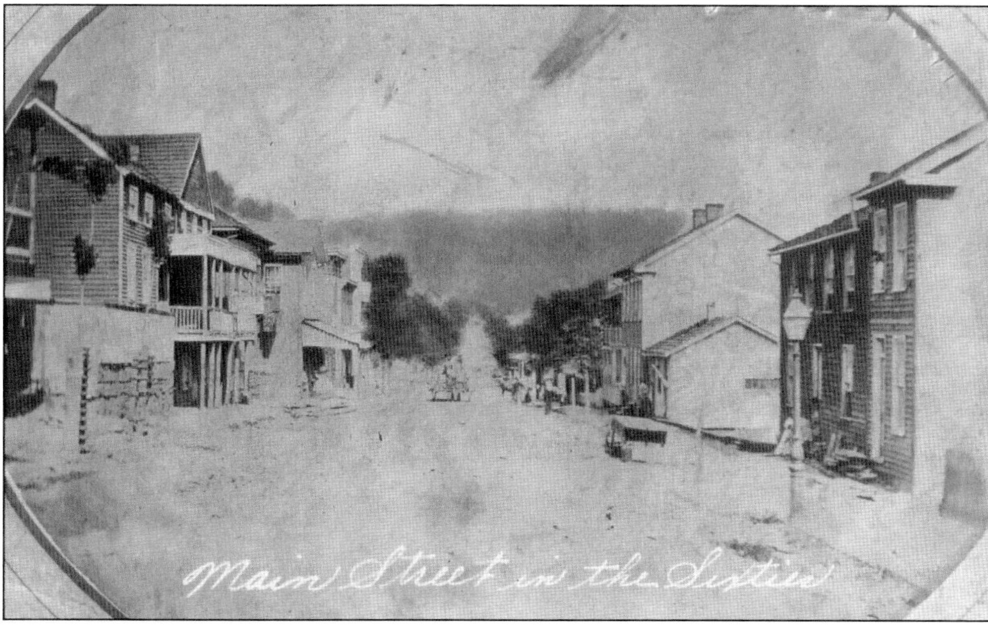

Main Street, 1860s. Grafton's main street was called Elizabeth Street until 1872, when it was renamed Main by an amendment to the town charter. Notice the dirt roadway and the early street light in this photo. Grafton was located on the main line of the Baltimore & Ohio Railroad, 100 miles east of Wheeling and 250 miles from the eastern seaboard. It was a division line for four of the branches of the B&O, the Cumberland Division, the Wheeling Division, the Parkersburg Division, and the Belington Division. (Photo courtesy of James Bolliger.)

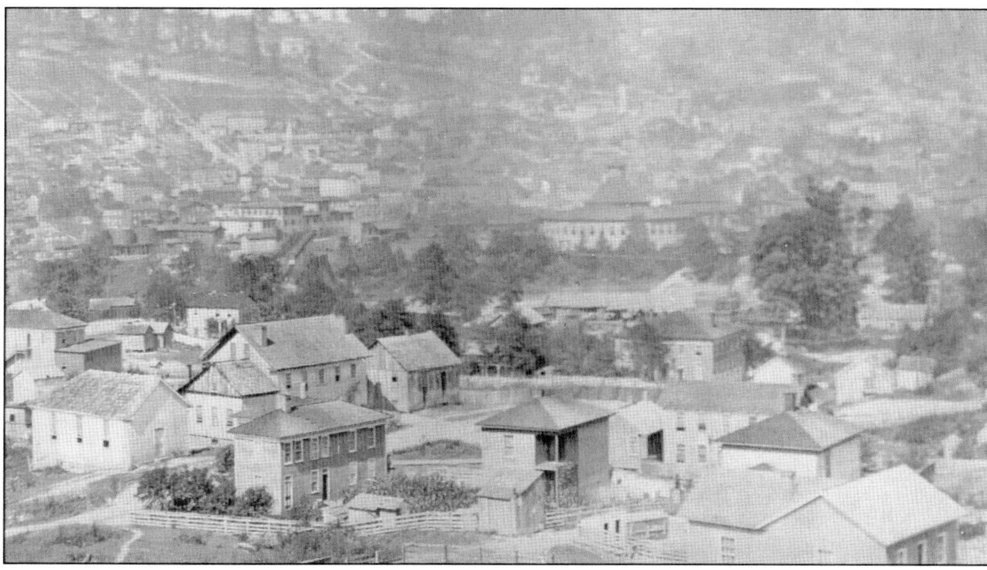

Early Grafton. By the time the country had reached its 100th birthday, Grafton had grown into a respectable community. Located here were two steam furniture mills, a steam excelsior mattress factory, foundry, and machine shop, the B&O repair shops, a wood pump factory, three shook factories, two steam planing, sash and door factories, and a cigar factory. Besides being a major railroad center, Grafton was a leading lumber processing center with large booms across the Tygart Valley River. (Photo courtesy of James Bolliger.)

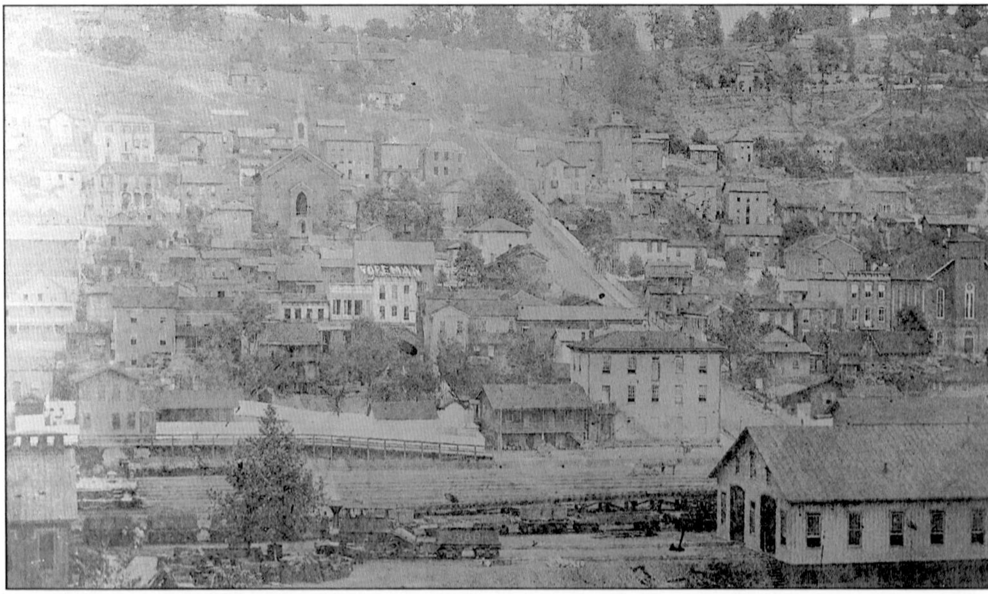

Early Grafton. In the early days of the Civil War, the importance of the Grafton rail center made the city a strategic point in the maneuvering of the Union and Confederate Armies. However, once the Union took control, no major skirmishes occurred here. In 1872, with the state capitol moving back and forth between Charleston and Wheeling, a six- to eight-county delegation met in Grafton and drafted a set of resolutions calling for Grafton to become the state capitol. The effort failed however. (Photo courtesy of Peggy Robinson.)

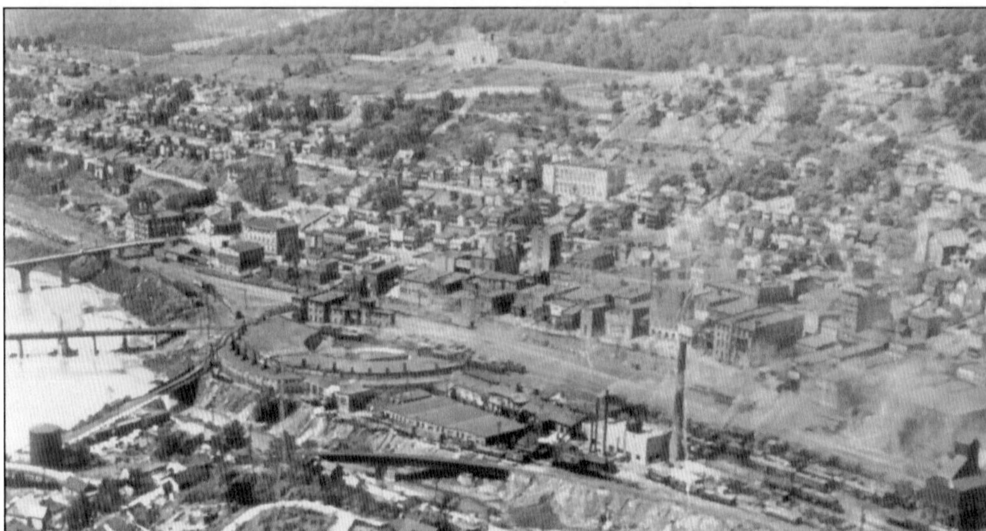

Overview of Grafton. In 1916, the defunct Columbia Tile Company was bought by the Hazel-Atlas Glass Company of Wheeling and the bankrupt Consolidated Manufactures Company was sold and soon became the Carr-China Company. Hazel-Atlas became Grafton's second largest industry and Carr China became the third largest employer until it closed in 1952. By 1920, the more accessible reserves of coal and timber were depleted around Grafton and this lead to declines in industries dependent on these raw resources. (Photo courtesy of Danny Moore.).

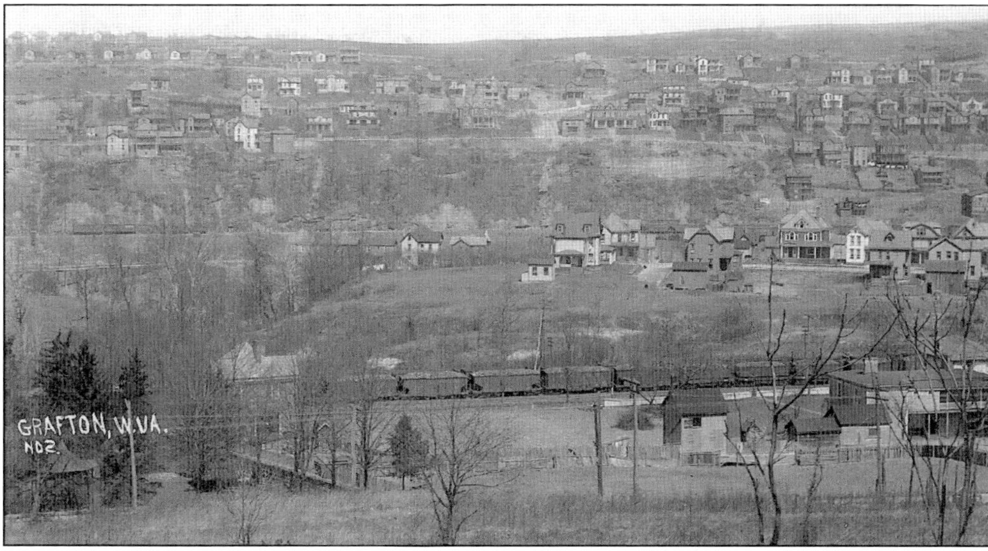

VIEW OF GRAFTON. Construction of homes and businesses expanded over the years. West Grafton formed a government and operated as a town until later being incorporated into Grafton. The B&O Railroad remained the city's leading industry, but it also inhibited growth. Studies showed that no other rail center had developed its business district immediately adjacent to the railroad. High hills and low wind held in the smoke and soot from rail engines and gave Grafton the reputation of a dirty city. (Photo courtesy of Lois Heflin.).

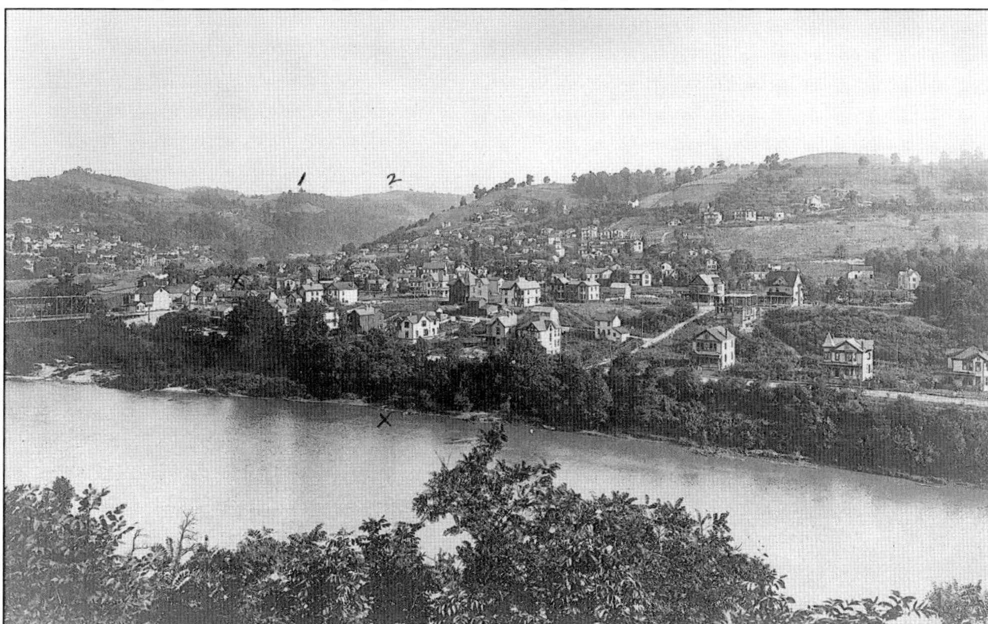

VIEW OF GRAFTON. The beauty of the gently flowing Tygart Valley River is shown in this photo. However, before construction of the Tygart Dam, the river would flood sections along the river. This photo was donated to the Taylor County Historical and Genealogical Society. The original owner marked a "1" at the top left of the photo to show the location of a cemetery. The "2" shows location of a water well. One of the spots marked with an "x" was a family home and the other mark along the river shows a vacant lot that the family had purchased.

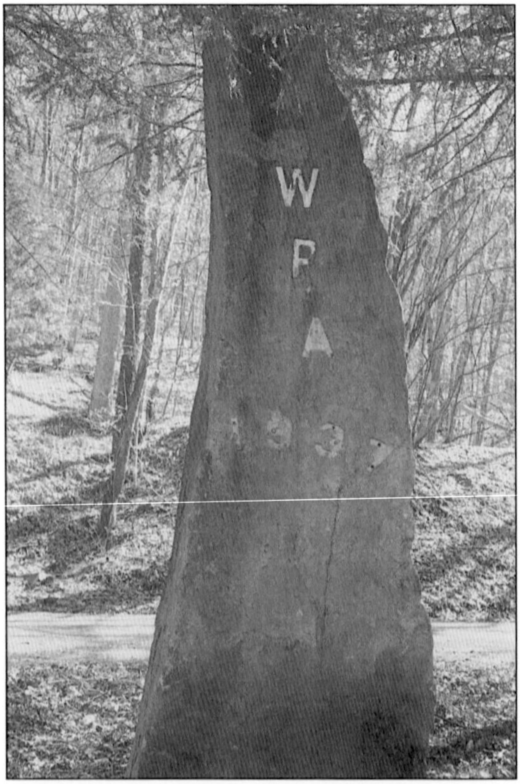

WPA STONE. Located in the Hardman section in northeastern Taylor County, this stone marker is almost in Preston County. It recalls work done in the 1930s by employees of President Franklin D. Roosevelt's Works Progress Administration program. (Photo courtesy of Peggy Robinson.)

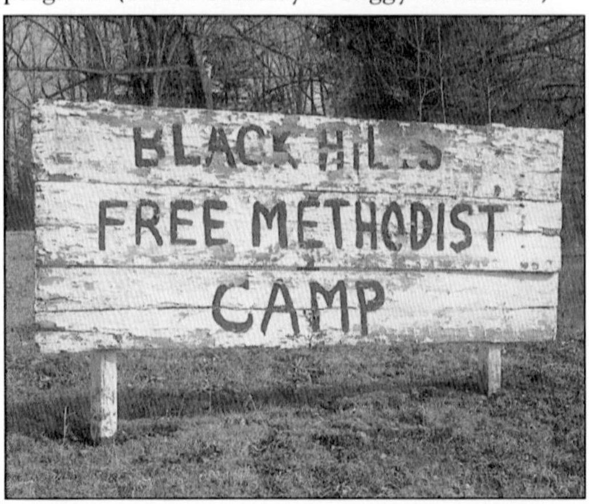

FREE METHODIST CAMP. Located along U.S. Route 119 North between Grafton and Morgantown, this camping area has served the Methodist Church for years. The area is now called Black Mountain. (Photo courtesy of Peggy Robinson.)

TIMELINE

1750s—First white men visit area

1760s—First pioneer settlers arrive

1844—Taylor County created and named for Virginia statesman John Taylor (1753–1824)

1856—City of Grafton chartered

1868—First Memorial Day observance

1878—Grafton becomes the county seat, replacing Pruntytown

1887—Fire almost destroys the city

1888—Great flood

1890—Grafton officially the 6th largest city in West Virginia

1908—First Mother's Day observance

1920s—Population decline starts

1935—Construction begins on Tygart Dam

1960s—Grafton revived due to efforts of its citizens

1963—Grafton selected as an All American City

Taylor County Historical and Genealogical Society: PO Box 522, Grafton, WV 26354

Grafton/Taylor County Convention and Visitors Bureau: PO Box 355, Grafton, WV 26354
Phone: 304-265-0164
Web page: www.taylorcounty.com

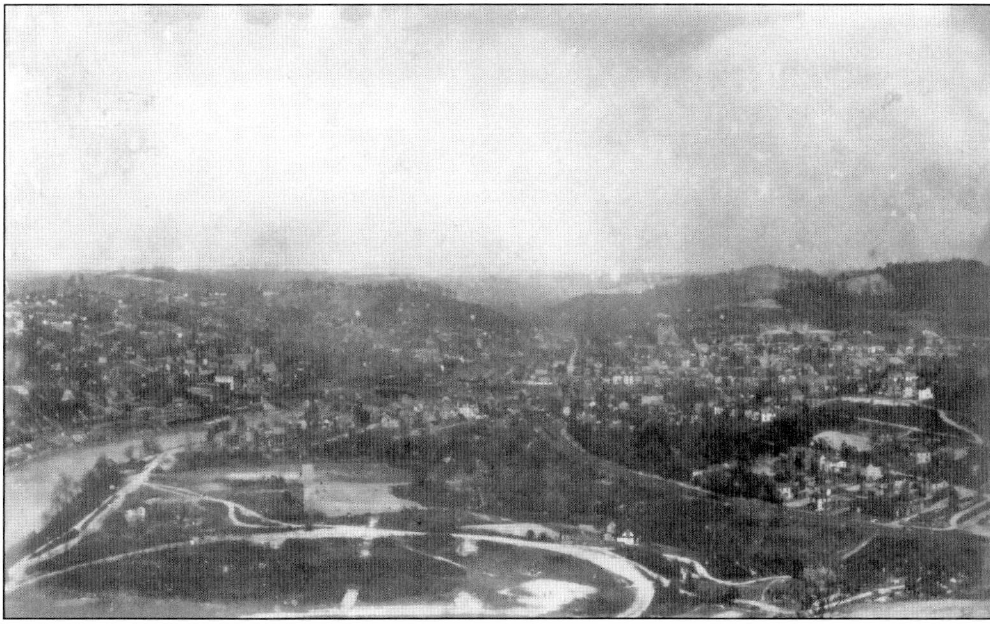

OLD FAIRGROUNDS. In 1870, representatives from Taylor County and Grafton organized an association, the Taylor County Agricultural and Mechanical Society, in order to revive the farm animal business. The association purchased 17 acres of land for $333.33 an acre from Alexander Yates in West Grafton, the site formerly known as Buffalo Flats. A half-mile race track was graded, and a grandstand, and two-story exhibition hall, were constructed. The first fair was sponsored in October 1870. (Photo courtesy of Norma Wyckoff.)

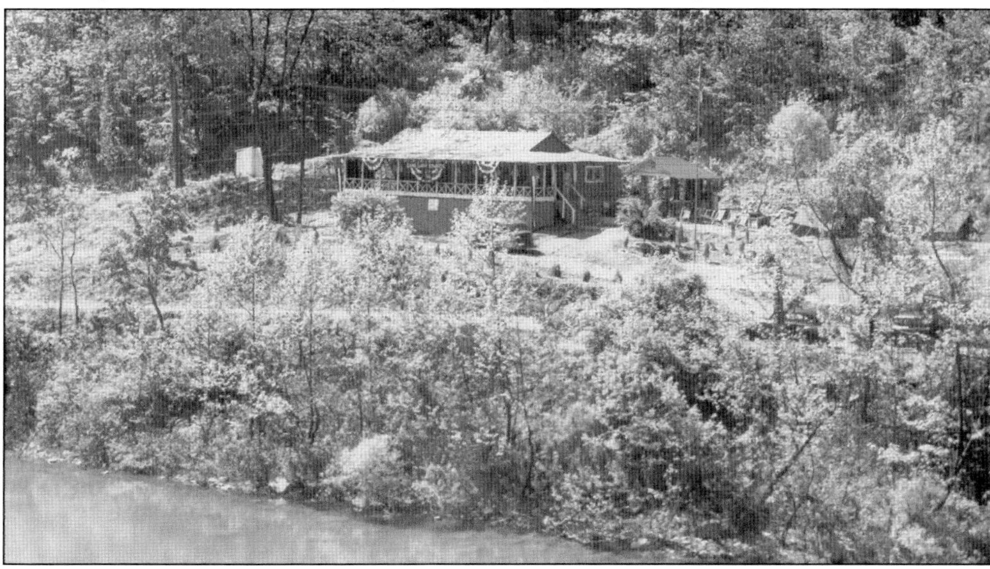

BOY SCOUT CAMP. Known as Camp Leroy Edwards, this Boy Scout camp was dedicated May 31, 1947, in memorial to the Boy Scouts who had served in World War II. The dedication was by Rotary Club Troop No. 3 of Grafton. The camp was named in honor of LeRoy Edwards, who had lived in the house across the river from the Carr China Plant. Edwards was killed in World War II. The camp was located on the defunct Wabash Railroad property along upper Maple Avenue. Renovated in 1967, it closed shortly thereafter. (Photo courtesy of Wayne McDevitt.).

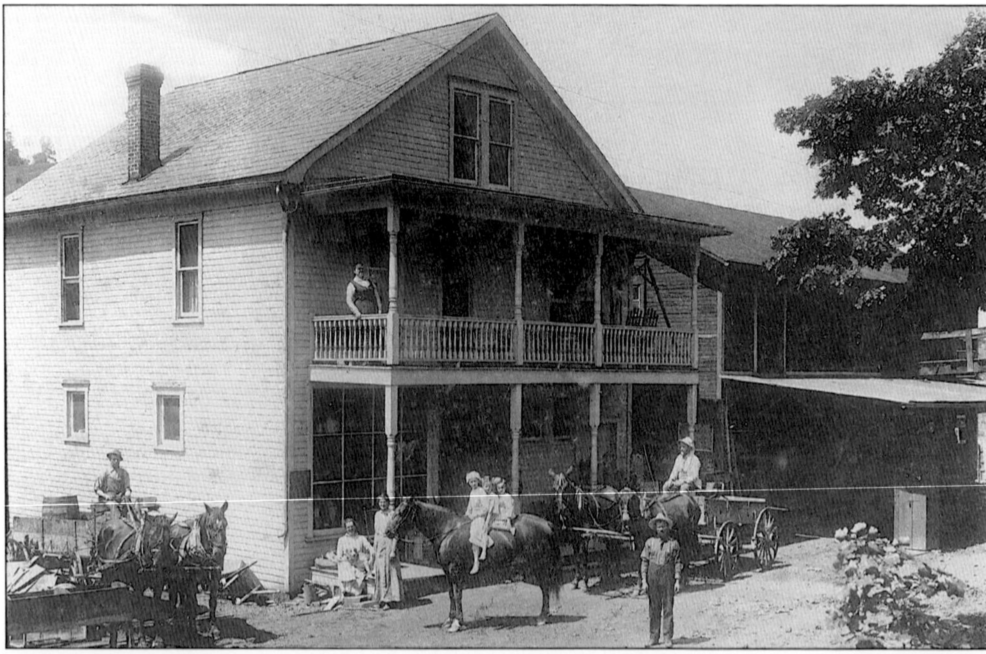

E. Lodge Ross House. Recently razed, the E. Lodge Ross house was located in the Simpson community. The structure had been used as a home, a mercantile store, feed mill, and post office. Zelma Eleanor Ross and Edna Ross are shown. The name of the horse was Della, while the names of the mules were Jack and Jimmy. A walkway was located on the right side of the structure and used for bringing in supplies of feed and other items when the building was used as a store, mill, and post office. (Photo courtesy of Geneva Phelps.)

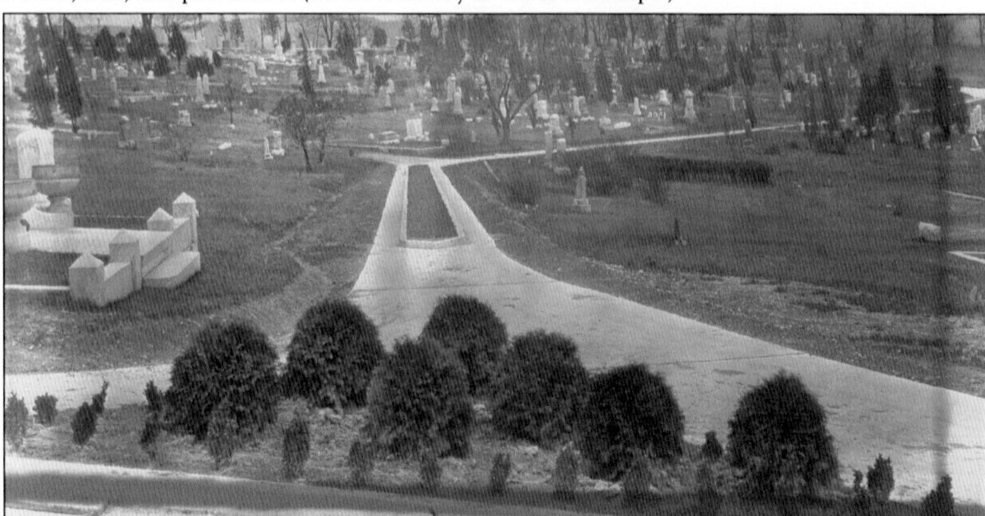

Bluemont Cemetery. The Blueville area of Grafton was named for John Wolverton Blue. He came to the area in 1835 and served as a foreman or inspector of the Northwestern turnpike as it was built from Cheat Mountain in Preston County to Clarksburg in Harrison County. After the Civil War, the Blues turned over to Grafton what is now known as Bluemont Cemetery. It has been described as one of nature's beauty spots and one of the most picturesque cemeteries in northern West Virginia. (Photo courtesy of the Bluemont Cemetery Historical Collection.).

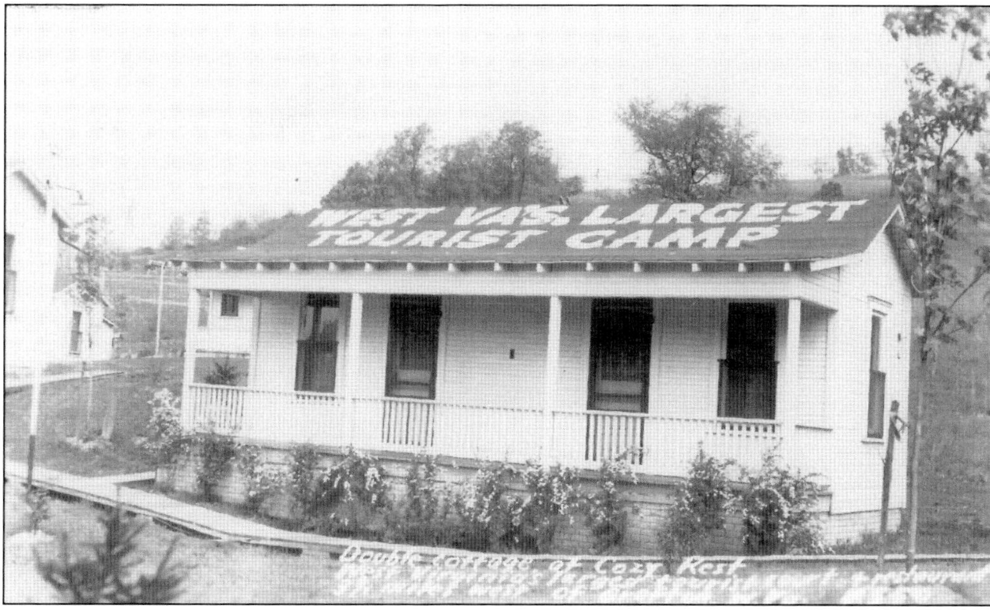

Cozy Rest. In 1939, Debendarfer's Inc., was created to provide eating establishments, lodging, and filling station services. The corporation owned Cozy Rest. Located along U.S. Route 50 near Pruntytown, it was known as "West Virginia's largest tourist Camp." D.W. Dudley was the first manager. In 1961, the corporation name was changed to Cozy Rest. The business included 40 cottages with private baths, the former Bartlett's Motel, and a restaurant. The restaurant was struck by lightning and destroyed on July 1, 1969. (Photo courtesy of Wayne McDevitt.)

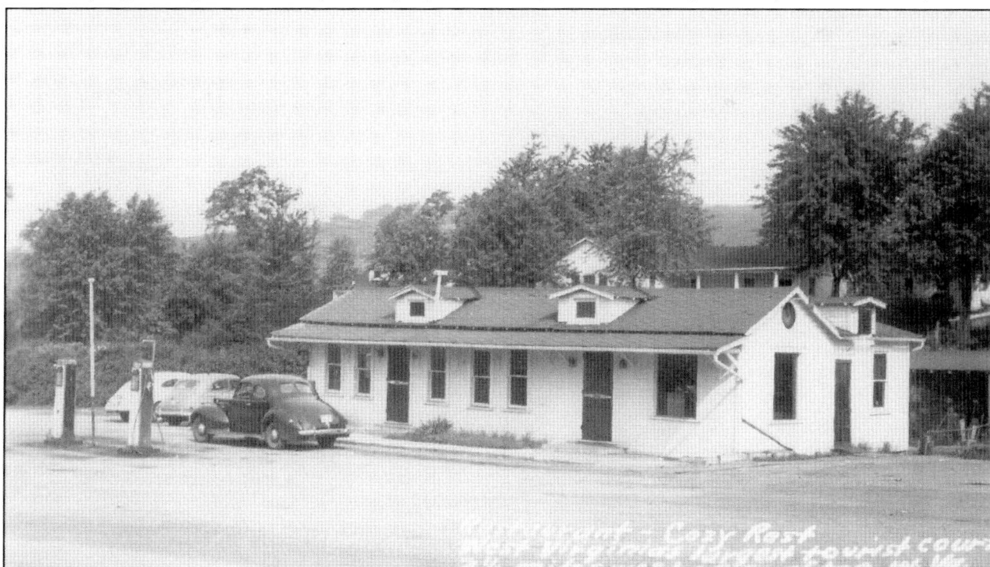

Cozy Rest. Shown above is the former Cozy Rest. The business was a popular stop for tourists and other travelers in the days prior to the opening of the interstate system in West Virginia. With the restaurant, service station, and cabins for lodging the business was a one-stop center for travelers along Route 50. As with most such businesses, the arrival of modern interstate highway systems diverted too much business for the establishment to remain open. (Photo courtesy of Wayne McDevitt.)

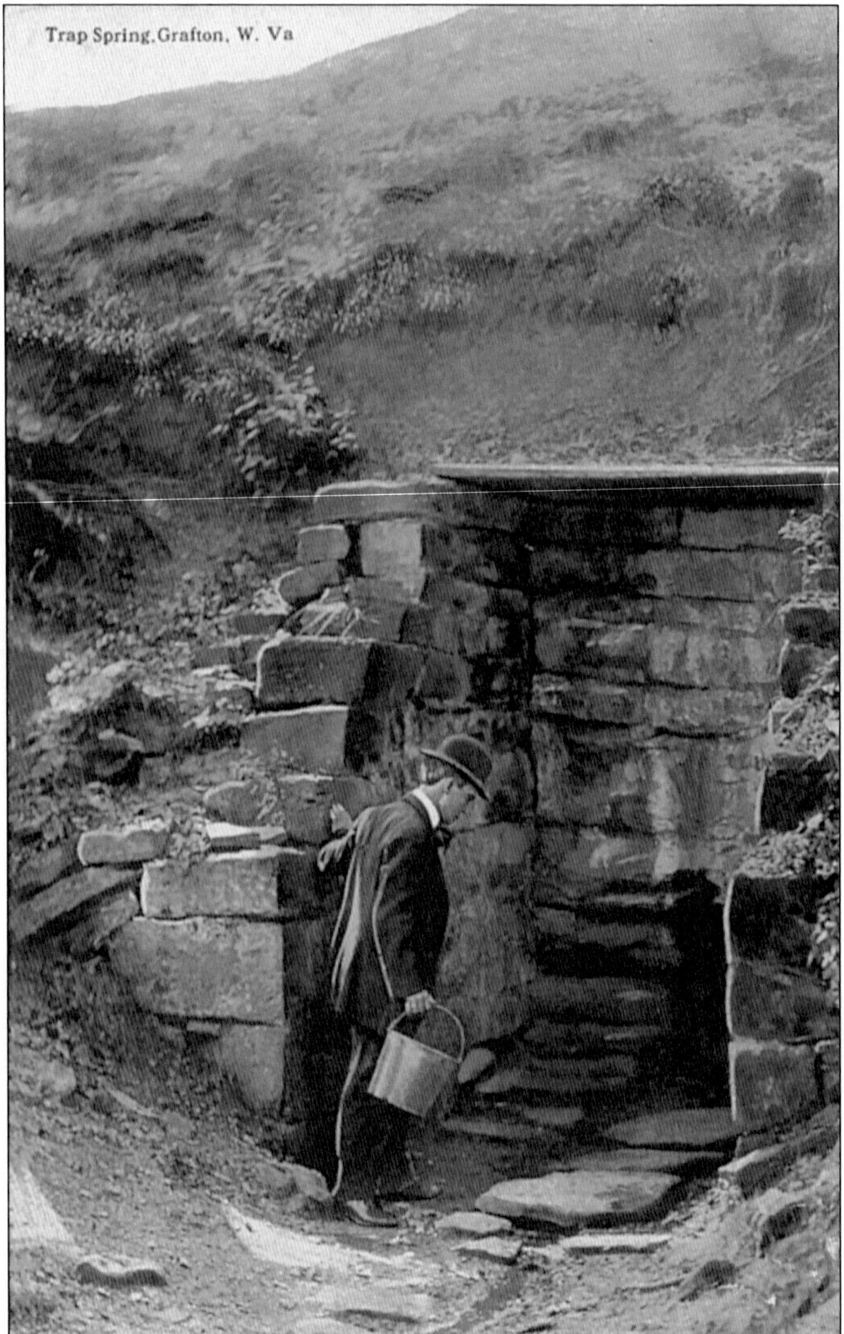

TRAP SPRING. This area is southeast of Pruntytown. Today both the roadway and the area are called Trap Spring after the water spring. In the days of stagecoach travel, the road made a sharp bend adjacent to the spring and the roadway embankment cut off view of the roadway beyond the bend. Robbers would block the roadway in the bend and the stagecoach driver could not see the "trap" until it was too late. Stagecoach drivers were helplessly stopped by the blockades. (Photo courtesy of Wayne McDevitt.)

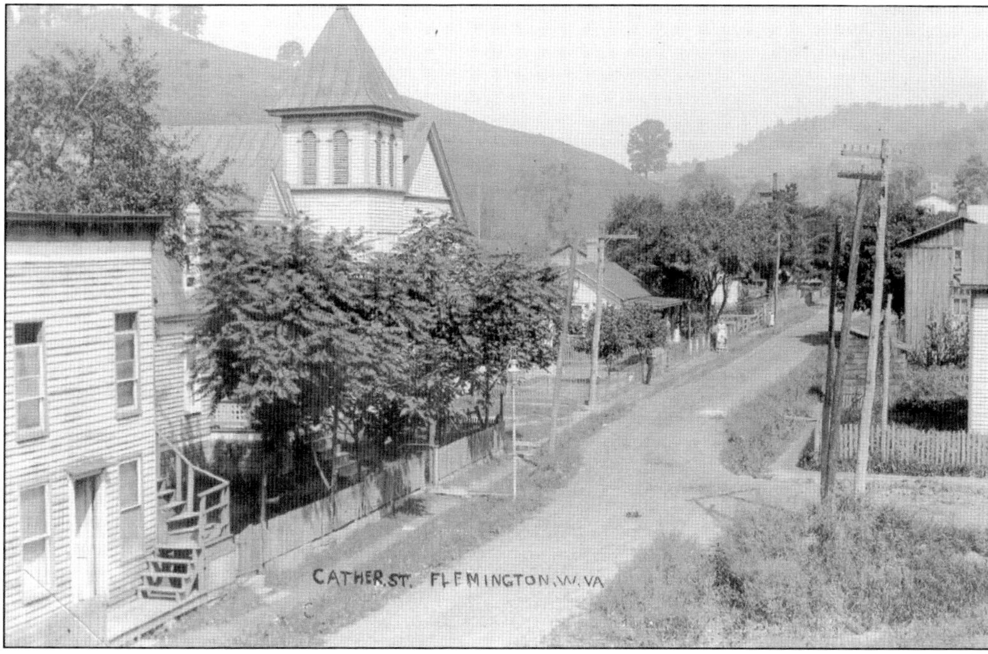

TOWN OF FLEMINGTON. Located in the Western District of Taylor County, Flemington was incorporated as a municipality in 1922. However, it traces its roots to the mid-1800s, when it was a thriving village. A rail line laid through the town paved the way for the development of coal, farming, cattle, sheep, and educational industries. Ground-breaking for a tomato plant, known as the West Virginia Best Corporation, took place on September 17, 1969. The facility later operated as a greenhouse under several owners. (Photo courtesy of Wayne McDevitt.)

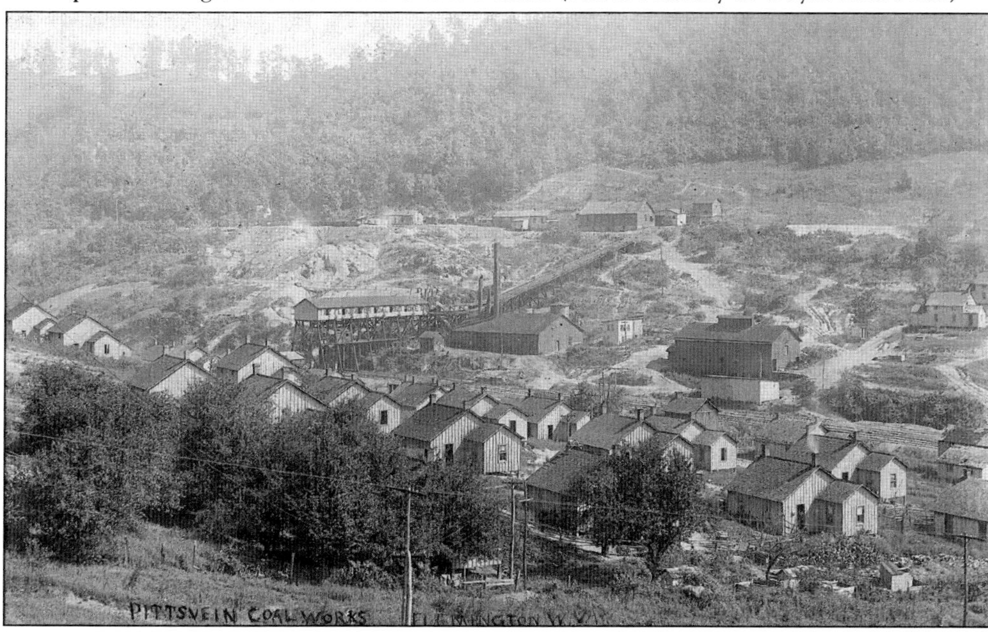

PITTSVEIN COAL WORKS. The Pittsvein Coal Company, one of the larger mines in the Dogtown section of Flemington, was owned and operated by the Pittsvein Coal Company. The company was incorporated on April 19, 1904, to operate a coal mine at Flemington.

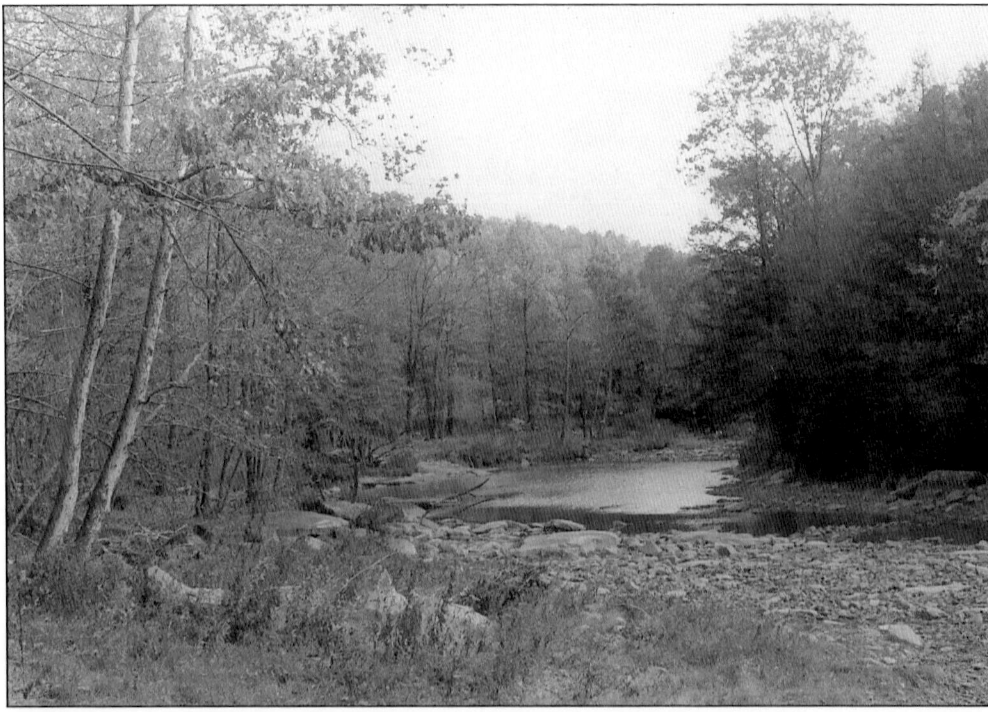

Blue Deep. Located on Sandy Creek separating Taylor and Barbour Counties, the area known as Blue Deep was a popular swimming and recreational area for many years. However, acid mine drainage from old abandoned coal mines upstream eventually entered the waters and killed off all of the aquatic life. In recent years the area is no longer accessible to the general public. Tygart Lake State Park has a swimming beach and the city of Grafton operates a municipal pool at the Fetterman Park. (Photo courtesy of Peggy Robinson.).

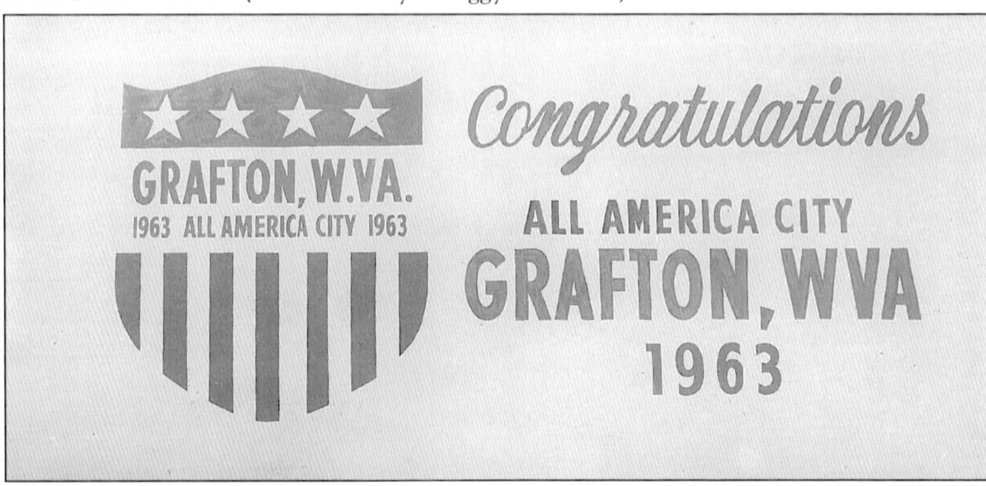

Grafton, an All American City. When the city's industrial plants started closing in the late 1950s, the people fought back. Operation Survival was formed and the citizens got behind a Grafton industrial development movement. The women of Grafton received national press coverage of a December 12, 1958 "March for Industries." New businesses, such as St. Regis and Baby World, opened operations here. In 1963, Grafton was the smallest city to be honored as an All American City by *Look* magazine. (Photo courtesy of Marvin Gelhausen.)